QUICK SOLUTIONS

BOOKS BY THOMAS L. QUICK

QUICK SOLUTIONS

500 PEOPLE PROBLEMS

MANAGERS FACE

AND HOW TO

SOLVE THEM

THOMAS L. QUICK

New York, New York

JOHN WILEY & SONS

New York   Chichester   Brisbane   Toronto   Singapore

Library of Congress Cataloging in Publication Data:

Quick, Thomas L.
  Quick solutions: 500 people problems managers
face and how to solve them.

  Bibliography: p.
  1. Problem solving. 2. Management. I. Title.
II. Title: Quick solutions: Five hundred people problems
managers face and how to solve them.

HD3Q.29.Q53 1987   658.4'03   87-10540
ISBN 0-471-85229-5
ISBN 0-471-85228-7 (pbk.)

Printed in the United States of America

10 9 8 7 6 5 4 3 2 1

To Terry

PREFACE

I anticipate your questions—some of them, anyway. For example:
Are the questions/situations/problems contained in this book real?

Yes.

How and where did you get them?

I managed to collect more than a few of them during my 30 years in organizational life, many of which I spent as a line manager. In addition to my own managerial experience, my tenure on the professional staff of the Research Institute of America was quite valuable. We were accustomed to having problems and questions sent to us by the managers who were members of our programs. For the past 12 years I've traveled widely, giving lectures, seminars, and workshops, each with its question-and-answer period. Finally, in hundreds of conversations, managers have expressed their concerns and described their experiences to me.

The idea for this book originated in two separate but related events. In the latter part of the 1970s, Philip Farish, the editor of *Industrial Relations News*, suggested, in a review of one of my books, that I could well become the Ann Landers of the management world. I was delighted with the compliment but thought little more about it. About three years ago, I spent nearly four hours in a meeting in Rochester, New York, simply answering questions from managers about managing. It occurred to me then that there might be a need for a book to cover, in Ann Landers style, the hundreds of minor though important concerns of managers that never find their way into the scores of management books published each year.

So, if you are a manager, want to be one, or simply want to get along with one, there is, I suspect, something in this book for you.

THOMAS L. QUICK

New York, New York
July 1987

CONTENTS

QUICK SOLUTIONS

ONE

SPECIAL PROBLEMS AND PROBLEM EMPLOYEES
1–104

Criticism and Feedback

▷ **1**

How do you criticize an employee who gets very uptight and defensive when you say one negative word?

The temptation may be to take time and use soft words to prepare the defensive employee for the bad news. I advise the opposite: Get right to the point, using the most direct language possible. For example, "I have to tell you I'm very upset that your report is so sketchy and incomplete. It is not what I understood we had agreed to."

The defensive person will talk a lot, show anger and embarrassment, and will often produce excuses and charges that the problem is not his or her fault. The employee may even suggest that there is no problem at all, that you are being unreasonable.

Through the torrent of words and emotions, you have to be firm. Keep interjecting the evidence that there is indeed a problem: "We agreed at the outset that your report would cover the feasibility of a regional distribution system, and there is almost nothing on this. I also asked you to include sources of further information in all the areas you covered, and that part is very incomplete. Overall, this report is not useful. Now, how is this problem going to be corrected?"

You'll probably get more emotion, excuses, and rationalizations. Listen. Don't agree, unless you find that his or her explanations do warrant your attention. Keep coming back to the question, "How are you going to rectify this?" Don't be swayed. And don't stop the session until you have the answer you want.

◊ 2

One woman in my department always comes up with a list of reasons why she couldn't complete this job on time or do that the way I wanted. There's always some excuse. Sometimes I think that trying to give her feedback is too frustrating to bother.

She's probably hoping that is exactly what you think, and you'll give up trying. Apparently she has been successful in frustrating you; otherwise she wouldn't keep working her little list.

Change your tactics. Spell out in detail what you want from her in her performance. Then, as she gives you her reasons why she can't fulfill your requirements, you respond, "I understand what you're saying, but I want this change made." You may have to respond several times before she realizes that you're no longer playing her game. Don't vary your response. Keep repeating the change you want and that you have already described to her. Remember that if the change is reasonable, you have every right to expect her to make it. As she begins to show confusion or less confidence in the validity of her excuses, you add, "Now, how are you going to accomplish this change?"

If you keep your eye on the objective—the change of behavior—and if you believe you have a right to expect that change, you'll make headway. Don't let her walk out of your office until she has offered a plan for improvement. In the days following, make sure she follows that plan. Otherwise, another session of criticism, or even counseling, is due.

One word of caution: You have to make sure that none of her excuses constitutes a real barrier to performance that you should investigate. It's always possible that she can't perform well due to a departmental problem of which you are not aware.

⇩ 3
I've criticized and criticized, and he still doesn't produce. How do I know when I'm justified in firing him?

If you are sure he understands what he is supposed to do, and if you have explicitly and specifically criticized his failure on two or three occasions, you ought to take one more step: counseling. Schedule some time when you will not be interrupted. Sit down with him and get his agreement that he has not done what you've required him to do. Emphasize that your counseling session with him is the last resort. Either he improves satisfactorily within a reasonable time—set a time frame such as three months—or you will have to terminate him. Make sure he understands he is on probation. The next recommended action: a plan of improvement that he understands, and, preferably, to which he agrees. If he doesn't agree to it, find out why. Don't just impose the plan on him. He may see an impediment about which he is not being open. If the hesitation to agree is arbitrary on his part, and if you are satisfied that he has the ability and the skills to do the job as you want it done, then make it clear to him that either he improves accordingly or he is out. If there is an impediment, such as lack of know-how or conflict within the department, work on that and schedule a follow-up session when the problem has been eliminated.

▷ 4

I followed the One-Minute Reprimand by saying something nice about the employee, but the criticism hasn't taken. I think he must have heard only what was pleasant.

The danger of mixing negative and positive feedback is that the positive may dilute the negative to the point where it is not taken seriously or remembered. But managers still try to soften the pain of criticism—for themselves as well as for the employees being criticized—by saying something nice about the people whose performance is deficient.

Because I believe that most employees want to do well, that they don't want to fumble and stumble, I am convinced they will accept criticism if it is straightforward and helpful. The manager should confine the criticism to the behavior that is wrong, and should describe how it can be changed. I don't think that employees need to be assured that their managers still love them, even if they have been naughty. After criticism, a manager's interactions with an erring employee should be normal, constituting assurance that the manager was objecting only to a specific action or behavior, not to the employee.

By the same token, when a manager praises, he or she shouldn't be tempted to slip in a little bit of criticism.

▷ 5

I have a subordinate who just doesn't seem to take my criticism seriously. I mention one problem; he listens, goes away, and forgets it. What do I have to do to impress him—bring out a whole laundry list of complaints I have against him?

It seems like a logical thing to do in your frustration. Ironically, the result may be the same as when you talk about only one problem: Nothing will happen, because he'll walk away from the interview convinced he can't do well, or confused about where he should start (so he may not start anywhere).

Stick with one problem at a time. Insist on a change—and a schedule of change. He is to make improvements by such and such a time. Otherwise you'll have another session with him, less pleasant than this time. It's unfortunate that you have to supply the memory for such a forgetful employee. Through discipline and warnings you'll have to make it important for him to start remembering on his own.

▷ 6

One of my employees has a strong body odor. I hate to get involved, but other employees have complained.

Apparently none of his coworkers feels close enough to this employee to give him some friendly advice. That would actually be preferable to the boss stepping in. You might try to convince one of your other subordinates to pull this person aside and give him the word. He would be far less embarrassed to hear it from a peer.

If you must take action, be as matter-of-fact about it as you can. Simply say something such as, "Some people have more sensitive noses than others. You're probably one of the less sensitive noses, and you're not aware that you are giving off an odor. It's probable that you, in addition to having a less sensitive nose, have a stronger body scent than others. I wanted to tell you about this so you wouldn't be embarrassed if you found out later. You can take steps to correct the situation. I hesitated to tell you, but then I thought if I were in your shoes, I'd want to know."

He'll be embarrassed, but if you act naturally, you'll make the ordeal less painful for him—and eventually for others.

⬦ 7

When I have a serious talk with one of my subordinates, to criticize her performance and to find out where her head is, she gives me the silent treatment. I feel so frustrated.

And angry, no doubt, too. I suspect that she's found a good way to express her aggressions toward you. It works every time.

Try not to talk so much. Say what you have to say, then ask her to respond. Once you've asked for her response, be silent. Look at her. She'll probably begin to feel the stress that you've felt from her silence. Don't break it, otherwise you'll rescue her. She'll eventually realize that she can't leave until she says something to you.

⬦ 8

When I criticize a certain female employee, she gets weepy and emotional. I usually cut the session short. How can I do a good job of getting my message across?

Her crying serves her well, although it's probably not a conscious desire to keep you from saying all that you want to say. She will continue to tear up when you give her negative feedback because so far you have rewarded her behavior by terminating the interview.

The answer, therefore, is not to terminate the criticism session. Buy a box of tissues and have it on your desk. When she cries, give her time to compose herself, then resume. Don't stop until you have said what you believe is necessary, and especially not until you have secured an agreement from her on how to correct the problem behavior for which you've criticized her.

Every time you feel tempted to quit, remember that you are being manipulated, even if it is unconscious on her part.

⬧ 9

How do I schedule a counseling session with one of my people who has a serious performance problem that she hasn't corrected? I want to do it with as little hassle as possible.

Your concern is well placed if you don't want the employee coming to your office with a long list of reasons why she can't do the job. It's best to schedule a counseling session on the spur of the moment, when there is no time for the employee to fret and rehearse. However, the last-minute scheduling doesn't mean that you shouldn't be thoroughly prepared with your documentation—evidence of her poor performance and your previous admonitions to her.

I prefer first thing in the morning, early in the week, for counseling. You have the time to give, and it may indeed take some time. Furthermore, you have the rest of the day in which to have more normal contact with her and show her that you have no wish to isolate or otherwise punish her. If you treat her in a normal fashion, with no discrimination, you'll also provide time for any follow-up session if she feels the need for one. She may, after all, have some additional thoughts, or want clarification on something you said during the session.

Don't counsel on Friday afternoon. It's doubtful that you will have an effective employee on Monday after she has spent the weekend brooding.

⊅ **10**
I have to counsel a problem employee whose attitude makes me so angry. In fact, I lost my temper during a previous session with him and really botched it. I'm afraid I'll do the same thing again.

If you need to counsel him, pick a time when you are least emotional. Because you dread the session, you may put it off until you are driven to it. You will then be so resentful that you are sure to be angry.

Even so, you may be a bit heated when you sit down with him. Don't try to deny your emotions. Tell him right off that you are upset with his behavior, and you want him to know it.

If his behavior has continued, and since he has been counseled before, put him on notice. Tell him if he does not straighten up by such and such a time, you will terminate him. Once you have taken decisive action with a time limit, you'll probably find that you are much relieved.

⊅ **11**
He wants supervisory training, but I don't think he has what it takes to go into management. I certainly don't

**want to waste my money, but how can I level with
him?**

What are his other options? If there is another career step you
believe he can take, sit down with him and counsel him. He
may want to try management because it's the only prospect he
sees.

If you can't guide him toward formal advancement, try giving
him increased responsibility. He may be able to handle it very
well, and it will give him a sense of progress.

You owe him your evaluation that he is not suited for a managerial position, at least at this time. If you don't level with him,
you risk having him nurse the hope and later resent you because
he feels that you misled him.

⇨ 12
**One of my subordinates generally performs very well,
but on a recent assignment she wasn't quite up to snuff.
I don't want to make a big deal of it, but I need to
point out that she was less than perfect. How do I do
this tactfully?**

Ask her how she felt about her work, whether she would have
done anything different, or how could she have improved what
she did. She'll probably open up with a bit of self-criticism, and
then you ask, "Would you like to hear my assessment?" She'll
say yes, and you can add your own criticism.

An alternate approach is to ask her, "On a scale of one to
one hundred, how would you rate your success on the project?"
If she says something such as 85, you might say, "Well, I'd agree.
Let's compare notes. You tell me why you chose eighty-five,
and I'll you how I see it."

⬦ 13

I have one subordinate who is arrogant. The other day, while I was criticizing some work he did, he said, "The problem is that I'm smarter than you, and you know it." How should I respond to a stupid statement like that?

Respond seriously. You might say, "I know you're smart, and that's why I believe you can be one of my best assets. Here's the way I'd like you to do the work. If you can come up with a more effective way, I'd be happy to hear it." Of course, you have to be the judge, and he may not always be happy about that. But you are the manager. You have the right to expect certain kinds of work. You are always open to suggestions, however.

Don't fight with his perception of himself, which, after all, may be true. Emphasize instead that you both have obligations: You are responsible for results, and he must exercise his intelligence to get better results.

⬦ 14

Remember the cartoon character Sad Sack? Well, I have a Sad Sack in my department. There are so many things I need to straighten out with him, I don't know where to start. Should I just call him in and read off the list to him?

How did you let this employee accumulate such a record? I don't know the full story, but I have to suspect that someone wasn't giving him proper feedback as he fouled up.

If you read off your laundry list, you'll overwhelm him. His reaction may well be, "What's the use? I can't do anything right," or, "My boss really has it in for me." You'll have a hard time building constructive action on either base.

Start with the most serious performance deficiency, and work to improve that. When you've succeeded, pick the next most serious and repeat the process. As he corrects the problem, give him a lot of praise. The satisfaction he gets from his achievement may encourage him to take action on some of his deficiencies without waiting for your intervention.

▷ 15

I have to cut the salary of a salesman who hasn't been doing well, and I'll be giving him the news on my regular visit. When's the best time to tell him? I hate to affect his selling.

There's no clear answer on this. If you schedule time to tell him in the morning, you're probably pushing up against his appointments with prospects. You won't be able to spend time if he wants to discuss it at length. The news may also put him off his selling stride.

Lower the boom in the evening. Give him time to get over the shock. Be loose in your schedule. Allow him to express his feelings and to ask you to help him make improvements. You may miss your plane, but you can't rush this session.

▷ 16

One of my subordinates frequently brings me suggestions, but only once in a great while is there one I can use. I don't want to turn him off, but how do I

soften the news that I don't find many of his suggestions worthwhile?

Give him a hearing each time so he feels satisfied that he had a chance to explain his new idea. Thank him warmly for having taken the time and effort to think through the suggestion. Tell him that, of course, you need to evaluate the suggestion. Then say something such as, "You know, I really appreciate your coming up with ideas, even though we can't use them all for one reason or another. I especially remember that idea to do. . . ." Describe one of his rare winning ideas. He'll feel genuinely complimented, and he'll be reminded of the time he won distinction for himself. He'll also feel encouraged to continue to come up with ideas to satisfy the law of averages.

Appraisals

▷ **17**

One supervisor tends to give very negative appraisals to his people. He says his evaluations spur people to better and better performance. But I think his people are sore at him.

Show him how consistently negative appraisals can backfire. They tell probably more about him than about his employees. If his employees show no substantial improvement between appraisals, the lack of improvement reflects on the supervisor. Obviously he is not giving them guidance between appraisals. Even if he thinks he is, but they are not responding, his ineffectuality gives him a black eye.

He should get a strong message.

◊ 18

Appraisal time is coming up. I heard the other day that one of my employees has been regularly disappearing from his workplace for long periods of time. I think I have to confront him on this. He knows he's not supposed to leave for any length of time without getting my permission.

I don't recommend that you appraise an employee's performance on hearsay or circumstantial evidence. That resembles a kangaroo court. Confine your evaluation to evidence you have collected as a witness. As I usually say, evaluate the behavior that you have observed.

You might want to keep an eye open for further infractions of the rules by this employee. When you have the firsthand evidence that he disappears without permission, criticize him. Don't wait until the next evaluation.

Firing

◊ 19

I'm terminating an employee for misappropriation of funds. He wants me to tell everyone that he is resigning to take a better job offer. That's simply not true, but I hate to pile on more hurt.

Your terminated employee may be accustomed to fooling himself and trying to fool others, but there's no need for you to reinforce his charade. In fact, there is need for you not to do so. People may know about his theft. They'll wonder why you are covering up the incident.

At the same time, you don't need to, as you say, pile on more hurt. Confine your announcement to, "David Burns is leaving us. I know you all wish him well." Your words won't fool anyone, and they won't hurt, either.

⇨ 20

When I terminated one of my people, I offered her an office for the time being so she could conduct a job search. But the search goes on, and she's still here. It's embarrassing.

You know now that next time you should put a time limit on the occupancy. Do so in this case. Call her in and say that you need the office, and that you'll let her have, say, three more days. To soften the blow, offer to forward her mail and to have someone in the office take messages and relay them to her. That way it will look as if she is still part of your operation.

⇨ 21

I have to fire a nice guy who hasn't worked out well. I don't want him hurt any more than necessary. How do I tactfully announce his termination?

It would be considerate to ask him how he'd like it announced, but stay within the boundaries of reality. If he hasn't been successful on the job, other people know that, too. It's almost a parody to state, as some managers do, "I regret to announce that Ted will be leaving. We'll all miss him very much," and so on, and so on. If his leaving has to do with poor performance that is common knowledge, the following terse but considerate message does the job: "Craig is leaving us. I know you all join with me in wishing him the best."

Sometimes the terminated employee doesn't want any announcement. If other employees ask you what is happening, confine your comments to, "Craig's leaving." No embellishment is necessary.

Whatever announcement you decide on, stay with it. That's the big reason why you'll want to make sure at the outset that it is something you can stick with.

◊ 22

An employee whom I'm terminating because of poor performance wants me to issue a statement that implies he is leaving voluntarily, to take another job. I can't see any harm in it; still I'm hesitant.

Of course you're hesitant, because you know that no one will believe you. Why expose yourself to snickers? Since everyone knows the circumstances, the terminated employee won't gain anything except to fool himself. How about, "Seymour is leaving us. He's been with us a long time and made a lot of friends here. We all wish him the very best in his next position."

The primary considerations in the case of termination—never a painless situation—are dignity and credibility: the employee's dignity and your credibility.

◊ 23

I've fired a employee for rotten performance. Because he has been with the company for a long time, I gave him a grace period during which he was to start looking

for another job. But every couple of days he comes into my office trying to argue me out of the termination. I've had it.

I assume that by grace period you mean you have kept him on the payroll. That is a generous act, but you've apparently simply prolonged the pain—for both of you. You need to talk clearly with him. For example, "Chuck, if I didn't make myself understandable the other day, let me do it now. My decision to terminate you was irreversible. Nothing you can say will cause me to rescind it. Knowing that, you can decide whether you want to spend the remaining time in an exercise in futility or in getting another job."

If he persists in the futile exercise, arrange for him to take the rest of his pay in a lump sum and let him look for a job from home. At least threaten that action. Perhaps he'll finally give up.

Unacceptable Performance

⬦ **24**

My new salespeople undergo training in the home office before being sent back to their territories. Much of it is self-training. That is, the trainees know what they have to learn. It's up to them to get what they need. But my latest trainee is hanging back. He seems to believe that people are going to come to him and hand him what he needs.

Your new trainee may have problems taking responsibility for his own learning. Much of the education and training in this country are passive. Lecturers or trainers talk, and learners listen. If he is a product of such a system, he'll need more orientation. He may also have to be weaned from dependency. Explain clearly what you expect of him. Make sure he understands what the alternative will be, that he will certainly fail in his training. Then, as he tentatively begins to take some steps to learn, compliment him. If he doesn't heed your counsel, give him one more warning that you will have to terminate him if he doesn't take charge. You can't afford to send him back to the field if he won't take responsibility for himself.

◊ 25
I always hear from one subordinate, "No problem," when I ask him about a job he is doing. But almost every job gets fouled up.

If you have evidence—and you should—of such previous fumbling, present him with it: dates and results. Remind him that each time he had assured you there would be no problem. Tell him that in that department he no longer has credibility. You don't want him to answer your inquiries with, "No problem." From now on, you tell him, you'll expect a detailed and accurate report of progress as well as any potential or actual problems, and any further concealing of problems with glib and vague responses will be noted in his performance evaluation.

◊ 26
My supervisors all seem to be firefighters. They spend more time focusing on crises than on developing their

subordinates' talents and skills. Consequently, we have a lot of people who are underqualified.

Putting out fires is a reactive stance. It doesn't call for much leadership. In fact, the manager who is a firefighter is often avoiding taking leadership responsibility. If you want your supervisors to take the initiative in developing their subordinates' skills, you would be well advised to provide them with a model. Show them how you believe their people should be developed by developing your own supervisors. Then make it clear that you expect them to go and do likewise. Furthermore, let them understand that you will be evaluating them on their success in bringing their people up to qualification.

At the present time they probably don't know how to do what you want, and don't feel rewarded for trying to do their jobs. You can change all that.

⇨ 27
She's a bright subordinate, but she tends to get bogged down in details. She can't seem to see the forest for the trees. As a result, her work is often very late and incomplete.

She has what I call a worm's-eye view rather than a bird's-eye view. You're going to have to train her to see contexts. The first step is to impress on her that her effectiveness depends on her ability to develop a holistic perspective. She can't expect to receive good performance evaluations if her work continues to be late and incomplete.

The second step is to work with her in achieving this understanding of context. You could outline the objectives and goals for her at the time of assignment, but she needs to be independent of you. Thus, when you assign a task, try to get her to explain to you what it will look like at its successful completion, and what she believes she will have accomplished. Once she understands the overall picture, send her off to start the work, but agree to meet periodically to reassess and perhaps redefine the total picture. The meetings will also serve to enable you to monitor the time factor: Is she on schedule?

⇩ **28**

He had a good track record before I hired him, and superb references. But since he's been here, about six months, his work has been just plain mediocre.

Are you absolutely certain he had a good track record, or could it be that he did a good selling job? Those who backed him up are either his friends or people who were glad to be rid of him. I've seen people go from job to job with the ability to do a fantastic selling job—but with no talent for producing anything other than hype for themselves. Often, the people who had hired them were so embarrassed over having fallen for a con game that they gave good references to conceal the mistake, or out of relief at the departure of the nonproducer.

You have to consider the possibility. You also have to make absolutely sure that you have given him every chance. He needs a counseling session. Be prepared to take a great deal of time. You want to find out things he may not be happy to talk about. For example, what may have happened in his private life in the past six months that interfered with his ability to produce for you? What about the change in environment that may impede his effectiveness? Is there a problem in the working relationship between the two of you?

Insist on a specific plan for improvement. No vague promises are acceptable. Let the new man know that you believe the trial period is over, the transition has been long enough, and that if he wishes to make this job permanent, he must show desired results within such and such a time. Otherwise, you will become one of his next references.

▷ 29

Is there such a word as "excusaholic"? Because I have one employee who always has excuses for not giving me the work I want, or for missing important deadlines.

This employee will continue to offer excuses as long as he thinks they will keep him out of trouble. Of course, there is always the possibility that a reason for not getting the work done is beyond his control, and you might want to see whether it indicates a departmental problem you should correct. Otherwise, you have to be firm about what you want. Each time he offers a reason why he couldn't do what you wanted, impress on him the standard or goal that you've set. For example, he gives his excuse, and you respond, "I'm sorry to hear that you've had that trouble. I need to have this report done on Tuesday morning. Now, how are we going to get this done by the deadline?" He may have a suggestion that you can take seriously. If he does not, tell him he must agree to finish and deliver the assignment by Tuesday morning.

You're always ready to remove barriers that are real, and you're always open to suggestions to improve the work methods, but you are also always firm. You have a right to expect the work to be done how and when you want it done. Don't deviate from that message.

If he continues to be deficient, you must counsel and threaten discipline such as probation or termination. When he begins to understand that the old excuses won't carry him any farther, he'll drop them. Otherwise you'll drop him.

⋄ 30

I feel certain an employee is going to fail on an important job I gave him. I've made suggestions that would help, but he seems determined to do it his way. I can't afford to have this project fail.

If you have not done so already, set some subgoals for the remaining time period of the project. You need to have clear indicators that the work is progressing well or poorly. If the employee can't make the subgoals on schedule, you have an undisputed right to intervene with your suggested ways of doing the work. If the employee resists after having missed deadlines, you have an obligation to insist that your alternative suggestions be tried.

Subgoals and schedules are indispensable when an important job is delegated.

⋄ 31

When I hired Jack, I was convinced that he showed extraordinary promise. But on two special assignments I've given him, he's done mediocre work. I'm wondering whether I misjudged his potential.

You may not have misjudged his potential, but you may have overestimated his confidence or the speed at which he could realize that potential. Back up. Don't give him special assignments that may stretch him too far too fast. Let him take on more usual tasks and see how he does on those. If he does well, you can add more challenge gradually. Your expectations may have gotten you—and him—into trouble.

⬦ 32

A key employee failed miserably on a project, and now I see him shying away from taking risks. I'd like to help him get over the defeatism he feels.

Keep him working on tasks and responsibilities that you're sure he can handle. They'll form the basis of his confidence. Gradually, but very gradually, add more responsibility and risk. As he completes those successfully, positively reinforce him. You may have to let him know that you are there, available to him, as a resource in case he gets the jitters. It may take time, but he'll rebuild much of his confidence, unless he suffers another substantial setback.

It's very important that he not be made to feel guilty for his failure, even if he was responsible. Thus, the fewer references to what happened, the better. It's a subject you probably should never bring up, unless it serves an an important learning reference for the future.

⬦ 33

A salesman who has always been a leader in production has been slipping lately. He's a very proud man, and I hesitate to offend him by stepping in.

If he is proud, he undoubtedly knows he is in trouble and it hurts. Being proud, he doesn't ask you for help. But your obligations as a manager won't let you sit by and let him flounder simply because you worry about offending him. A manager I know, in a similar situation, finally did intervene, and the troubled employee said, "I wondered when you were going to say something." Your man may be wondering the same thing. It's not the time for cat and mouse, a game which, unfortunately, some managers unwittingly play.

Relieve as much of the stress as possible. Tell the salesman you want to come out for a talk—and to work, if you have time. I recommend that you get your discussion out of the way before working. In your conversation, stick to the future: "What has to happen for you to meet your goals?" Don't accept vague assurances, even from this veteran. Both of you need more specific antidotes.

⇨ 34

One of my supervisors has an employee who's a real loser, but the supervisor always wants to give this fellow one more chance. How can I move this supervisor to draw a line?

If the employee's performance is deficient, you have a right to require the supervisor to justify his treatment of the employee. Ask him to come to your office with his documentation on the employee. Have him show you where his methods have worked. If they have not, and the supervisor pleads for more time, you have at least two options: One, you can grant the time with a limit; or two, you can insist that the supervisor take immediate action to discipline, impose probation, or terminate. Of the two options, I would favor a time limit, after which it is clearly agreed that, if there is no improvement, more drastic action be taken. Get an agreement from the supervisor on both the time limit and the specific action to be taken.

◊ 35

One of our salespeople is great at submitting ideas for increasing sales to our field newsletter, but his own production record is mediocre. I hate to stop publishing good ideas, but I think we're encouraging him to devote more time to getting his name in print than to his selling.

If your other salespeople know about this fellow's mediocre production, they may not take his ideas very seriously. They may say to themselves, "If this guy's ideas are so great, why doesn't he apply them himself?"

Right now you are rewarding him for coming up with good ideas. You'll have to make it clear that, henceforth, your rewards will be based on good sales performance. For the moment, don't publish his contributions. Hint that you'll resume feeding them to the field when he turns in a better record.

For the long run, you might consider this man a potential sales trainer or manager. If his ideas are indeed useful for others, and if he can work well with them, he may be wasted as a salesperson.

◊ 36

One of my employees is a perfectionist, and it drives me crazy. She doesn't meet deadlines. I can't get finished work out of her until she is satisfied with it. How can I change her?

You can try to change her, but I don't think you'll get results other than more frustration for yourself. I would look for at least three kinds of tasks for this woman: One, give her detailed, demanding work for which other people don't have patience. This woman, I'm sure, has much patience. Two, give her long-term work that doesn't require her to meet a short deadline—reports, analyses, projections, the kind of work that you keep putting off because you don't have the time to do it, and work that other employees are not suited to do. Third, put her on committees where she can apply her brightness and ability to analyze.

Be careful, however, not to assign her to collaborative work with other employees whose methods are different. She will drive them crazy, too.

Perfectionists can be strong assets if you can match them with the work they do better than other people.

⇨ **37**

A very bright subordinate often disagrees with the way I want things done. I have to order her to follow instructions. Her work doesn't come out right, even though she says she did it my way. I suspect she's secretly screwing things up to get even with me, but I can't prove it.

Was it Oscar Wilde who said the gods punish us by answering our prayers? One explanation for the disappointing results could be that she *is* doing the work exactly the way you wanted it done and thereby showing you that she had reasons to disagree with you. Her way might indeed have been more effective.

There is, of course, the possibility that she is providing you with a textbook case of passive-aggressive behavior. She consents to do it your way, but finds ways of making it fail or not work.

If you can't prove either hypothesis, why don't you try bending a little? Listen to her more carefully and with less resistance than I suspect you show now. Find out why she wants to do things differently from your specifications. Why not let her have a crack at doing things her way for once, so long as she understands that you expect certain standards of performance and results to be followed? For example, her way shouldn't be expensively longer or require more resources to achieve the same results she'd get following your methods.

If she succeeds, you have a happy employee with desired results. If she does not, you have solid evidence on which to evaluate her and to convince her that you know what you're talking about.

⇩ 38

For 15 years one of my salespeople has been in the top three rankings. Now he's just turning in an average performance. How do I get him going again?

It may be a question of his having done essentially the same thing for all those years. He could be tired of it. There's little challenge left for him. He's made all the calls, heard all the objections, and recited all the presentations. What can you do for him now to enrich his work? It's time for you or someone he trusts and respects to sit down with him and find out what he wants to do, what would turn him on again. Perhaps his life has changed, or his health isn't what it was. His needs are probably different. For example, he has enough money and he has enjoyed enough glory. Now he'd like a different kind of responsibility. Can you use him as an internal consultant? Would he be good at providing training for others? Is he suitable for a management position?

Or does he just want to stay an average salesperson? Can you afford to let him? One solution might be to split his territory and give a portion to a young tiger.

He sounds as if he is very much worth salvaging. It also sounds as if someone should have sat down with him some time ago to learn what he wants to do with the rest of his life.

▷ 39

Lately the quality of his work has really fallen off substantially. The trouble is, he's my friend. It makes it awfully hard for me.

He makes it hard for you, not it. And he has to know that. You must deal with him as you would any other employee—for his sake, for yours, and for that of all the other employees who will be watching to see how you treat your friend.

If the performance problems have multiplied as you say, you must counsel this person, and right away. Perhaps the first thing you ought to do is let him know that you are dealing with him no differently from anyone else, just in case he thought he could ride on the friendship. But you can also let him know that, as a friend, you want to help him any way you can. However, don't use the friendship as a threat; that is, don't say that if he doesn't shape up, your friendship is at stake. He has a performance deficiency, and you must approach it as you would any such deficiency. He must know that if he does not improve, you will have to consider probation or termination, and you can add that, as a friend, that would cause you special anguish.

▷ 40

I have several unmotivated employees. How do I motivate them?

First, let me clear up some misconceptions you seem to have. The only unmotivated people are dead people. Thus, what you're really saying is that your subordinates are not motivated to do what you want them to do. And you don't motivate anyone but yourself. You can, however, stimulate motivating forces in others.

Here are five guidelines for managers who want to increase the motivation of employees:

1. **Tell employees what you expect them to do.** State your goals and your standards clearly so employees know what you expect of them. Do this on a periodic basis.

2. **Make the work valuable.** As much as possible, assign the kind of work that you believe the employee enjoys doing the most, and that will help employees achieve their personal goals as well as yours.

3. **Make the work doable.** Make sure that employees have confidence in their ability to do the work well. If they worry about this, they become demotivated.

4. **As employees try to do what you expect, give them feedback.** They need to know what to continue to do and what not to continue to do. So give them positive and negative feedback consistently.

5. **When they've done what you expected them to do, reward them—always.** Praise them, give them perks, more money, more responsibility, and let them know that their reward is for their performance.

Motivation is complex, but if you follow the above guidelines, you'll never go wrong.

◊ 41

Recently I instituted a weekly performance reporting system for my supervisors. But the reports don't come in on time, and some don't come in at all unless I go to the supervisors and stand there while they complete them—and then they're often inaccurate. How can I make these supervisors give me what I'm entitled to?

It sounds to me as if what you're getting is what your supervisors believe you are entitled to. My sense of it is that they're registering their unhappiness with either the reporting system, the way you instituted it, or both. You can continue to insist and to stand over them, but I suspect you will also continue to be frustrated.

Try sitting down with your supervisors as a group and explaining what you want and why. Then ask them to help you design a reporting system that will give you what you want and won't be an unbearable burden on them. Bringing them into the decision-making process will give them ownership of the new system and eliminate their need to rebel against what they seem to consider your imposition.

⬦ 42

I've just replaced a manager who left the company. Bill, one of his key people, enjoyed a close relationship with him. Unfortunately, Bill's work is not up to my standards. Yet he continues to believe he is special. In fact, he's a headache.

The antidote for this kind of headache is not as fast-working as aspirin. Bill continues to work at the old level of performance because he believes it is acceptable. No doubt your predecessor did accept it. You have to tell Bill, and everyone else in the department, what you expect—your goals and standards. After a time, preferably sooner than later, Bill will realize that he will not be rewarded for working at a lower level. Continue to emphasize your goals and standards, criticize Bill when he doesn't meet them, counsel him if the problem becomes habitual, and terminate him if he proves he won't do the job. Don't single out Bill. That's the way you should treat everyone in your department.

If you don't want Bill's friendship, which he is likely to exploit, maintain a strict working relationship with him. He'll be looking for favored treatment, such as privileges and extra time with you. If you do extend such treatment to him, make sure it is because Bill has learned to work according to your standards, not because he's a nice guy and plays up to you. In time, Bill will learn how to truly get on your good side, and you'll both benefit.

Unacceptable Behavior

⬦ **43**
I hired a bright young MBA who does fine work, but who is abrasive and arrogant with other employees. How can I take the cutting edge off his behavior?

Young people tend to develop sensitivity toward others when they find that it helps them to accomplish what they want. Unfortunately, for many it is a trial-and-error experience. If you have a mature work group, one that deals effectively and collaboratively with one another, they'll eventually blunt that cutting edge so long as they don't see you trying to protect him in any way. They may test you at first, to see how you might react to their approaches with him. For example, one of your employees who feels comfortable with you will mention him critically. If you seem to agree that the problem is real, the word will get around that it's okay to give him a little feedback on his offensive behavior.

Coach him on behavior you see as offensive. Don't, however, try to sandbag him with what you've heard from others. He probably displays some abrasive behavior even with you, and you can tell him what impact it has on you.

◊ 44

One of my supervisors hoards jobs instead of delegating them to his people. He says he can do them better and faster than his subordinates. Meanwhile, I think his people are underworked and he is overworked.

This man does not seem to understand that a high-priority aspect of any manager's job is to help his or her employees be effective. But it sounds very much as if they do not get to do the work they are capable of doing, and they don't get a chance to stretch themselves. This manager's people are probably already suffering from demotivation, and he can't recognize the danger.

You'll have to persuade him to recognize it. Set goals with him that involve giving extra assignments to his people. Once the goal is set for delegating, you have to evaluate his performance at the next appraisal time. When he sees that his rating as a supervisor depends in large part on his distributing his heretofore hoarded jobs, he'll have to change.

Don't, however, wait until the next appraisal to give him feedback on how well or poorly he delegates. He needs monitoring and interim feedback. After all, he's been behaving in a certain way for a long time, and it's going to take a lot of encouragement—and pushing, perhaps—to get him to change his ways.

◊ 45

One of my employees, who has a sales business on the side, takes orders and solicits over the office phone. He's a good man, but I can't allow this.

He probably doesn't realize that he is engaged in a form of stealing: He steals time and telephone costs. He is also undoubtedly angering the people he works with by taking time away from his job to make extra money.

If you've observed him doing personal business, tell him that it won't be permitted. If you've heard about it but not seen it, ask whether he has been doing it. If he admits it, give him the message: No longer. If he hasn't been, tell him you're sorry that you acted on a rumor, but that you thought it was important to check. He'll get the message.

⊳ 46
What's your advice on coping with an employee who comes into my office and loses his temper?

The first thing you do is close the door. You don't want the rest of the office to witness the spectacle.

If the tirade seems to be unfocused, you might regard it as symptomatic of a bigger problem. The employee has experienced an overload, and it may take patience on your part to sit out the blast to find out what the background might be. The trigger might be quite incidental and minor.

Let the employee get it all out before you start probing for the cause. Listen. Accept the person's feelings. Encourage the employee to express everything that's causing pain and anger. Then get the employee's help in finding out what's causing the disturbance. If the reason is legitimate, you can change the situation. If it is not something you have control over, the employee has at least gained a little self-knowledge. Perhaps the employee can begin to work on a personal problem.

Admittedly, it is tough to sit there calmly while you are the target. Your consolation, and your calming device, is the knowledge that you may, in fact, not be the target. You and the employee both need to define what the real problem is.

▷ 47

She's always making excuses for being late to work—car trouble, late baby-sitter. How can I get her to come to work on time?

When she comes in late, call her to remind her that you want her to arrive on time. When she offers her excuse, you respond, "Yes, I understand, but I want you to be here on time." Repeat that each time she presents an excuse. Eventually she'll stop the excuses. If she says, "I'll try," you reply, "I want you here on time. Trying is not enough."

She may say, desperately, "I'll do my best. I can't do better than that." If so, you say, "I want you here on time. I won't accept less. If you continue to be late, I'll have to suspend (terminate) you. Do you understand?"

Make a record of the interview. You should have documentation covering each previous warning.

If her lateness continues, take the action you promised.

▷ 48

An employee got mad at me because I didn't give her an assignment she thought she ought to have, and she told me off. That's insubordination. Am I justified in firing her?

In my lexicon, insubordination means that an employee refuses to do what the manager requests. If this employee performs well, she isn't insubordinate just because she loses her temper in her disappointment. You may feel she is disrespectful, but that's not necessarily a firing offense.

Perhaps you ought to look more closely at her complaint. If she feels that strongly about that kind of work, she may well be suited for it. And ask yourself why she thought she ought to have it. Did she misconstrue your words to imply that she would get the assignment?

◊ 49
My department has a washroom lawyer who is always advising people or giving them the "real story." He's a nuisance and full of baloney. I'd like to find a way to silence this know-it-all.

I think you have to ask yourself why this person is listened to, even though he is wrong now and then. He couldn't function unless he told people what they want to hear. Either they don't believe they are getting information from management, or they don't trust what they do get. It's also possible that this man gives an antimanagement slant to the information he passes along.

All of which should give you much to think about. If you want to undercut his importance and effectiveness, don't move against him directly. He sounds as if he is already a hero; don't make him a martyr. Go into competition with him, instead. Be more free with your information, which should be more accurate than his. If you are open and on target, people will grow to trust your pipeline. Be more accessible to your employees. They must be able to come to you when they have a problem or a question. And when they come, treat their problems and questions with respect, even if their concerns are short of the mark.

It may not be so easy to counteract the antimanagement sentiments, if they exist. It will take you time to learn whether they do exist, and on what they are based. The us-versus-them resentment and suspicion take time to eliminate. You can make a good start by being open and receptive.

◊ 50

One of my supervisors frequently cries wolf. He comes to me with crises—at least he thinks that's what they are. I calm him down by showing him that things are not as serious as he thinks. But a couple of days later he's back with another crisis.

And he'll probably continue to come to you with his crises so long as you are willing to reward him for doing so. He gets to sit there watching you do all the work, figuring out what he should do. Next time he comes to you with the cry of wolf, make him explain to you why he thinks he is facing a crisis. Then ask him to tell you what he plans to do about the situation. Refrain from suggesting options yourself. When he comes up with possible solutions, reinforce them and encourage him to apply them. When he does apply them, reward his accomplishment with some praise.

It may be that he lacks confidence. You can help him to build up confidence by encouraging him to develop solutions that work, which you won't do if, like the villagers in the fable, you rush to his aid.

◊ 51

He's a smart supervisor; that is, he knows the work inside out. But he's insensitive and upsets the people with whom he works. I've tried to discuss it with him, but he doesn't understand what I'm talking about.

Sometimes it's difficult for people who are insensitive to others to know what you mean by telling them they should be sensitive, and why they should care.

Your feedback to him should involve specific experiences in which he has been involved, has shown insensitivity, and has not achieved the right results. Then you must also be prepared to show him the kind of behavior that might have done a better job. He'll probably be resistant, but if you can show him how and why he has been ineffective, he'll begin to listen to you. Don't give him too many examples to work on at one time; you'll overload and demoralize him.

The closer the examples of less-than-desirable results are tied to performance evaluation, the greater the impact you'll have on him.

It will take time, but you have to unfreeze the old behavior, which he believes has been rewarded, and substitute a new behavior, which you will reward him for practicing.

◊ 52

One of the engineers in my department has become so active in his professional association that he is taking a lot of time off from work. He's brilliant, and the recognition he gets professionally is great for his ego. But sometimes he's not around for me, and I resent it.

Some managers resolve this conflict by simply banning outside involvement, but I've always thought that such peremptory action was shortsighted and self-defeating. The active professional not only provides good PR for his organization, but often has channels of communication that bring technical and competitive information back to the organization. In my field, training, people who are active in the American Society for Training and Development often hear about the latest tools and trends and leading-edge developments ahead of their more isolated peers.

At the same time, you have a right to expect a certain level of performance from your celebrity. Assuming that you'd like to enjoy some of the benefits I've suggested in the preceding paragraph, and that he wants to retain his job, it seems that some negotiation is in order. Sit down with him and ask him to tell you how he sees his outside involvement helping him on the job and increasing his value to you. He is obliged to think along those lines. Then explain what you need from him in the way of performance. Finally, ask, "How can we both get what we want?" He wants his outside activity, and you want his inside expertise. Agree on how much time he needs outside and how much time you can afford to give him. That agreement should constitute a contract between you, and barring unforeseen circumstances and emergencies, you should both be prepared to abide by it. You may both emerge as winners; you will be seen by others in the profession as a very enlightened boss, a person for whom it would be great to work.

⯈ 53
My assistant has become very pushy. I think ambition is getting the best of him. I'm sure he'd like to take over my job, but I'm not ready to let him.

Why don't you create a new place for him? He's flexing his muscles. He wants to show off. Let him. Give him a job to do that you haven't been able to give to anyone else because it would require special drive and talent. Think of a serious or nagging problem on which you'd like to concentrate some brains, or a possible innovation you just haven't had time to map out. Here's a man who is lusting for additional responsibility so he can prove he's ready to move up. Many managers would make the mistake of trying to put a cap on his ambition. You should, instead, turn him loose to apply all that energy to something for which you'll get the glory. If he thinks he is ready to move up, and he doesn't get that chance with you, he'll probably move out in time. But while you've got him, get the most you can from him.

⇨ 54
One of my supervisors is far too democratic for my taste. I think he's going to extend too much power and freedom to his people and get himself in trouble. Then I'm going to have to clean up his mess.

I can only assume that if you haven't had to clean up any messes so far, this man must be delivering for you. Thus, it isn't his record of mistakes or failures that you have to contend with, but your anxiety over what might happen. Why not share your concerns with him? You don't want to fix an operation that isn't broken—yet. Let him know that even though you don't much care for his style of managing, you still respect the fact that he is doing a good job. However, if his style of managing is ever the reason for his getting into trouble, you'll hold him accountable. That's a fair statement. Of course, if a problem does occur in his operation, you must take care to be sure that it occurred primarily because of the way he deals with his people before you do hold him accountable.

The responsibility rests on both of your shoulders: his, to make sure that his style doesn't create trouble; and yours, to ascertain that the troubles that do occur are indeed the result of his managing style.

◇ 55

An employee goofed seriously on an assignment. Now he talks and rationalizes about it a lot. I'd like to steer him away from his obsession.

Give him some reasonable listening time. But as he talks, especially as he tries to rationalize his mistakes, insist that he answer the question, "What did you learn that will help you in the future?" Don't argue with his rationalizations. That won't do him any good, and it will waste your time. Keep him focused on what he can salvage from the experience. Eventually he'll tire of the repetition. Hasten that time by keeping him busy.

◇ 56

I'm about to get an employee on a transfer from another department. I've heard he can be very troublesome and hard to manage. I've thought about letting him know from the outset that I won't tolerate any problems from him.

You're about to convict him on hearsay. You don't really know the conditions that surrounded his work, and the relationships that may have contributed to any troublesome behavior. If you start him off with your negative expectations, he may very likely fulfill them. He'll say, "There's no way I can win here. I'm already judged."

Give him the same starting breaks you give everyone else. Tell him what standards of performance you expect. Let him know that if he performs well, he'll be recognized and rewarded. You needn't add that if he doesn't turn in a good performance, you'll take corrective action. He'll hear that message anyway.

He may be looking for a brand-new chance. You may be surprised to find that you have an exceptional performer because you gave him that chance.

If he demonstrates the behavior you've already heard about, you know how to deal with him—but you may not have to.

⬦ 57
How do I approach one of my subordinates who is always talking with another employee or reading a newspaper or a magazine? I just don't think it looks good in an office.

The first question you should deal with is this: Is the employee doing the work you expect him to do? If the answer is no, then you must approach him on his inadequate performance. Require him to meet your standards, or face discipline or termination. If he is performing up to par, then he may be capable of taking on more. But don't just pile work on him; that may be seen as punishment on your part. Find some interesting, challenging tasks for him to do. Consider that he may be bored with his present work load. If, after doing well for you, he still has time for socializing and reading, let those activities be his reward for the good work.

⬦ 58
Two of my subordinates have been feuding so long they don't remember what started it all. I think it's childish, and I'd like to put a stop to it.

If their feuding disrupts their effectiveness and/or that of the department, you should take steps to stop it. Call each subordinate in for a private session. Explain what you see going on that creates a deficiency in performance. Then describe the changes in behavior that you want. Stay away from any adjectives that imply attitudes or motivations, for example, "You are stubborn," or, "You are contentious." Discuss only behaviors—those you see now, and those you want. Let each know that their next good appraisal depends on their changing.

But don't try to persuade them to like each other. It isn't necessary, and it may not be possible.

◊ 59

A subordinate is furious with me because I didn't give her a raise. She's a mediocre performer who has always gotten increases from other managers. But I've tied raises to performance, and she didn't merit one. I can't afford to have her sulking in my department.

Neither can she afford such behavior, if her future raises are tied to performance. You might gently let her know that. Then explain to her clearly what she has to do to get an increase. If she is still operating at her old level of performance, believing that level to be adequate, she needs to be educated. Offer her whatever help she needs that is reasonable: coaching, training, guidance, and so on. She's a potentially valuable resource you'd like to upgrade.

If it's possible, set another appraisal session for an earlier date than what would be usual. Perhaps you can give her a token raise at that time if she improves sufficiently. Between now and then, praise her attempts to raise her level of quality and quantity. After all, you have to overcome years of conditioning and acceptance of mediocrity.

▷ 60

What do I do about an employee who is forever coming into my office complaining about minor things? Nothing seems to satisfy her.

If she complains about different things as opposed to one thing over and over again, I suspect that the substance of the complaints is not as important as her need to get your attention. If she does good work, do you let her know on a regular basis that you appreciate that good work? If you compliment her on her work, and reward the performance, you'll probably find that her complaints will fall off.

If the complaints don't fall off, and if you're confident that they are not serious or well founded, make it more difficult for her to take up your time. Explain to her that you are in the middle of a task, that you cannot stop to listen to her, and suggest that she try later when you might have some time. You may not be able to shut the complaints off entirely—and you shouldn't. Some may be worth investigating. But you will stop rewarding her by listening each time to her apparent bids for attention.

▷ 61

One supervisor I inherited when I took over this department is an old-fashioned, bull-of-the-woods type. He gets the job done, but his style is so offensive to me that I want him to change it.

Why do you insist that he change? If he is doing the job in his autocratic manner, the fact that you have a different managerial style is not sufficient reason for you to try to make him do his work differently. It's probable that he has built a trusting relationship with his people. They know him. He is predictable. They may even believe he is fair in his own tough manner.

The most important consideration is whether or not he meets your standards of performance. It sounds as if he does. If it isn't broken. . . .

▷ 62

I have an employee who thinks he's a clown. He can be funny, but the problem is that most of his jokes are directed at me—in public. At first I went along with it, and laughed like everyone else. But I'm worried that he's ridiculing me, although he plays innocent. On the other hand, I don't want to come across as a prig.

I hope you're no longer laughing at his little jokes, because, when you do, you encourage him to continue. If you don't laugh, other employees will soon get the message that you don't regard him as funny, and they will stop laughing, too. Soon he won't feel that he is seen as a jolly fellow. He may stop.

But he may not. If he doesn't, it's a pretty good sign that he is expressing something—hostility, envy, discontent, and so on. It may be a message you need to hear, but since it is cloaked in humor, you can't understand it clearly. Call him in for a private chat. You might say something such as, "Al, when you crack your jokes about me, I get uncomfortable because I think you're trying to tell me something about me or the operation that I need to hear. But I'm not sure what it is. So why don't you tell me straight out what's on your mind? If something is wrong, maybe we can fix it." You may shake loose some useful information. You may not. But you'll put Al on notice that his humor isn't working with you.

If Al persists, assume that he is working out some hostility toward you. He won't tell you what it is, but you can tell him his behavior is creating some bias in you, even though out of fairness you're fighting it. If that doesn't work, suggest that he might wish you to put in a transfer for him.

Promoting

⌂ 63
I promoted a woman beyond her competence. But each time I give her feedback on her failures and mistakes, she tells me I'm treating her unfairly because she is a woman, that I would be more tolerant if she were a man.

In the early days of the feminist movement, many women came to believe that they were promoted to fail, that men would give them more responsibility, confident that the women really couldn't handle it. The women would fail, and the men would say, "Well, you see, women aren't cut out for this."

Your woman subordinate may have concerns that you are setting her up to fail. Your protests aren't sufficient, should she decide to file an action against you for discrimination. Your records must tell the story. Build up documentation of your criticism and counseling sessions with her. You'll need some corroboration that the males in similar positions have indeed performed better and taken hold of their new responsibilities faster. If you don't have clear corroboration, I would advise you to exhaust every possible avenue of assistance for this woman before you demote or terminate her.

Your conscience and good intentions are not enough. You may need to prove you gave her every chance you'd give a man.

⇨ **64**

Last year I promoted an excellent salesman to district manager, but he isn't working out. How can I get him to go back to the field where I need him? I'd hate to embarrass him.

How do you believe he feels right now? I suppose by now he is aware that he is not making the grade. Therefore, he is frustrated, embarrassed, and perhaps angry at himself and at you for getting him into this fix.

Most likely he could use some straight, caring talk—straight in the message that he isn't cut out for the job. It was a gamble for both of you, and it didn't turn out right. There's no shame in that. There's probably never any way to predict managerial success.

That having been said, now comes the caring: "We want you. Nothing would grieve us more than to lose a good man." What are your options? New business development? National accounts manager? Or a very desirable territory? Make the announcement something like this: "We're very pleased to tell you that Charles Phillips is assuming the Atlanta territory. He's making the choice because, as Charlie tells us and has proved beyond doubt, selling is his first love. We're happy to have Charlie where he's happy."

After the move, find ways to treat Charlie in a special way. Call him now and then to chat, or to ask his opinion on something. Visit him and treat him to dinner. Ask him to conduct part of the program at the next sales meeting. Make him feel exceptional, because, you see, he really is, having been able to step aside gracefully.

⇨ **65**

One of my best salespeople has just turned down my second invitation to be promoted. He says he likes the

trenches and want to stay there. I think he'd be a superb manager, but I don't know how to persuade him.

I wouldn't try. He knows himself better than you know him, and he's doing what he wants to do—and obviously doing it quite well. He'll continue to sell well until he grows tired of it. Watch for signs of fatigue in his declining performance. In the meantime, let him know in a nonpressuring way that you'll be glad to talk to him about a job change whenever he wants. And while you can't promise him that you'll have a position open at that moment, you're always ready to talk.

⇨ 66

I'm thinking about promoting Jean to section supervisor, but Marge, who I think would like the job, has told me that Jean is great in getting other people to do her work for her and that the other women don't like her. I don't know how much to believe. I'm not sure now whether I should go through with the promotion, although I need a supervisor.

No matter how much you need a supervisor, you're not ready to promote Jean. You don't know enough about her. It may be true that Marge is passing along some half truths, especially if, as you suspect, she would like the job. What is puzzling is what persuaded you to believe that Jean has supervisory potential. If she has genuinely demonstrated an ability to manage the work of others, then you might want to test that ability a bit more before you make a final decision. If you could give Jean a piece of supervisory responsibility on a temporary basis, you might be able to see how well she can perform in that capacity. Ask her to take on a special temporary project that would require her to work with others, or ask her to train an employee, or to act as supervisor, until you've made a decision. Of course, everyone, including Jean, would have to understand that the acting supervisor might not be the one to be promoted ultimately. (The problem with the last option is that, if you don't decide on Jean, you may lose her. But then you might have discovered that she is indeed expendable).

Monitor Jean's work while she is performing the temporary task or is serving as acting supervisor. You'll be able to tell how well she can supervise others by the results she achieves—or doesn't achieve. And if the women are averse to working for her, they'll find a way to let you know.

▷ **67**
How do you handle an employee who asks to be promoted to a job for which she isn't qualified? She's a good worker now, and I don't want to demotivate her.

I suggest that your speech go something like this: "I know you want the promotion, but I can't do it. You don't have the qualifications for that position. Here's what I mean." Then describe the necessary qualifications. If she insists that she does have them, you can respond, "I haven't seen them." Perhaps the two of you should decide on how she can demonstrate the qualifications by having her agree to take on certain kinds of responsibilities that will give you the chance to see her talents in action.

On the other hand, you may be satisfied that she does not have the skills to handle the job. If you suspect she has the potential, offer to work with her to develop it. If you're convinced the job she wants is all wrong for her, give her help in planning for another kind of advancement. For example, you could say,

"You're much better qualified for this other kind of promotion. There's no opening now, but I'd be willing to help you prepare for such a promotion when it does open up."

⬦ 68

A supervisor I promoted from the clerical staff six months ago constantly brings her problems to me. How can I discourage her from always running to me to solve her problems?

One thing you might do is to stop solving her problems for her. People do what they feel rewarded for doing. In her case, the reward is that she doesn't have to deal with her own troubles or challenges. She has a friendly, accommodating boss who will do that for her.

The next time she comes to you and describes a difficulty, listen without commenting while she talks, and then say, "What do you think is the best way to handle that?" You may have to coach her through the solution-finding process, but make her do the actual solving. Eventually she may come to realize that you're not going to do her job for her anymore. She'll probably cut down on the visits to your office.

If she continues, however, you must make clear at her next evaluation that she needs to develop the ability to solve problems and experiment with solutions on her own. You will have substituted a new reward for her: a good evaluation if she acts on her own.

⬦ 69

I promoted one of my best claims clerks to claims supervisor. But she continues to spend time doing her

former kind of work when I think she should be supervising, checking, and training. How can I get her to start functioning as a supervisor?

Chances are that the reason she won't let go of her former job is either that she doesn't know what she is supposed to do as a supervisor, or that she doesn't feel confident she can do the job.

Your first step is to sit down with her and explain what you expect of her—your goals and standards, or rather, your *joint* goals and *your* standards. Be detailed and take time to make sure she understands her new duties. Then ask her to tell you how she intends to work—her methods and techniques. You'll be able to get some idea of how confident she is. If she seems hesitant to talk or has reservations about aspects of her new responsibility, you may want to provide some training or coaching. Don't let her walk out of your office not knowing where to turn.

After your interview, you'll have to monitor her activity. If she continues to fail to do her proper job, you'll have to call her in for criticism and a reminder of the goals and standards on which she will be appraised. If your informal criticism doesn't work, schedule a counseling session. If that isn't successful, you must choose to demote or terminate. You cannot leave her in a job she can't or won't handle.

⇩ 70

I have a promising, ambitious employee I cannot promote for a time. I worry that I will lose him in the interim.

You are less likely to lose him if you keep him challenged while he waits for a promotion. One possibility is to let him head up a task force to work on an important problem or project. That way you can give him authority he wouldn't otherwise have.

Another is to make him an unofficial assistant and delegate some of your responsibility to him. A third is to provide him with some training that he regards as valuable to him in building knowledge and skills. If he is truly on a fast track, you do indeed risk losing him if you cannot eventually promote him. But you may forestall that possibility if you can keep him in a challenging, exciting job that provides learning and growth for him.

⊅ 71

I promoted an excellent field sales manager to national sales manager. But now that he's in the home office, I can't get him out. He's always pleading that he has too much work to do inside to get out in the field.

It's not unusual for salespeople to come in from the cold and find that they like the warmth of the home office. He has fallen into an activity trap, and chances are he will continue to find good reasons not to leave his desk.

You're going to have to establish some performance standards with him. He needs to know what you consider to be a reasonable proportion of field versus home office time. Once he realizes that his evaluation will be based in part on his activities in the field, he should respond. Incidentally, he may not be using his administrative resources in the home office. He may not be delegating work to his subordinates. If so, that's something else on which you will have to coach him.

There is a more serious problem you should be prepared to face: The new national job may appear too big for him to handle. It probably isn't, but you'll have to deal with his perception that it is. You're the coach. Help him work out the right moves that will build his confidence. You'll probably have to stay close to him during the initial period while he learns he can do the job.

Employee Resistance

⇩ 72

How do you deal with a man who is just plain hostile? He can do good work, but if I ask him to do something different, he's very stubborn.

It's important not to take the hostility personally. He's probably carrying around a lot of old baggage. If he speaks harshly and offensively to you, say, "I'm sorry you feel that way. I don't see how you'll benefit by offending me. Think that over."

You don't have to turn the other cheek, but don't respond in kind. For hostile people, hostility from others often helps them justify their own negative outlook and reaction.

If he resists, let him know the negative consequences of that resistance. He isn't privileged. He's just bad-tempered. He can't arbitrarily turn down responsibilities. But if he does well, give him lots of praise.

⇩ 73

Some people seem to hate deadlines. They just won't meet them, and it drives me crazy.

Me, too. With a known deadline-misser, I set the time limit early, giving us both a cushion. Thus, if I need the work done by Friday, I'll set the deadline for Tuesday or Wednesday. Sometimes it works.

An additional step may be needed. Set subgoals or interim deadlines so that you can monitor the progress. You may not always be able to enforce the deadline, but you can see by how much you might miss it. There's no point waiting till the last minute to find out how late your subordinate will be. And you can apply a bit of pressure at each time marker.

Of course, for some people the pressure will not work. As you say, there are those who are constitutionally unable to bring the work in on time, even though their quality of performance is otherwise superb. For others, the problem could stem from carelessness and/or laziness. In such cases, the progress markers or subgoals will be helpful, and the knowledge that an employee's observance of deadlines will be a matter for the performance evaluation may bring about a desirable change in behavior.

⇨ 74

One of my better employees resists having work delegated to her. She says her regular workload is all she can handle. I don't agree. I think she is quite able to handle more, and should.

Often when employees resist delegated work, they do so for one of two reasons. The first is that they see the tasks primarily as simply more work. Their perception is that, "Around here if you do a good job, they let you do more." Present the work as a reward for what she has done in the past, and show her how it can contribute to increased status and esteem. Not only will others respect her more highly, but she'll have an enhanced feeling about herself. You might want to say that she is under no obligation to accept the increased responsibility, but that your esteem for her is sufficiently high that you wanted to give her the first choice.

Another reason why employees duck delegated work is that they are secretly worried they cannot handle it successfully. They don't want to fail or look foolish. You may want to provide some coaching or training, or direct her to resources that will back her up, or present yourself as someone always available to guide her. If you can remove her self-doubts, you'll probably find she is eager to take on more challenging assignments.

Of course, if she continues to resist despite your best efforts, you have to decide whether she is sufficiently valuable to you just doing her regular work.

⬦ 75

One subordinate is very reluctant to take on anything new. She's always protesting she won't do a very good job, and I ought to give it to someone who is sure to do a better job than she.

Back in the days of Transactional Analysis, this game was called "kick me." Basically the player felt incompetent and begged off. Because you want the job done well, you might unwittingly have become a player.

Here's how not to be sucked in. First, don't rush to agree with the employee's self-assessment. Ask questions about what she means when she says she can't do the job. Insist on her being specific with you: "Where do these negative feelings come from?" She'll probably answer that her record isn't good, that she does dumb things or fouls up. You respond that there's nothing unique about that. Everyone does dumb things and fouls up.

If she is incompetent, she has to understand that you can't tolerate that. She'll have to show you a plan for improvement. And you can start with how she will do the job you originally wanted her to do. Insist on it.

⬦ 76

When I took over this department a short time ago, my predecessor told me about one employee "who's a real

pain," and said I should keep an eye on him. How much of the employee's past should I consider in judging his present performance?

If this employee has had a bad relationship with your predecessor, he'll be looking for signs of suspicion and distrust in you. Start from scratch, giving him the same chance you give everyone else. Reserve your judgment until you see how he performs for you. When you evaluate him, don't refer to past appraisals. Incidentally, convey your belief that this man wants to do a good job. Your positive approach may encourage him to fulfill your expectation.

Even after your fairness and hopeful outlook, the employee may repeat many of the troublesome behaviors that he demonstrated with his previous boss. But you'll have the consolation that his failure to change is truly his, and can't be traced to your prejudice.

⇨ 77

Some time ago, I took an employee from another department where his manager thought he was inept. Under me he performed moderately well, and he and I were both pleased. Maybe I praised him too much, but now he is so puffed up, I can't tell him anything. I think I've created a monster.

It's possible that you praised him extravagantly, but it's more probable that he was just so parched for that praise that he would have soaked up any amount. Now he has found a way to compensate for the negative feelings he must have had about himself before by cloaking himself in your remembered praise.

If he is not performing well, you're going to have to explain what he should be doing that he is not. Don't try to penetrate his cloak with a detailed discussion of where he is falling down. Start from the point of what you expect, then explain the gap between that and what he is doing now.

He'll probably argue with you. Keep repeating what you insist he do. Don't let him sidetrack you with his protests. Stay on the track: "I understand how you feel, but this is what you must do." Then fire the last zinger: "I have to warn you that if you do not perform the way I want, I'm going to have to put you on probation (terminate you)." Follow up to make sure he does as you wish. If he doesn't, make good on your threats. Otherwise, he—and others—will not believe you again.

▷ 78
How do you deal with an employee who does good work but always needs specific directions and is defensive about it?

Try letting her tell you how she will do the job. When she has finished, question those methods or steps you don't agree with or suspect may not be as effective as she anticipates. Your attitude should be one of negotiation: "Let's see how we can work together to get this job done in a cost-effective manner." There's not much point in being firm and unilateral unless you know that her suggested way of doing things will not work. Give her the room you can afford to give her, and that means also giving her the benefit of any doubt.

Set subgoals so that you can measure progress. That schedule will also help you to monitor the success of her methods. If they are plainly linked to delay and error, you can show her that they are not working and recommend an alternative.

⬦ 79

I've made certain rules that I believe help the operation to run more smoothly. Most people observe them without any problem, but one man makes a fuss. He doesn't always follow the rules. He says they are not practical, that he doesn't think it's worth the fuss I make.

I'd make a deal with him. If he can come up with rules that do the job better, substitute his for yours. But you'd have to be convinced that they are better. If he can't come up with superior alternatives, you have a right to expect him to observe your rules. End of discussion.

⬦ 80

I like to do postmortems after mistakes, to learn from what we did wrong. One of my key people, however, says that we ought to bury them and go on. How can I convince him that what we learn from the past we apply in the future?

He may be nervous because many postmortems become "whodunnits." Finger-pointing may inhibit the learning. The question that should be asked is not so much, "What went wrong and how?" but rather, "What can we learn from the mistake that we can apply or avoid in the future?" If you keep the focus on the future, you're less likely to aggravate old wounds, or to make people believe you're witch-hunting.

Another approach is to announce that you're less concerned with the causes of the failure than with what alternative you'd follow in a similar situation next time.

◇ 81

He's a good employee, but he won't take directions from me. He wants to do things his way. We have a lot of conflict over my insistence that he follow instructions.

It sounds as if there is no middle course between the path he wants to follow and the one you believe he should take. Perhaps there *is* room for some negotiating: "Okay, tell me how you want to do it, I'll tell you how I want you to do it, and we'll see if we can compromise."

If that isn't feasible, you can look forward to continuing conflict. You may have to let him risk failure. A wise man said to me once, "You can't know what you can do until you know what you can't do." He might have to fail before he understands the value of listening to you. Give him free rein on a project the failure of which won't mean disaster. If he can't pull if off his way, the two of you should have a talk about where he went wrong. This man sounds as if he doesn't like failure. He seems proud. One failure ought to soften him up, make him more open to your suggestions, so long as you go easy on the I-told-you-so stuff.

If he succeeds using his own methods, then perhaps you ought to listen to him more carefully and generously.

◇ 82

One of my employees frequently comes to me for suggestions on how to do this or that, but he never seems to put any of them to work. I think I'm going to tell him next time that if he doesn't take any of my advice, he should stop taking up my time.

You probably need to offer the time without the suggestions. If he doesn't apply your suggestions, he must think they are not as good as he can get elsewhere, or as good as his own. Cut down on your exasperation by encouraging him to talk about what he needs and how he sees the job. With your help, he'll probably come up with solutions on his own. You know enough to help him think things through. You also provide a nice sounding board, and you have enough experience to tell him whether or not what he wants to do is practical. Stop feeding him your answers and nourish his looking for his own.

Remember, he respects and values you; otherwise he wouldn't come to you.

Older Employees

▷ 83
I'm a young manager in my 30s, saddled with a department with a number of employees in their late 50s or early 60s. They are not my best workers.

There's no reason why you should have to put up with performance that is below reasonable standards. It's true that old-timers slack off sometimes, but it's also true that they get away with it only if the managers allow it. You may not be able to stoke up their former enthusiasm, but you can certainly shake them out of their torpor.

First, let them know your standards and your goals, and that you expect them to make the contribution they're capable of making. Many of these people are security-conscious, holding onto their jobs to increase their pensions. They aren't blind to the possibility that you can build a case against them if they don't produce.

Next, expose these people to new stimuli. They may well have been frozen doing the same kinds of things for years. Find new responsibilities for them. Don't exclude them from training. They have a lot to offer any training group. And perhaps some of them would be suitable as trainers.

Third, get these people in positions where they interact with younger people. Some of these old-timers not only have much knowledge and skill to pass on, they have wisdom. Young people are usually vacant in that department.

Monitor and evaluate the senior employees' work just as you would any other person's. Hold them to the standards you've set. It may take a while for them to realize you mean business: Not only are you not going to give up on them, you intend to use their resources constructively for the remainder of their time with you.

⟡ **84**

A number of older employees in my company seem to coast the last years to retirement. Is that a common problem among old-timers? If so, why?

I would judge that it is, since so many managers complain about the phenomenon. There are several contributing factors. First is the probability that the older employee doesn't want to take any risks that might threaten his or her job, hence the pension that will follow. Next is the feeling in a lot of senior employees that they have been passed over, that there's no real future for which to work hard. so they have no incentive to work hard. Their competitive days are over. It's probably true that as the employee gets older, his or her resistance to change hardens. After all, why should they disturb themselves and learn new ways of doing things when they have established competence doing the job in the old way? Finally, many old-timers may see their reduced efforts as a reward for having put in all those years of loyal service.

Managers frequently reinforce these nonproductive attitudes by simply shrugging and saying, "What're you going to do?"

⟡ 85
I've taken over a department in which there are a number of old-timers, men in their late 50s or early 60s. I'm not certain how best to manage them.

The best way for me to answer is to put myself in their shoes, since I'm in that age range. If you're my boss and a much younger person, I'd like to be consulted on some matters involving the department. I've been here for a time. I know the operation better, I'm sure, than you. It's not that I expect to be asked to make the decisions, but I'd be complimented to be consulted and brought into the process.

Knowing that you'll want to make changes as new broom, I would hope that you would ask me what you could do to help me be more effective. What I would like you to remember is that I also need challenge and, even though I'm getting to be a senior, I want to have a sense of growth in my work. Don't give up on me just because you suspect I'm over the hill. I want to feel important to the operation—and to myself—until the day I retire.

I'd want you to take charge confidently in those areas in which you are an expert. I'm prepared to respect your credentials, and I want you to respect mine.

⇨ 86

One of my subordinates is 62 and seems to be coasting the rest of the way to retirement. He does just what he has to do and no more. I can't afford to have him doing this level of work for the next three years.

Make that clear to him. If you don't do something, he'll regard the next three years with a light workload to be a reward for years of service.

Keep in mind, however, the possibility that he is doing now what he has been doing for a long time. He might be unchallenged. Look at his years of experience, knowledge of the organization, skills, and talents. How can you use them? Could he take on special jobs that no one else is as qualified to do? Can he coach up-and-coming managerial talent? Could he train employees?

What a resource he may be for you. Your imagination will tell you just how rich a resource he is.

He must understand, though, that you expect him to meet performance standards. Otherwise, he may find himself retiring earlier than he expected. You'll have to keep strict documentation on this man's productivity.

Personal Problems

⇨ 87

I've watched one of my finest employees destroy himself with booze. I've begged him to lay off the stuff and get help. I'm at my wits' end.

You've been a good friend and an understanding, patient manager. Now you must become a firm, impatient boss. Insist that he get help and begin to straighten himself out. There must be no evidence of drinking on the job. He mustn't show up hung over. If he does any of these things, you will suspend or fire him. Explain to him that you will fire him not for the drinking itself, but for the poor performance that results. Don't let him tell you that he can handle it. Show him that he hasn't been able to in the past. Documentation will help you at this point. You should have a record of the work that has not been done well or at all, as well as a schedule of all the times you have talked with him about the problem.

Repeat the admonition: He stays sober or he goes. If he fails even once, take action: Suspend or terminate him. Perhaps you can't save his job, but you might save his life.

⇨ 88

A longtime employee of mine has marital difficulties and a delinquent child who may be into drugs. His work is suffering. He arrives in the morning looking like hell, and sometimes he can't concentrate. The other employees are sympathetic, but they're beginning to complain that he isn't doing his share.

Managers have to make choices, and some of those choices are quite unpleasant. You have a loyalty to your employee, but you also have a loyalty to yourself and to the organization. And you have to be concerned about the impact of this man's low productivity on the other employees.

Undoubtedly you hate to add to the man's burdens, but you must. You must point out the man's performance to him, how it deviates from what you believe you have a right to ask, and that you expect him to come up with a solution to his low productivity. He may respond with vague assurances: "I'll just have to try harder." If he does, you'll have to be firm: "I can't be satisfied with 'try.' I need you to do the job we're paying you to do." It sounds heartless, but it's questionable whether the employee will work to find a solution unless he feels the situation is desperate. Get some plan of action, something to which the man can commit himself.

You may consider suggesting that there is professional help available. But that's about as far as you can go.

⇨ 89

I never quite know how to handle employees who come to me with a personal or a confidential problem. I don't want to cut them off, but I don't know how far to go.

Listen. Create an atmosphere in which the employee feels encouraged to talk. Show understanding. All you have to do is realize and accept that the employee is going through a stressful time. You may not agree with the employee's perception of what is wrong, but there's no question in your mind that a problem exists. It does little good—and it can do harm—to say, soothingly, "I'm sure you're exaggerating all this."

Don't play judge. If the employee discusses things and behaviors of which you disapprove, try not to show how you feel.

Give information as information, not advice. For example, if you believe the employee could use professional help, don't suggest that. Simply point out that there is help available if he wants it.

⇨ **90**

I talked with an employee who is having some problems doing his job and found that there is a lot of stress between him and his wife. I know his wife very well, and I think if I talked with her it might have some value. She may not realize how much their marital problems are affecting him on the job.

The nature of the marital problem is not your business, and regardless of how well you know her, she may resent your getting involved, especially since you've heard only the husband's side. Of course, you could open yourself to hearing her side. Then what do you do? Mediate. If you decide in favor of the husband, you'll probably exacerbate the stress that exists now. If you come down on the side of the wife, you risk alienating your subordinate. And you may not extricate yourself easily from the mire you've walked into. One manager who did precisely what you're planning found to his distress that every time the husband and wife had words, he appeared in the boss's office to complain, and she followed up with long telephone calls to tell her story.

You can empathize with the subordinate. You can even, within bounds, sympathize, although you don't want your sympathy to be an open door for his confidences. But you must, at the same time, insist that he perform according to your expectations. Yes, you can understand and tolerate a setback now and then, but you can't afford to have less-than-productive people working for you. Encourage your subordinate to seek out someone who is more qualified than you—a clergyman, a counselor, a psychologist. Your role is to manage his work—not his personal life—and that is what you must do.

⟡ 91

I like to have lunch away from the office periodically with each of my key supervisors. But one of them is a heavy drinker. The two times I've taken him out, he's come back bagged. I don't want to encourage this sort of thing.

You can always order in lunch. And you might consider that for all your people now and then. You don't always have to go out. At least if you have your lunches in from time to time, your drinking manager may be disappointed but won't necessarily feel discriminated against so long as others have to eat in as well.

If you take him out to a restaurant, order as soon as you sit down, thereby eliminating a long period of drinking before the food is served. If you regulate the time, you may be able to keep him to a drink or two, not enough to put him out of commission.

Special Problems

⟡ 92

A subordinate is about to transfer, at his request, to another department. He's disruptive and a troublemaker. Needless to say, I'm glad to see him go. I'm wondering whether the decent thing for me to do is warn his new manager what he's getting.

It's the decent thing to do only if the manager asks you for an evaluation of the employee. Otherwise, you're making two assumptions that may not be justified. First, you assume that the employee will continue the same offensive behavior in the new department; and second, that if he does, the new manager will find it as objectionable as you did. It may, understandably, not be a possibility that you want to consider, but the conditions that spawned his behavior in your department may not exist in another. Or the employee may wish to make a favorable impression on his new boss, who may think you a bit strange if you describe an employee who doesn't resemble the one he or she has just received.

The employee, no matter how offensive, has the right to establish a relationship with his new boss that is not tainted with your advance warning.

If the new manager asks you to tell him about the employee, stick to describing the employee's behavior. Don't talk about what you believe are the employee's attitudes, motives, or psychological problems. You're not a mind reader or a psychologist (unless, of course, you are). And be as evenhanded as possible. Mention the employee's good points even though you are biased.

▷ 93

One of my best engineers has told me that he has a job offer that will pay him more money. I don't know whether I can match that offer. Should I try to offer something?

It depends greatly on why he is leaving. If the reason is that he wants to make more money, I'd be hesitant to try to match the offer. It won't buy loyalty to you. In fact, it may erode what he feels now, because he'll ask himself why he had to force the money out of you if he is indeed worth it. The next offer that comes along, paying even more money, he'll probably grab.

He might be leaving for reasons other than the money—challenge, excitement, or more recognition. If in your discussions with him you can determine this, you might be able to restructure his job to provide him with more of what he wants. And you can find ways to give him more recognition when he deserves it, as he must since you are unhappy about losing him. Let him know that you are willing to provide more money, if you can, at the usual time. That way you won't be seen as yielding to the blackmail.

⇨ 94

I was asked to take on a manager from an operation that has been phased out by the company. I gave her the job of supervisor, reporting to me. But she's had more rank than the other supervisors, and I'm sure she feels it's a comedown. I've thought about giving her the title of assistant manager.

That may be fine, but only if you give her the job as well as the title. Are you prepared to give up some of your managerial functions to her? If you're not, she'll quickly discover that it's a make-believe job—and everyone else will, too. It can be humiliating to have an empty title.

Even a genuine promotion, complete with responsibility, can cause you problems with your other supervisors, who may have had their eyes on such a position. They may not look kindly on your promoting an outsider, even if she has been a manager.

Still, if you are willing to share the management, and if you believe she has the qualities to make a good assistant, the move sounds like a good one.

If you decide against a formal promotion at this time, let her be an unofficial assistant. Consult with her on issues and decisions. Give her a bit more access to you than you provide the others. Give her the opportunity to share her experience and knowledge with you. She's a valued resource. No doubt, in her disappointment over the loss of her position, she'll respond favorably to your sensitivity and attention.

⇨ 95
A few weeks ago, I was upset when one of my key people left me for what he said was a better job. Now he wants to come back. I have mixed feelings about rehiring him. I don't think I could ever trust him again.

How did he betray your trust in trying to better his career? His first obligation is to himself, just as yours is to you. If he didn't have a contract with you, verbal or written, he was exercising his right and obligation. Interestingly, you can probably trust him more now than you should have before, actually more than you can trust the others who report to you, who might leave you at any minute. He has left for what he thought were greener pastures, and he now believes he has made a mistake. He'll probably be much more wary of future attempts to seduce him away. If he's a good man, as you say, bring him back. He'll be grateful to you and more loyal than before. In addition, he'll serve as a reminder to others that often what is delivered is not as attractive as what is promised. They'll also be wary of outside offers.

When he returns, make him feel welcome. You don't have to make a big fuss, and you certainly shouldn't remind him that you also believe he made a big mistake. Just make it clear that you want him to perform well, as he did before he left.

⇩ 96

An older secretary in my department is the butt of jokes by the younger women. She is finicky and set in her ways, and she complains a lot, but she is very conscientious and a good secretary. I worry that all the joking by the others will hurt her.

How do you know about the joking? You must have had it repeated to you or overheard it. If you smiled or laughed or consented to hear more of it, you were giving your sanction to it. If, on the other hand, you frowned or said, "That's cruel," or, "That's tacky," you would have conveyed the message that you don't appreciate such joking.

Not that your implied disapproval would have stopped it— probably nothing you can do will stop it. But you might pass along the word to the younger secretaries' bosses that you hope they won't encourage such cruelty.

In time, people will stop thinking it's funny. Meanwhile, if the older secretary wants to complain about the jokes, let her talk to you and get it out of her system.

This sort of thing will go on in the workplace, and you can't order it stopped. Just don't collude.

⇩ 97

I've hired a bright, attractive, pleasant woman for an editorial job, only to discover that she lied about having a college degree. I have mixed feelings about her now.

Consider the possibility that you will always have mixed feelings. In short, how will you know when you can trust her? Trust is essential to a good boss-subordinate relationship. Her coworkers will have problems trusting and liking her. Perhaps she can do the job, but it does sound as if a sound education is a requisite for this kind of work. She may not have it.

I can't see many pluses in retaining her, and there are a lot of minuses. Terminate her as quickly as possible.

◊ 98

I've heard a rumor that one of my more important subordinates is seriously looking around for another job. Naturally, I'm upset. Should I let him know that I know?

There's no easy answer to this problem. He may have hoped that the rumor would reach you. On the other hand, he might have hoped to keep it a secret, since he is embarrassed or reluctant to offend you. His game plan, if the latter is true, is that he would come to you, job offer in hand, and say that he had received this terrific deal that he couldn't turn down. Nothing, of course, about the long search he had initiated.

If you believe you have a good working relationship with this man, why not let him know what you've heard? That is, if you can do so without compromising your source of information. If he admits it, then you can talk about what has prompted the job search. You might be able to find out and eliminate the problem he's trying to get away from. Or if he wants more challenge on the job, perhaps you can supply it.

He may deny the search. If so, make a little speech about how you hope that if his work with you is not satisfying, he'll tell you in time for you to make some changes, if possible. Beyond that, there's not much you can do in the absence of some specific information from him. You can, however, keep in closer touch with him.

You have to ask yourself, when a situation such as this arises, whether you've been close enough to your key people. You may have allowed too much of a gap to grow between you and them, and you'll want to rectify that.

⇗ 99
I have a very promising subordinate. How do I nourish that promise without inflating her ego, which is already big enough?

It seems to me that the promise is a more important consideration than her ego. Give her growth jobs, assignments that stretch her capability and encourage change and progress. When she completes them to your satisfaction, give her the recognition that is due her. Her ego will work in your favor, because she won't want to fail. Her ego may work against both her and you, however, if she begins to take her ability for granted and does mediocre work. When that happens, show her how she has failed to perform satisfactorily. You probably won't have to make a big deal of it. She'll correct herself not so much because of you but because of her pride in herself.

⇗ 100
I gave one of my employees a very difficult job to do. I'm worried that he is botching it, but he's awfully proud. I don't know how to check up without offending and possibly demotivating him.

You're the boss, and you have a right to know everything that is going on. Still, your concern for this employee is understandable. Call the employee in for a progress report. Let him tell you what he is doing, and how. Ask questions. If you see signs of trouble, suggest that the employee give you the pros and cons of doing things the way he has chosen to do them. He may be reluctant to give you any minuses, but you must gently insist that there are always possible pitfalls in any choice. Once the employee acknowledges that possibility, then you can make suggestions for more sound approaches.

Next time you make a difficult assignment, let the employee know what you expect in the way of results—and when. Also, make it clear that you will want progress reports from time to time. When the employee knows what is coming, there's less room for him to develop resentment over your watchfulness.

⋄ **101**

He has always seemed to me to be an achiever. I've offered him an interesting new project that carries a certain risk to it, but he says it will overload him. I think he's really scared.

You may be taking for granted that achievers like risk. Most research into achievement motivation shows that achievers are motivated by moderate risk, but they aren't gamblers going for the long shot.

Approach this challenge on two fronts. First, how can you reduce the risk he perceives? Can you train or coach him? Offer yourself as a resource? What other resources can you make available? How about loosening the schedule for completion? Can you break the task into segments that don't seem so formidable as the complete package? At the moment, if your analysis is correct, he may see a reward in taking the assignment, but he worries that he won't be successful.

The other part of the problem is his present workload. Don't assume he is covering up the truth. One obstacle to success on the project may well be the amount of work he has now. What can you do to lighten the load at the same time that you move on the first front? Can you give some duties to others? Can you extend deadlines? Can you provide some assistance for him?

◊ 102
I've just learned that one of my star salesmen has an interest in a tavern. Do I have grounds to object?

If the tavern is strictly an investment, I think you'd have a hard time prescribing where he may or may not put his money. If he works there part-time, you have a case if you have a contract with him that proscribes other employment. If you don't, your recourse is to watch his production. If it flags, you may have an indicator that his outside activity is absorbing his time and energy. Then you have a right to step in, but not to accuse him of working in the tavern. You can't know for sure that bartending or whatever is the culprit. Thus, stick with the performance: It isn't up to par, and it must be. Leave it up to him to make the correction.

◊ 103
This employee is a wimp. Everyone walks all over him. I'm thinking of sending him to assertiveness training. Is that a good idea?

It depends greatly on how you present the training prospect to him. If you suggest that he needs to have a correction in his personality, you probably won't see many results. No one likes to be told he or she is deficient, and therefore needs training.

Have a serious talk with him in which you suggest that perhaps he doesn't often get the results he wants in dealing with other people. If you show some empathy, or at least sympathy, you may persuade him to open up and admit that occasionally he gets frustrated because people take advantage of him. Then offer him the opportunity to attend an assertiveness workshop at which he'll be helped to identify his needs and wants, and to express them effectively with other people. If he sees the training as a way to get more of the results he wants more often, he'll probably jump at the offer. He'll also probably want you to keep confidential the kind of training you're giving him. There's no point in exposing him to teasing around the department.

He—and you—should understand that the workshop is only a beginning. But it can be an important beginning in any effort to change behavior.

▷ 104
I have an employee who is bright but very passive. I've suggested to him that he take an assertiveness training program for which I will pay. But he doesn't seem receptive. How do I persuade him to do something that I know will help him?

What he's probably hearing from you is this: You're deficient, and I want you to go get trained so you won't be deficient anymore. At the same time, he surely knows that other people take advantage of him. But to admit that publicly by taking the program is something he is reluctant to do.

Where possible, training should be presented to employees as a way for them to get more of the results they want more often. After all, no one is always as effective in every situation as he or she would like to be. That's a nonthreatening message. In addition, again where possible, training should be seen as a reward for good performance. As a manager, you recognize someone's contribution by suggesting that that person increase his or her skills or knowledge.

It might be too late for you to take those steps. Consider sending not only your nonassertive employee but one or two others as well. That way he won't have to bear the stigma. He'll be camouflaged among the other employees. You may also suggest to all three that, while they take the program, they should evaluate its potential value for others in the department.

TWO

PEOPLE IN MEETINGS
105–157

Objectionable Behavior in Groups

⇨ **105**

I've noticed a tendency in our meetings to jump at the first solution that even seems feasible. Discussion stops, and we're into talking about how it will be implemented. Sometimes I think we jump too fast.

Groups have a tendency to settle quickly on an option and run with it. Sometimes, I suspect, it is an avoidance phenomenon. People are uncomfortable with open-ended discussions that range about looking for as many possible options as possible. Most people are probably more comfortable when they don't sail out of sight of land. Once the option seems to have been accepted, someone can be depended upon to insist that the *how* be answered. Thereupon, people will sketch out the implementation and probably succeed in quashing any lurking doubts that they should discuss the *what* and *whether* further. After all, when you're busy, and you think you know what you're doing, you must be doing it right. Yes? No?

Often I choose no. If you have this gnawing feeling that your group is too precipitate, call a halt to the how-to activity. You won't be a hero with some of your colleagues, but you might be surprised to find that one or more will agree with you that further discussion is desirable to find other options. You may be challenged: What other options? for example. You don't have to have one ready. Stick with your argument that you know there have to be other choices. You'll move the group, grudgingly perhaps.

◊ 106

I have a colleague who smirks at meetings, and I wonder whether he feels as superior as he looks. It's very distracting when you're trying to get your point across, and he looks as if it couldn't possibly be important.

If his body language baffles and distracts you, why not call attention to it? Many people are not aware of their nonverbal messages. You might say, "Al, you look as though you don't agree with what I'm saying." If he acknowledges that he doesn't, follow up with, "Well, the way you looked—your body language—made me suspect it, but I think it would be more helpful to all of us if you told us what you disagree with." That's a clear message, but it may have to be repeated a few times before he realizes that he's not going to continue to get away with his silent expressions of opposition.

On the other hand, he may reply, "No, I don't disagree." You can then explain that his body language seemed to convey otherwise. Follow his disclaimer with, "Well, you must have some opinions about what I've been talking about. Perhaps you'd share them with us."

Again, you may have to repeat this kind of action until Al understands that his smirking draws some possible disapproval.

⋄ 107

One of my brightest subordinates is an absolute clam in meetings. I know he has much to offer, but if I call on him, he says he has nothing to add. I want to get him involved.

There are several steps you can take to open this man's shell. First, if the clam has a specialized area of knowledge that could be useful, call on him when you want the kind of input he can make. He may regard himself as useless in general topics of deliberation, but he probably has much to say when you're on his turf.

Assign him a report to give at the next meeting, and ask him to be prepared to take questions. Or notify him in advance of a meeting as to the subject, and ask him to develop some ideas to put on the table.

It may be that the clam has trouble being spontaneous. If so, during the meeting, when you want to hear from him, say something such as, "Peter, I'd like to get your thoughts on this, but I think Hank was first. Let's hear from him and get back to you." The advance notice may help the clam to prepare his thoughts.

⋄ 108

I recently was promoted to management. I meet regularly with my division's management group. Everyone seems to be very polite. No one disagrees directly. I've always been plainspoken, but maybe I'm wrong in thinking people should be more direct in meetings. Do you consider this group to be a healthy one?

There are many people, I suspect, who regard politeness as the sign of a healthy, effective group. My opinion is that that is not necessarily so. I like directness in a group. I appreciate openness. When I hear an opinion, I like to think that I'm hearing what the person really thinks. I can tolerate anger and impatience, as long as it does not turn into rudeness or hostility.

I have seen many so-called polite groups that were, in my view, dishonest and withholding. I do not understand why people who may not think as I do are hesitant to say so. If they are more concerned with protecting my feelings than with getting on with the group's business, I cannot believe they are effective members of the group.

My suggestion to you is that you be yourself, that you do not subscribe to the elaborate rituals of the group. You will, of course, be taking a risk. But you may eventually have a positive impact on the group's behavior. Practice saying what you believe without much display of emotion, at least in the beginning. These people sound from your description as if they would find emotional participation a bit hard to handle. But, in time, you will no doubt be seen as a direct, honest person, although in the beginning you will probably be seen as a threat. If you remain honest without showing any desire to injure others, if you can take the disagreement from others as well as express it, you will be accepted, and quite possibly respected, for what you've brought to the group.

▷ 109
I hate it when I'm talking in a group and someone says, "I think we're off the subject." I feel put down and sometimes get very angry. How can I deal with this kind of petty dictator?

Discipline yourself to stay cool and—to use one of my favorite expressions—make it a group issue. Here's how you might rescue yourself: "The point I'm making is. . . . Here's how it fits in, I believe. Do the rest of you think I'm off the subject? If so, I'll withdraw my point. But if you agree with me that it is relevant, I'd like to see us discuss my point."

Go with the group's decision. Very often, it will be favorable to you.

▷ 110

We have a product line that's been in trouble for a couple of years. I think it can be modified to be competitive, but for the past several months, the marketing committee, of which I'm a member, meets regularly to talk about supplementing it with a new product line. But nothing has jelled. Meanwhile, our sales grow worse. No one else seems to feel any urgency.

From your description, I suggest that your committee is locked into some classic avoidance behavior. There's an old saying in management: When you don't want to deal with an old issue, invent a new one. I suspect that the new product line idea was conceived to avoid having to face the painful reality that the old one is no longer selling.

Sound out some of your colleagues on the committee. You'll probably find at least one other who is experiencing your brand of frustration. You may find more potential allies than you imagined. Prepare a little speech for the next meeting. It might go something like this: "I have to say that I'm frustrated and worried. Our sales are slipping constantly, and our response has been to come up with a new product line. But we haven't yet, and even if we could, it's going to take a lot of time and redesigning. I ask that we look at what we're doing, because I wonder whether it's cost-effective. At any rate, I wanted to share my worries with you."

Stay with the "we" tone. You share the burden with everyone else. If the group is committing an error, assume your part of the responsibility. It's less accusatory. Also, express your opinions in terms of your feelings: You're "frustrated" and "worried."

Ask the group to give you their reactions. If you've already cultivated friends there, you'll get support for confronting the real and old issues that your group has been avoiding.

▷ 111

Sometimes in meetings it takes me a long time to say what I want to say, and people interrupt me. Often they go on talking as if I hadn't said anything.

I suspect that if you don't capture people's attention in 15 or 20 seconds, you've lost your audience. It may be an exaggeration, but the fact is that most people don't have much patience when it comes to listening. You'll have to learn to be effective immediately when you speak up. Train yourself to offer the key point first, something you probably haven't been doing. Follow it up with supporting arguments or explanations. Like many other people, you build up to your key point or thesis, and by the time you manage to get there, you don't have ears tuned in.

People are often reluctant to offer their key point first, because they fear that someone else will cut them off with an argument. If that happens to you, say, "Let me explain why I think this way." In your case, it may be also that you don't think well under pressure. An antidote for this is to do much of your thinking before the meeting. Write down your key points ahead of time, so that you don't take up the group's time thinking your way through to them.

◊ 112

Occasionally I write detailed, analytical memos concerning our operation for our management group that meets every two weeks. But the group never seems to want to discuss these memos. I'm really ticked off.

I read the sample memo you sent me, and I found that a critical element is missing. Nowhere in the memo did you tell your colleagues what you want them do with the memo. From now on, state in the memo that you would like it to be entered on the agenda for the next meeting.

At the moment, they probably expect you to bring up the memo, and you just sit there waiting for them to do it. Quite an impasse.

◊ 113

Another manager bulls his way through meeting after meeting. But people seem to regard him highly. All I hear are clouds of words. Is this the way to get ahead?

You've provided no evidence that the bull artist is on a fast track. Don't assume that his colleagues admire him for his loquacity. It may be the total person they like, and as for the talking, they tolerate it. People who talk excessively in meetings usually signal to others that they have problems. Some talkers are uncomfortable because they have nothing of substance to say, and they try to conceal the fact behind, as you put it, clouds of words. Others are unable to organize their thoughts, and consequently they ramble as they try to think aloud.

It's obvious that you don't admire this style (and you may be surprised to find that some of your colleagues also secretly dislike it). Thus, if you try to practice it, you won't admire yourself, and others will suspect you of imitating. Respect comes with being authentic, the real you with which people are probably very comfortable. That doesn't mean that you can't hone your articulateness. Most conferees appreciate the person who can discuss substantive issues clearly, and who not only helps the group stay on track but provides much of the locomotion toward achievement of the group's task. So, as you sit listening to your colleague's long speeches, ask yourself, How can I help this group to get what it wants? Then act on that. You'll find your colleagues' respect for you increasing.

⇨ **114**

Today I sat in a meeting with our vice-president and the other managers on my level. At one point an argument developed between one manager and the vice-president. It got heated and dragged on, so I stepped in to try to get us back on the track and to help out the manager. He was taking quite a beating. I wasn't surprised when the v-p turned on me for interrupting, but I was flabbergasted when the other manager bawled me out. I thought he'd appreciate somebody stepping in.

I've had the same experience in my consulting. One notable case involved an executive who I decided was sadistic, and his subordinate manager, who I decided was masochistic. The rest of the group sat there seemingly embarrassed while the executive took the junior man to the woodshed. But when, as a consultant, I intervened, I got it just as heavily from the victim as from the persecutor.

I wouldn't want to suggest that everyone in such a situation suffers from a psychological malady. There may be a number of more harmless interpretations one could put on a scene like this. One is that the participants, even the bloodied one, feel embarrassed at being chastised for taking up the time of the group. Another possible explanation is that the two of them are so caught up in the moment that they can't see how the dispute between them is going or is perceived by others. There's always the chance that the disputants love the grandstanding.

My suggestion is that next time you make it a group issue. Don't attempt a rescue all by yourself. Ask the group whether they share in your confusion or belief that the discussion has taken the group off its track. You may not be seen by the combatants as a hero, but you may be lauded as such by your suffering coworkers.

⇨ 115

The management group in my department meets on a regular basis. Everyone is so elaborately polite—on the surface. For example, when I offer an idea, someone else responds by thanking me for submitting the idea, complimenting me on how well thought-out it is, but then tearing it apart. It makes me angry.

You have reason to be angry. You are being *yes-but*-ed. The essence of the yes-but response is: *Yes*, I hear what you're saying, and it's an important contribution; thank you for saying it. *But* you're all wrong. It seems polite, but in fact it's not. It can be a put-down by discounting what you've said, especially when the responder seems to build you up for your supposed contribution and then, when you least suspect, he tears you down. It's a rejection of your thinking under the guise of acceptance.

If most people in your group are guilty of yes-but-ing, it's probably because they've felt it was unwise to be direct. If you want to be more direct, you'll have to gauge the risk for yourself in simply saying, without polite prelude and softening up, that a member's idea is not workable. You can lessen the risk by saying, "I have some positive and negative reactions to that proposal. I'll give both if you wish." However, after you have done so, if you feel preponderantly negative, make that clear. Don't seem to straddle the fence. When you have no positive reactions, respond with your negative feelings and reasons.

◊ 116

In meetings, another manager often argues against something I didn't say. We waste a lot of time with I-didn't-say-thats and Yes-you-dids.

You're telling him that he didn't listen to you, and no one likes to be told that. Next time he misquotes or misunderstands you, simply say, "I'm sorry I didn't make myself clear. Let me correct that." You've taken the responsibility on yourself and avoided accusing him of not hearing you right. Repeat your point and ask the group, "Am I making myself clear?" If he then argues without having understood you, someone else may intervene with, "Charlie, Alice has already made it clear that that's not what she said."

Exercising Leadership

◊ 117

Sometimes when our meetings seem to ramble on, I get very impatient, and yet I don't know how to get the meeting on track.

Enlist the aid of other members of the group in getting the meeting to go where it should. Say something such as, "Let me throw out an idea and see what kinds of reactions you have." Once you have the group's consent to do that, you may get help from others who want the group to move as you do. Keep your idea very basic and simple. Don't give people the impression that you've come in with a full agenda already worked out. You can always flesh out the picture as others begin to show interest in the idea.

Look for help. You don't want people to believe you are trying to take over. Encourage others to discuss what you've proposed.

If you sense opposition, back off. Don't press your idea; you'll have another chance later.

⇨ **118**

Recently I sat on a committee that had a lot of problems getting itself organized and working. From the beginning I took a strong leadership role—the chairman did not. We cut through the bull and got a lot done. But later, I began hearing that people saw me not as a leader but a steamroller. I don't understand this.

In the initial phase of a group, there's what I call "garbage time." People do ramble, seeming perplexed, even confused, and leadership may be obscure and hard to find. It seems as if nothing is happening, but it is. The members of the committee are trying to figure out what roles they are to play in the group. They have an ambivalence about strong leadership at this point. On the one hand, they may seem relieved when someone, such as you, steps in to take control. On the other hand, they may grow to resent the intervention because they haven't quite figured out their relationship to you. Once they begin to assert themselves and to play a more defined role, they may see you as having imposed yourself on them. That explains why you were initially a hero, but then later became a villain.

Next time, play a guide rather than a pusher. You guide the group with its consent. A guide suggests, recommends, and points the way. But a guide does not take forceful action. A guide does not take over and push the group into what it may see later as premature action.

▷ 119

I'm in charge of a special committee that meets one day each month. The problem is that we never get through my agenda; others are always adding to it before we can get started talking.

Share your proposed agenda with them sufficiently in advance so that they can make suggestions for including their items. It sounds as if they are insisting on that right at the outset of your meetings, anyway. You might as well build in their wish lists ahead of time.

When you have, with their help, completed a workable agenda ahead of time, ask the participants to think through the various items before they meet. It's possible that your colleagues are doing so much thinking during your meeting that they take up a lot of evaluation and discussion time. A little premeeting organization of their thoughts will cut down on the rambling.

Take a few minutes at the beginning of each session to achieve consensus on the time allotments for each topic. Once the group has decided on the appropriate time limits, they'll help you take responsibility for seeing that the agenda is completed in one day.

⋄ 120

Frequently people in the meetings I attend don't seem to listen to one another. Someone will say, "A is B," and someone else will jump in and argue with him as if he'd just said, "A is C."

There's a constructive role you can play that is called mediating. Say that Carl has advanced his proposal, and Ted criticizes what he thinks that proposal is, but which it isn't, according to your understanding. When Ted finishes, you intervene with something such as this: "Let me see if I understand what your viewpoints are. Carl, what I heard you say is. . . . Is that pretty much on target?" Carl says it is. You turn to Ted. "What I heard you say is. . . . Is that reasonably correct?" Ted agrees. You continue: "Well, it seems to me that you two are talking about different things." Explain the difference as you see it. If you want group support, you turn to the others and ask them whether your interpretation is what they heard.

Another approach is to say to Ted, "But what you're arguing is not what I heard Carl say." Then explain what you heard, check it with Carl, and if you're correct, you have clarified the issue and given a message to Ted that he didn't hear correctly.

⋄ 121

I sit on a committee that takes endless time to discuss trivia. One man, especially, who is not the chairman, seems to love the sound of his own voice, and just takes over the meetings.

Your chairman needs help. Your description indicates that he has abdicated leadership to the windbag.

There are at least two ways you can go. The first is to talk with the chairman about some of the more substantive issues that the committee could deal with. Offer to help the chairman draw up an agenda for the next meeting. He may be very happy that you've come forward; he may have assumed that the boorish member represents the will of the group. True, he's not much of a leader, but there's nothing in committee tradition that says you can't exercise a little informal leadership.

Another way, instead of, or in tandem with, the above, is to caucus with some other committee members. Don't approach them with the theme, "What's going on is terrible. Don't you agree?" They may think so but be intimidated by the dominator. Further, some people hesitate to speak out in their own behalf. So they go along. Instead, do an informal survey about some of the issues they'd like to see the committee tackle. Settle on two or three of the most popular items and ask them to support you when you suggest that the issues be included on the agenda at the next meeting.

There is a riskier way: confronting the dominator. His artillery of words may wipe you out, however. Confronting is the least-recommended way, unless you are assured in advance that others will reinforce you.

◊ 122

One of the members of my task force doesn't contribute much during the meetings, but he seems to have plenty to say after them. The word gets back to me that he frequently criticizes our inefficiency. It irks me that he doesn't take any risks during the meetings when the others do.

At your next meeting, before you adjourn, make a point of saying, "I want to give everyone in here one last opportunity to talk about what has happened here today. I'm sure that all of us have thoughts afterward about what we did or did not do. So I'm going to go around the room and ask each of you to give us your final thoughts." When you come to the fellow who does the postmortems, you might say, "John, I know you do much valuable thinking between meetings. We'd especially like to have your impressions." Whether or not he cooperates at that time, add, "Well, John, if you do have some thoughts after the fact, would you please be prepared to give them to us at the start of the next meeting?" Expand the responsibility to others: "That applies to all of us. If any one of us has further thoughts, we should jot them down and be prepared to discuss them next time. I'm sure that all of us have good thoughts that we don't bring back into the meetings. That way they're wasted. So from now on, I'm going to open each meeting with time for each of us to report those between-meetings ideas."

You thereby create the possibility that the next time John expresses himself privately but not publicly, some member of the group will say at the meeting, "John, you were talking to me the other day. . . . "And John will have to contribute.

⬦ 123

I head a committee that is looking at the feasibility of a new field organization. From time to time we've invited certain department heads, other executives, and specialists to join us. But now people come without invitation. The meeting room is filled with people, and it's just not manageable. Still, if I tell some of these people not to come next time, they're going to be insulted. How do I shrink this monster?

Stop meeting. After a time, when the schedule has been broken, start up again without announcement. Invite only your committee members at first. That way, all others will see that they are getting equal treatment and will not feel so offended as they might have had you disinvited them. If people begin to ask to come or show up, simply advise that, for the time being, you are running closed sessions. Eventually you can begin to again invite people you need.

⇩ **124**

I'm chair of a task force, and as such, I meet regularly with higher management to keep them informed of our progress. Some of the other members of the task force seem a bit jealous of my contacts, and even suspicious of my accounts of the conversations I have with management.

You might pardon them if they wonder whether you are trying to shut them out of the glory and the visibility. After all, you are in an enviable position as the conduit to higher management, and you enjoy a great deal of prestige.

Find ways to cut the others in on the action. Instead of your reporting alone to management, have management come to the task force meetings occasionally so that all task force members can have some communication with the powers. In addition, you might take a different group member with you each time you visit higher management. From time to time, submit a written report to management, signed by all the task force participants.

You can't blame the others for wanting some of the exposure and credit that you have heretofore kept to yourself.

▷ 125

I sit on an interdepartmental committee that was formed to explore ways of working better with one another. We meet every other week, and I can't tell you how boring it is. We never seem to discuss anything of substance.

It sounds to me as if you have no formal leadership, and no one wants to risk moving into the leadership vacuum. If that situation continues, nothing much is going to happen, except that you will become even more bored and frustrated.

You might try exercising a bit of informal leadership by saying to the group something such as, "I'm a little confused about what we should be doing in these meetings, and perhaps some of you can help me out. I keep thinking that we are not discussing all the issues that we might. Maybe I'm mistaken, and that's why I ask your opinion. Does anyone here agree, or am I the only one who feels this way?" Expect a silence. After all, you have interrupted the pattern and even appear to criticize, although very diplomatically. Your intervention may likely produce one of two reactions. The first is that someone will ask you what kind of issue you have in mind. Thus, it would be helpful if you could think of one that the group hasn't discussed that you believe should be on the table. The other reaction you should expect is some hesitant support from others. Let them talk; you've done your part for the moment. But if the support falters, turn to others and ask them how they feel. You may be able to fan a little flame.

Be positive and tentative. Don't come on strong with your opinion that the group is wasting its time. You don't want an argument. So let it be known that you very much want to hear from others. And if you are prepared to define some issues that you believe the group should be working on, you will have filled a yawning gap. People might even begin to look to you for leadership, and that won't do you any harm.

◊ **126**
When I call people together for a problem-solving session, many of them just sit there. Two or three of us wind up doing much of the work. How can I get more participation?

It's probable that if the two or three of you are willing to do the work, others may feel they don't have to worry.

The first thing to check is the size of your group. Problem-solving groups, to be effective, tend to be small—say, five to nine. If your group is considerably larger, you may never get the open, full participation you're looking for. Larger groups are fine for collecting and disseminating information, but not for the intense interactions that problem-solving requires.

My second recommendation is to tell all participants the nature of the problem to be discussed and that you want them to come to the meeting with suggested solutions. Keep the definition of the problem as loose and general as possible so that you don't foreclose the possibility of some worthwhile options. At the outset of the meeting, conduct a round robin. Go around the room and ask each person to come up with the ideas that he or she has generated before the meeting. All ideas should be recorded. There should be no discussion or evaluation of these ideas until everyone has contributed. Groups are better at evaluating ideas than in generating them.

⇨ 127

In our interdepartmental meetings, another manager often just takes over the meeting. The boss lets him. He's very bright and very abrasive. So when he takes over, people shut up. I think some of his decisions have been lousy. What do you do with a steamroller like that?

There are at least two steps you do not take with a dominator: the first is to compete with him, and the second is to take him on one-to-one. You probably can't outdominate him—he's a pro—and you may come off second in a debate, so why risk it?

Get some help from the group. After the dominator makes one of his speeches, turn to the rest of the people in the meeting and say, "I'd be interested in going around the room and finding out what others think about this." What you're doing is perfectly in order. If the dominator tries to take the floor again, you say, "You've been very clear as to where you are. I want to know where everyone else is."

Dominators are very fond of pushing for a vote, to which you can say, "I wonder if we've covered all our options. Let's go around the table and have people comment."

Unless you want to address the dominator directly, make your comments to the boss and to the group. When you address the group, avoid eye contact with the dominator. You're saying it is a group matter.

⇨ 128

One of my task force members, a peer, is consistently five or ten minutes late to meetings. It annoys me,

especially since I think it's a power play on his part. How can I make him get there on time?

You may not be able to make him be on time if, as you suspect, he's playing a power game with you. You can, however, lessen the reward he feels for disrupting your meeting. The less attention his late entrances earn, the less gratification there is for him. When he walks in, go right on with your business. If he tries to explain or excuse, don't respond. You can talk to him privately, of course, but if he is indeed playing power games, your discussion could be seen as a plea on your part. A better bet is to make it a group issue. After all, the other members of the task force are probably as annoyed as you. When, despite the lack of fanfare, he continues to be late, say, at the conclusion of the meeting, something such as, "Jack, I think all of us would appreciate your being on time for the next meeting. That way, you won't distract us, but more important, we'd have the benefit of your contributions from the outset."

If Jack makes excuses for his continued lateness, don't argue, just repeat, "It's very important to all of us that you be here when we start." Chances are, you'll get some support from others in the group. Jack will begin to realize that others are annoyed, just as you are.

⟡ 129
Sometimes in our meetings we can get endlessly hung up on trivia. I want to yell, "This is so much bull," but that's not a good thing when the boss is part of the scene. How else can I get people to talk about what is important?

Here are a couple of statements you can make: "Excuse me, but I've lost track of where we are in relation to the main discussion.

Can someone help me to connect what's being said now to what we're supposed to be deciding?" And another: "In all the discussion, I am having trouble remembering the main issue here. Can someone help me find my place?"

If you say these quietly, with no hint of impatience or scorn, and if you present yourself as being the one who is temporarily lost and appeal to the group for help, you may be a catalyst for the group's recognition that they are riding a merry-go-round.

⇨ 130
What's the best way to deal with a hidden agenda in a meeting?

I wouldn't rush to take action. Covert agendas sometimes surface and get taken care of without any special effort. Someone wants the next offsite meeting to be held in New Hampshire in February. You can figure that one out easily—he wants to ski. But New Hampshire in February, someone says, is too uncertain for traveling—and that takes care of that.

But agendas can become obstructive. One member of the group has a grudge against another in the group, and finds ways of sniping at the other person. If the remarks aren't clearly relevant, you can say to the sniper, "I'm having a hard time relating what you're saying to the general discussion. Would you help me out?" or, "You make most of your comments to Charlie. I wish you'd make them to the rest of us as well." Either remark discourages further sniping.

If you believe a person with a covert agenda is delaying the forward movement of the group, say so. But check with the group: "I sense that we're not making progress toward our goal.

Does anyone else share my feelings?" Now the person with the obstructive agenda is on the spot.

If, as a result of a hidden agenda, two people monopolize time with a private feud, intervene: "Robert, I suggest that you and Carl have some issues to work through that don't relate closely to what we're dealing with here. Perhaps the two of you should work through your differences in the privacy of your office."

Another tactic is to move around the obstacle. If the discussion seems not to go anywhere and is stuck on dead center, suggest that the group move to another item on the formal agenda and come back to this one later. The delay may serve to cool off the member with the personal agenda.

Time and Length

⋄ 131
I think we have too many meetings that run too long. They take too long to get going. What are some simple steps I can take that will reduce the number and hours?

The first simplifying step to take is to ask people to do most of their thinking before entering the conference room. Define the issue or problem to be discussed. Keep the definition sufficiently broad or general so as not to eliminate options or suggest a specific solution. Second, set a firm time limit, say, 90 minutes, on the meeting. People tend to work more efficiently within known time boundaries. Third, go around the room at the start of the meeting and ask people to record on a blackboard or flipchart all of their suggestions, with no evaluating permitted until all ideas are recorded. Fourth, aim for a consensus rather than a majority, since majority votes seem to spawn additional meetings on the same issue as people begin to wonder whether they voted correctly.

There's one other consideration that always helped me. I schedule a meeting in mid to late morning, hoping to catch everyone on an upswing in their energy curves. Morning people are still on an energy high, and others are just beginning to function effectively.

⇨ 132

I frequently get stuck in meetings that go on forever. The people who call them seem to like being in meetings, because they don't do anything to keep them to a reasonable time limit. What can I do about it other than get frustrated?

I assume that you feel you don't have enough influence to say to the chairs before a meeting, "Can we set a finish time on this, because I have some other obligations (appointments, deadlines, etc.)?" If you are stuck in a meeting that seems to be going on forever, you can try the same tactic. Look at the chair, and ask, "What time do you anticipate that we'll be winding up, because. . . ." If you want to be less direct, choose a time when the discussion is going in circles and summarize respective positions: "I'm getting a bit confused," you might say. "Maybe it would help if I summed up what's been said." After you've finished, you can say, "Where do we go from here?" or, "What do we need to arrive at a decision?"

Often such intervention puts new life and direction into an aimless discussion.

⇨ 133

Often we discuss a decision, take a vote on it, then, after people have second thoughts, we have another meeting, and take another vote that reverses or changes the decision we've already made. It seems like a waste of time to me.

Probably some of those people who apparently had second thoughts actually were still holding onto their first thoughts. They went along with the decision but were not really sold on it. Groups will often run with the first feasible solution or decision that comes along—and regret it later. Try taking more time in your meetings to provide everyone with a full say. If people push for a vote, tell them you want a consensus, in which everyone commits himself or herself to the solution. If you give enough time, insist that all the options be put on the table, and hold out for 100 percent agreement rather than a majority, you'll have fewer of your decisions unraveling after they're put together. Consensus decisions generally take more time, but they hold up better in the long run. And everyone commits to them.

⇨ 134

Our meetings exhaust me. I doubt whether we're efficient.

You're probably exhausted because you've exceeded your normal span of concentration and have to expend more energy to stay with it.

Usually an effective way to control the length of a meeting is to set a time limit, perhaps 60 to 90 minutes. That's about as long as most people can concentrate. However, you must start on time and end on time. When people know that you are serious about the time limit, they will help you to keep the meeting on target. Group members will police one another to keep the comments relevant and avoid excessive talking.

It also helps to have a clear agenda so that people don't flounder. If people know what they are expected to do, stay on the subject, and know they must complete the deliberation by a certain time, you'll see your meetings becoming more efficient and effective.

⬦ 135
We waste a lot of time in meetings because people don't listen. So we get into arguments about what was said and what was not said.

Here's a technique that you might use to help train people to listen better. Ask each respondent to repeat the point he or she heard the first person make before speaking to it. If the point has been misunderstood, the first person can correct the error before an inappropriate response is made that provokes an argument.

Negative/Unproductive Behavior

⬦ 136
The people in my group don't like to take risks, and they jump to say no whenever a new idea comes up. How can I get around their negativism?

Before the meeting at which the idea is presented, see whether you can line up an ally or two who will support you. Even if your ally doesn't agree with the idea, ask him or her to support at least the notion of giving the idea a full discussion.

Be prepared to clarify the risk. You may propose a project that sounds complicated, but one you know that, with the resources you have, poses comparatively little risk. You might also anticipate that if the step is taken, the consequences of doing nothing might be worse than attempting a project that falls short of complete success.

Sell the benefits, secondary as well as primary. For example, there may be some valuable fallout, such as information, even if the idea proves not to be a success. Whatever good things can come out of a risky decision should be emphasized and reemphasized.

Finally, single out the most negative opponents and put some straightforward questions to them: "Why the pressure to hold back?" "How do the dangers outweigh the benefits?" "What's the worst that can happen if a positive decision is made?" "Are you sure you are not closing out chances to consider the idea fairly?"

⇨ 137
One subordinate is always taking a contrary position in staff meetings. Then we have to listen to a long, rambling explanation of why he disagrees. He wastes everyone's time.

Many people are not able to organize their thinking. They may know generally where they want to go, or they have a piece of a premise, but after that they wander all over the landscape. You can probably help this man by breaking into his monologue and asking how he wants to tie what he is saying to the issue being discussed. For example, "John, I'm having problems relating what you say to the idea that Jim brought up. Could you help me out by showing me the relationship?" Or if you want to make it a group issue, ask, "Excuse me, John, I wondered whether anyone else here shared my problem in getting the link between Jim's idea and what you're saying."

You'll probably have to ask the question from time to time, since John may not know how to be relevant and concise without help. So far as the negativism is concerned, you might occasionally say, "Okay, John, that's your con. Now give us a pro."

John will very likely continue to play a limited role of naysayer or devil's advocate unless he is forced out of it.

▷ **138**

How do you deal with a brilliant subordinate who constantly shoots other people's ideas down in meetings? He's often right, but he's beginning to intimidate some of the others to the point where they won't offer suggestions.

One way you can hold him in check, at least until you get the ideas recorded, is to announce a round robin in your next meeting. You set aside a time in which you go around the table and ask for ideas, which you record on the blackboard or flipchart. During the round robin, participants are not to criticize or evaluate the ideas. They may ask questions for clarification only. You'll find that once people know they are not going to run into the buzz saw, they'll open up. Of course, once the evaluation of the ideas starts, you'll have to deal with your brilliant but abrasive subordinate. But at least you'll have ideas on paper, which seems to be a step further than you're getting now.

⇨ 139

He sits in meetings and his response to nearly every idea is, "The problem with that is. . . . " I get so sick of his being negative.

He probably believes that he plays an important role in evaluating the contributions of others. And he could be right. When you look at an idea, you should look at all sides of it. I agree that if it is your idea he's punching holes in, it can be demoralizing. Nonetheless, his behavior is predictable. Everyone knows what he will do. To that extent, your affront at his negativism should be lessened. It's not personal when it is applied to everyone.

You can encourage him to think in more balanced terms by waiting until he finishes with his criticism and asking, "Now what do you think might be useful about this idea?"

Of course you could always make a group rule that everyone must come up with a positive when he or she offers a negative. But that might limit group discussion, because if the idea had no merits, no one would be permitted to say anything.

⇨ 140

What do you do when someone in a meeting tears your idea apart? I didn't want to be defensive, so I kept quiet. But he just talked on about how stupid the idea was and made me look like a fool.

It's possible that others in the meeting felt sorry for you and wanted to help you, but didn't know how. Next time make it easier for them to come to your assistance. When your critic has gone on long enough to make his point, interrupt him: "Excuse me, Phil, you've expressed yourself clearly about my proposal. Now I'd like to hear how others feel about it. What are the reactions of the rest of you?" Look around the table as you speak. If your colleagues are sympathetic, or at least hold middle ground, your opening the door will make it easier for them to speak up.

▷ 141

I give regular reports to the R&D committee. One member of the group usually grills me. I regard him as hostile, and I get very defensive and rattled when he interrogates me.

When he questions you, look thoughtful and take time before you answer. A few seconds are sufficient. That gives time for one of his colleagues to rescue you, if anyone cares to do so. Frame your reply concisely before you open your mouth. If you think of your reply as you go along, you will probably ramble and become tense. As you answer, look around the group, and include everyone. Others may then be encouraged to join in the discussion. If you look just at your questioner, the others may stay on the sidelines and watch what happens between the two of you.

When you finish your answer, look at the others and ask for more questions or comments. If your antagonist wants to monopolize your time, suggest politely that you'd like to make sure that others get their questions answered or their comments recorded, and that you'll come back to him. If the others speak up more moderately, he may decide to temper his hostility.

Never show anger toward him. The group may feel obliged to come to his defense, and you will be in danger of losing them.

◊ 142

People who come up with ideas get picked off one by one in our meetings. Let's say that Ralph comes up with an idea. Someone is sure to shoot it down. There doesn't seem to be any general discussion—just, "bang, you're dead."

It's easier to come up with reasons why an idea won't work than to look for ways in which it might be made to work. Your subordinates seem to have settled into the easier of the two paths. Your first step is to discourage the one-to-one interactions. Anyone who wants to address a new idea must talk to the group as a whole, not to the contributor. You as chair must enforce this rule. You must also encourage a general discussion. Don't let one individual close out that possibility. If one person is negative, ask how others feel. People apparently have been sitting on the sideline without having to commit themselves.

Another tactic you might try is to ask members of the group what they find positive about the idea, after a negative opinion has been expressed. Up to now, people have felt rewarded for simply saying, "It's not a good idea." Make them feel rewarded now for giving the contribution a balanced hearing.

◊ 143

I can always depend on a certain other manager to throw cold water on ideas that I present in meetings. I get very defensive and get into arguments with him. Usually the boss cuts us off and nothing happens with my suggestions. How can I get my ideas considered?

Probably no one listens to either one of you anymore. Your roles have become predictable: You propose and he disposes. Next time, make your idea a group issue. Instead of debating with your colleague, turn to other members of the group and say, "I'd like to hear what other people think about this." Don't be surprised if you have to repeat your proposal, because the chances are that others have automatically tuned out the minute the other person began his rebuttal. If your antagonist insists on talking, you might respond with, "Yes, I understand how you feel. I need to know how others react." Then sit back and be quiet. Eventually others will begin to talk, and you may find yourself gaining allies to help you in your battle. Up to now, you've seemed to others to be quite willing to fight your wars all by yourself.

Making Presentations

◊ 144

I'm going to give a rather technical presentation to a committee and I'm not sure how many of them will understand it easily. How can I increase the chances of everyone getting my basic facts?

Go through your notes and circle every term that is technical, and be sure you define the term at least once. And it might not be a bad idea to repeat the definition the second time you use the same word or phrase.

Use visuals that are graphic and nonverbal to underscore the difficult and important parts of your presentation.

Rehearse your presentation before someone who doesn't know the subject matter, and ask your audience to stop you when he or she loses a point or becomes confused.

As you give the presentation, encourage questions. They will serve as a barometer, telling you whether the people understand you.

Finally, provide written follow-up so that people can refresh their memories later or fill in some possible gaps in your presentation.

◊ 145
What do you do to avoid the jitters before you give an important speech or presentation?

I don't try to avoid the tension altogether. I need it for the adrenaline, and to keep me properly alert. When I'm too relaxed, I'm not sufficiently sensitive to what's going on around me.

Obviously, I can reduce stage fright enormously by being confident that I have a well-constructed, meaningful speech for the audience. I prefer to have some quiet time before I'm announced, when I can think about what I'm going to do and say. For that reason, I dislike the banquet at which I have to sit and make conversation for an hour or more. Ten or fifteen minutes are usually sufficient for me to focus my thoughts on the speech and the occasion. When I go on, I want to be completely absorbed by the moment. The less I carry in from the outside, the better. I want to concentrate on this audience, to please them, and to meet at least some of their needs. I think about that during my quiet time alone.

◊ 146
How do I recover from a speech in which I bombed? I've always had stage fright. Now I think I'll be paralyzed.

I suppose it won't help you at all to know that skilled, experienced speechmakers bomb now and then. I had a very bad experience a few months ago that I'll never forget. Everything in the speech unraveled as I gave it. Right after the speech, I left the scene of the crime as fast as I could.

There are reasons why a speech bombs. As painful as it is, you must analyze the bad experience to find out what caused you to have problems. Frequent reasons for failure are inadequate preparations, misjudging the audience, not being in command of the material, or simply selecting inappropriate content. Once you've pinned down the offending reason, you consider how you can avoid it next time. In my case, I concluded there were two reasons: One, I agreed to give a certain kind of speech that I'm not accustomed to delivering—an inspirational kind; and two, I violated one of my commandments, don't try to be funny. What I thought was hilarious simply baffled most of my audience.

Once you've diagnosed the fault and decided how you will correct or avoid it in the future, take heart. You'll be a better speaker for the experience. Keep telling yourself that. It's true. Of course, you'll still have the jitters. Everyone does—or should. When you stop getting stage fright totally, you're not sensitive to the audience.

⇨ 147
I need to learn how to relax before I speak in public, even to a small group in my company.

Your best bet for relaxation, such as you can achieve, is knowing thoroughly what you are going to talk about. The more rehearsed and researched you are, the more confidently you'll begin to talk. Have extensive notes handy so you can refer to them instantly. I usually print my speech notes in large letters, using different color pens or markers for emphasis. You don't want to have to search through your notes when you're pressed. Take deep breaths before you begin. When you get up, look around the group and smile. Then talk slowly and deliberately, gradually increasing your tempo as you become more comfortable. Find a friendly face and talk to that face, but don't exclude others. That friendly face is an occasional refuge. When you sense yourself tightening up, focus briefly on that face. As you warm up, you'll probably begin to find other friendly faces, and you'll visibly relax.

▷ 148

I have to give a presentation to a group of higher level managers. I really don't do well on my feet.

One answer for you is to use visuals. Prepare some charts that summarize your main points. That way, if you are less effective in your speaking, the visuals will help carry you.

Another option is to prepare a handout that outlines your talk. Again, even if you are not a good speaker, your audience can follow your speech with the aid of the outline.

▷ 149

The executive committee has asked me to give them a rather technical presentation on some of the work my department is doing. I have some question about my ability to answer some of the detailed questions I might get, and I hate to look stupid.

Get the executive committee's permission to bring some backup in the form of subordinates who are more knowledgeable about certain aspects of the operation than you are. You might break up the presentation into sections and assign those sections to the appropriate subordinates. Rehearse your people, however.

They must understand the need for tight organization and strict time limits. You don't want to have unpleasant surprises handed to you by subordinates who ramble interminably.

Varying the presenters—with you in charge and coordinating—will usually make for a more interesting presentation. Members of the committee, having heard the experts, will feel more comfortable asking questions of the right people. The pressure will be off you, and your subordinates will appreciate the visibility you provide them.

⇨ 150
At my boss's invitation, I'm presenting a project that is very important to me to the executive committee. I already know that one vice-president is totally against the project, and I'm nervous about being able to handle his negativism.

You are probably already feeling defensive, but if you show it when you are questioned, you might sink yourself and your project. To begin with, he'll smell blood, and he'll feel confident moving in for the kill. Also, most people regard a show of defensiveness as a weakness. You may not get the sympathy you want.

When your antagonist questions you or voices objections, listen carefully and respectfully. Hesitate before you answer. Your thoughtfulness will compliment your questioner, and the pause will give someone else the chance to speak on your behalf. When you've finished with your answer, ask, "Does anyone else here have a thought or question on this subject?" You thereby open the door for others to join in, diluting the negative impact of your hostile v-p. Someone else may indeed come in with a reinforcement of your position.

People present will be measuring your respect and confidence. If you don't lose your cool or show your nervousness, and answer as if all the data are on your side, you'll make a favorable impression, even with the opposition.

▷ 151
What do you do when you give a presentation to a group and one person starts asking questions designed to show you up?

If you know the answers, and if the answers are positive and favorable to your position, snap them back. If people realize that the questioner is out to embarrass you, they'll admire your confidence.

If the questions do put you on the spot, you might look thoughtful and hesitate before answering. This creates time for someone else in the group to come to your aid. Your rescuer, who as a member of the group carries more credibility than you, may suggest that the question is not really relevant or of great importance, or was answered during your presentation.

Never put the questioner down. He or she is, after all, one of the group, and the group will resent the affront.

If the questioner threatens to take up all the time, say, "I wish you'd hold that question, and I'll come back to it. I want to be sure that the others who have questions get a chance to get them answered." If you have time, come back to the hostile questioner.

Special Problems

◊ 152

The other day I offered an idea in a staff meeting, and one of the other managers began to argue with me about my supporting data. He was pretty intense in his questioning, and I began to flounder. Finally I just shut up for the rest of the meeting. I know there has to be a better way of handling a situation like that.

You were not alone in the room. Other members of the staff were there also; yet you let the other manager isolate you. If he wanted to render you dead in the water, he succeeded.

In the future, when you realize you are floundering or are confused or otherwise not dealing well with another member of the group, stop and say to everyone else, "I'm not being very effective. Can someone else here help me out?" A plea for help when you are in distress will often result in someone coming to your aid, being articulate when you believe you are not and supplying information that you can't remember or do not have.

To repeat one of my favorite expressions, make it a group issue. Others are witness to what is happening, and are probably feeling for you and anxious to relieve the stress of the moment. Let them help you.

◊ 153

I don't think on my feet very well, so often in meetings I don't express myself clearly.

There are two relatively easy steps that can help you. The first is to think to yourself before speaking: What is the main point

I want to make? Then make it without preface or preamble. Don't open your mouth until you are clear on that key point. Then you can support your main point with explanation or elaboration. You may ramble a bit, but it won't hurt you seriously so long as people understand the point you are supporting.

The second step you can take when you suspect you are not being effective is to appeal to the group: "I'm not sure I'm making myself clear. Could any of you help me out?" People will usually step in and give you assistance in expressing yourself.

⇨ 154
What's the ideal size for a productive meeting?

That depends very much on what you want to get done. If you want the group to solve a problem or to make a decision, a smaller group, perhaps five to nine people, is better. The larger the group grows beyond that point, the less chance everyone will feel that he or she can talk freely. Larger groups are good for disseminating information, but not for free exchange between the attendees.

There has been some research suggesting that odd-numbered groups are more effective than even-numbered ones. The thinking is that people in the former realize that a majority is possible (the group won't split 50-50) and they are freer to express their beliefs. They don't worry about a stalemate. I favor consensus decisions, however, in which everyone agrees, so for my purposes it does not matter whether I have an odd or even number.

⇨ 155
Another manager called a meeting of several of us to discuss a project that he wanted to propose to top

management. I was very busy, and I sent an assistant to represent me. Now I hear that I offended the other people, especially the manager who called the meeting.

If you sent your assistant without having gotten permission from the manager who called the meeting, you sent a clear message that you didn't regard the project or meeting with the other managers as deserving of your time. And you probably exposed your assistant to a very cool reception at which he was made to feel he was an interloper.

In the future, explain the action you'd like to take before you take it. In this case, you would have discovered that sending a substitute would not be appreciated.

⬦ 156

I have to invite the company president for the big national sales meeting I'm holding this year. But he's a boring speaker, and I hate to schedule such a downer.

Have a "Meet the Press" format. Three or four people sit at a table and interview the president. If the president is worried about what kinds of questions he'll get, draw up the queries in advance and submit them so he can be prepared. Or let him suggest some. It's a change from the expected, and the format enlivens the event. So long as there are no unpleasant surprises, executives often find this kind of program more interesting to do than giving a straight speech.

⬦ 157

How do you get a consensus in meetings? Doesn't it take longer?

Yes, it takes longer, because everyone is encouraged to have a full say. That's why consensus decisions are usually superior to other kinds. More options are developed, and everyone commits himself or herself to the one option finally selected by the group.

You have to be prepared to take time. Keep emphasizing the positive contributions, the pluses. When criticism is offered, try to answer it with a positive. Find out how serious the negatives are. Sometimes people bring them up because they feel obliged to say everything they think about on the issue. Stress areas of agreement.

Between emphasizing the positive comments and areas of agreement, you start a movement. People feel they are heading for a resolution, and they want that resolution. They'll eventually overcome the negatives and fill in the gaps.

THREE

YOU AND YOUR BOSS
158–227

Objectionable Behavior

▷ **158**
I'm confused by my boss's appraisals of me. Sometimes they seem very arbitrary and contradictory.

You may have to help your boss to appraise you. Ask him, for the sake of your effectiveness to him, to discuss with you the criteria he uses in evaluation. Then ask him to tell you how well he believes you meet those criteria, and if you don't, what you need to do to match up better.

I'd make notes of what he says. Before the next appraisal time, make an appointment with him to discuss your progress and to review the criteria. It's possible that he never uses exactly the same criteria consecutively, so you may have to ask him whether there will be any further measurements he'll be using this time that you don't have in your notes.

You're making the evaluation more of a joint effort, while keeping him as honest and consistent as you can. Both of you will benefit. There will be more continuity in his appraisals, which is the only way they can be helpful in guiding your growth, and you'll have a clear idea of what his criteria are.

▷ 159

How do I handle a boss who is frequently sarcastic? I'm sure he thinks he is clever and funny, but his so-called humor is a pain.

Here's how you might get that message to him: "You know, Jerry, I often think you're trying to tell me something when you make a joke. I'm sure it's something I ought to know about managing my department, but since I'm not clear about what you're saying, I miss whatever you want me to hear. I think you'd get through to me better if you didn't use the humor. If you want to give me feedback, I'd prefer it straight." If he suggests that you're thin-skinned, you might add, "I'm concerned about understanding what you're trying to tell me. I suspect there's feedback there, but since I don't get a clear signal, I worry. And that affects my ability to work closely with you."

In the future, when Jerry pulls a funny, don't laugh. If you pretend to enjoy his attempts at humor or sarcasm, you simply reinforce him. You might ask him to translate what he just said. It's true, you may come across to Jerry as humorless, but that's better than seeming to be a willing target.

▷ 160

Lately I've had a lot of work loaded on me. I know the boss is complimenting me by delegating so much, but I'd like to relieve the pressure.

It's necessary for you and the boss to negotiate your deadlines. When the boss gives you an assignment, find out when he really needs it. Don't assume that he wants it yesterday; find out. He may in fact not be in the rush that you imagine him to be.

When the boss responds to your deadline query with, "Well, when can you have it?" give yourself enough comfort time. You may be surprised to find that the boss is agreeable to your extended deadline.

If the boss gives you more work while you're still trying to meet a previously set deadline, ask, "Is this more important than the other? Does this supersede the other deadline?" Once again, you'll find yourself negotiating. It's important that you negotiate time periods that ease your anxiety and permit you to do a good job.

Keep in mind that the boss probably doesn't keep a strict record of the deadlines on your assignments, and that he or she expects you to look out for your own interests.

⇨ 161
My manager hoards information. I have to go and ask for it. For example, I heard about a policy change. I asked my boss about it, and then he told me. It's very annoying.

Your boss is either forgetful, disorganized, or on a power trip. He can't remember to pass information along to you, or the clutter of it all buries him. At least your boss tells you what you want to know. It's no use getting upset. You probably won't change your boss's behavior. Give in a bit. Make sure you have fairly frequent informal chats with your boss where you trade opinions and information. Undoubtedly you hear gossip that you can also pass along. It's just that you will have to initiate the exchange.

Of course, when it comes to policy or urgent matters, you can try to convince your boss that your effectiveness and compliance are at risk. Perhaps that will wake him up.

⬦ 162

The boss is forever checking up on me. He does it to others, too, but I get upset by it. It's as if he doesn't trust me.

If your boss singled you out, I'd ask you to think about what you do that might create this lack of trust. But since the boss treats other subordinates in the same nervous way, I would recommend that you not react resentfully. When the boss checks up on your work, respond cheerfully. For example, answer "Did you finish that Texlite report?" with "Oh, sure, that was done this morning. It's being duplicated and circulated."

You might go even further. Volunteer information about your progress: "I know you're anxious to get those figures on the Warton bids. I rushed them a bit so you could have them this morning," or, "I sensed you were concerned about how I was getting along on the Septa study, and I wanted to tell you that I should have it wrapped up by the first of the week."

If his behavior is the result of a deeply ingrained habit and is general, you're not going to persuade him to stop it because you feel affronted. By voluntarily allaying his anxiety, you may be able to convince him that he doesn't have to check up on you. You'll usually beat him to it.

⬦ 163

My boss chews me out in front of my subordinates. How do I get him to stop this?

Schedule some private time with him, and give him a speech such as the following: "Yesterday, you called me down for not having made the assignment you wanted. I had some reasons for doing as I did, and I'd like to give those reasons to you. But first I want you to know that when you criticize me in public, I get very upset because I think that kind of thing should take place in the privacy of an office. I am embarrassed, and my employees are embarrassed. Their respect for me is important. They need to know that you respect me. If bawling me out before them reduces their respect for me, then I'll be less effective in dealing with them. You and I both want me to be as effective as I can. So I'd like to ask that you criticize me either in your office or mine. I know that you'll get a better response from me. I'll listen better because I won't be so upset."

The boss will probably agree. But if he or she begins to criticize you again before your employees, stop the boss and ask, "May we continue this in your office?" That's usually sufficient to remind the boss of the agreement between you.

▷ 164

How do you get a boss to respect closed doors? This morning he burst in on the middle of a counseling session I was holding with an employee. I've spoken with him about it, but he says that he doesn't believe in closed doors.

Regardless of his belief about closed doors, you and he agree on one important issue: your effectiveness. He needs you to be effective, and you want to be. But you cannot be as effective a manager as you would like when your manager interrupts an essential and private interview between you and your employee. Put the issue of your closed door, therefore, on this basis: Close your door when you are convinced that privacy is necessary for you to get the results you want. Furthermore, while you know that your boss respects his and your employees, his disruptiveness may broadcast a different message. And you wouldn't want employees believing something about your boss that is far from the truth.

It's doubtful that your boss could turn his back on such arguments. He will probably consent, at least grudgingly, to respect your closed doors.

⬦ 165
My manager always wants something done yesterday.

It's fine if you can deliver it yesterday, but that's a little tough if you have other work of your own. I'd be inclined to negotiate: "I can't give it to you yesterday. Would you settle for tomorrow?" It's interesting how many times I've received work with an immediate deadline, and when I indicated that I'd like more flexibility, I got it without any argument. I guess that proves my suspicion that people negotiate when they have to. If we don't make them negotiate, we buy their panic.

⬦ 166
I'm annoyed that my boss never has time to see me unless it is over lunch. I'm the only female in the office, and the only person who can't see him during regular hours. I know it's sexist on his part. I don't like to have to give up my lunch hours.

He can only see you at lunch if you make yourself available. Simply express your regrets that you have made previous plans that can't be set aside. And repeat your request for time. If the matter is urgent, say to him that you need to see him as quickly as possible, and state the amount of time you'll need. Pepper your request with a description of the problems that a delay in seeing him might cause.

This is an unfortunate pattern that you should break.

⇨ 167
My problem is that my boss likes to sit in on my staff meetings and take over. How can I stop him?

The intriguing question is not so much how you can control your boss, but rather why he wants to sit in on your meetings. That's quite an investment of his time. It seems to me that you'd want to know why he is there. You might try this approach: Since you recognize that his attending your meetings requires a lot of time away from performing other functions he undoubtedly regards as higher priority, perhaps he'd like you to prepare a summary of the business concluded in your staff meetings. Or you would be happy to meet with him after your meeting to give him a brief verbal report. Emphasize that you are thinking of his time and of the inconvenience to him in tying up his morning (or afternoon).

If he persists in wanting to attend, you'll have to be more direct. Recognize, further, that he must have certain concerns or interests connected with your staff meetings, and that you'd like to know what they are. If he answers that he enjoys attending, you can reply that some of your staff feel a bit inhibited when the big boss is there, that because of their inhibitions you don't get as much done as you'd like, and that perhaps, in the interest of your effectiveness, he might be agreeable to attending meetings on occasion rather than each time.

On the other hand, his answer to your question about why he attends may produce a more disturbing answer. For example, he does not trust you to get results on your own. You then have a deeper problem, and you must find out from your boss what you must do to inspire the proper amount of confidence.

⬦ 168

I have a boss who occasionally sits in on my staff meetings and scowls her way through them. It upsets everyone in the meeting because we think we're doing or saying things of which she disapproves.

Her scowling may have little or nothing to do with what is going on in your meeting. Sometimes people have unpleasant expressions on their faces of which they aren't aware. She may be thinking about matters entirely unrelated to your meeting (although that in itself may be a comment about the interest level of your meetings). But it's important that you find out. Periodically, when her face shows a scowl, say to her, "You look as if you're unhappy with what was just said," or, "Do you disapprove?" Chances are she will be surprised and deny being upset or disapproving. Then you can tell her about the facial expression that led you to check with her. After a few such comments by you, she may try to discipline her facial expressions. To reinforce your message, you may tell her privately that her scowling and frowning cause concern among your staff. She needs to be concerned about the issue because she's the boss, and everyone is trying to read her thoughts.

If, however, the scowls reflect her disapproval of things said or done in the meeting, you have to ask yourself what happened to the communications between the two of you that she conveys nonverbal rather than verbal messages.

⇩ 169

When my boss is out of the office on personal business, which is often, I think, he has his secretary transfer his phone calls to my office. I'm supposed to say he is in a meeting and can't speak on the phone at the moment. But I hate to lie.

You don't have to lie. When someone calls, you can reply, "I'm told he is tied up in a meeting (in conference)." That's no lie since that is what you've been told. If the caller presses for more information, you reply, "I don't know any more than that. May I take a message?" That's no lie, either, since you apparently don't know where he is or what he is doing.

⇩ 170

I do a lot of covering for the guy I report to. He has a drinking problem. I go to interdepartmental meetings in his place because he doesn't feel well. Sometimes I get incomplete work from him at the last minute because he's in no shape to finish it for the deadline. He leaves early, and I have to lie for him.

It's distasteful working for a man who is so out of control, as you describe. But it can have its benefits. You're doing work that is appropriate to a higher level. You have become your boss's surrogate. There are people in your organization who know you are doing the work. Your boss's drinking is no secret, although drinking managers often believe that their excesses are unknown to others.

How can you translate your accomplishment into progress for yourself? Instead of resenting the additional responsibility, you might look for even more. It's possible that you could start to perform some of your boss's tasks without having them delegated to you. Watch the boss's reaction. If he suddenly becomes suspicious, you know you've reached a boundary. Draw back. If he welcomes your taking on more, expand your boundary. The more you learn, the more you're worth to the organization, or to another.

But you don't want to be a surrogate forever. Remember that the organization tolerates your boss's incapacity for reasons you may not understand. It will be even easier for management to tolerate your boss as you become more proficient in doing his job. Eventually you are going to have to make a move. Since you've been dealing with higher management in your boss's stead, you must have one or two contacts whom you can approach discreetly and informally. Don't try to shoot down your boss in these conversations. Stick to describing your ambition and readiness to move ahead. See what kinds of responses you get. It may take time for the word to get around that you want your reward for having carried the extra burden. But if you don't get encouragement within a reasonable time, you can fairly well assume that management is happy having you where you are. Resume your job search elsewhere.

Usually I'm very cautious about advising people to go over the boss's head, but in the case of a drinking boss who has become dependent on a subordinate, there is no reason why the boss should want to help the subordinate if it means losing that person. Furthermore, the boss has probably weakened his or her own influence in the organization and couldn't help the subordinate much, anyway, even if the desire were there.

⬦ 171
When my division manager comes to work with me in my branch, we always wind up the day in a bar. He

looks for a woman to pick up. I'm a family man, and I don't care to be part of his hunting expedition. How can I let him know I disapprove?

Why antagonize your boss unnecessarily by criticizing his morals? No one likes to be preached at. Start finding reasons to have to go home after the working day. Since you're a family man, you have a number of obligations you can present as a reason for not drinking with him while he's on the prowl. If you believe it is in your interest to have a drink with him, make it clear that you have time for one only. Persuade him to talk with you about your day, about what is happening in the company, what he would suggest you do to sharpen your skills. After the drink, thank him warmly and excuse yourself. Incidentally, if you drive, you have a valid excuse for not drinking. You could wind up with a Driving While Impaired charge. This may result in your losing your license, at least temporarily; your boss would understand the disastrous consequences of that, to you and to the company. If you must join him and drive, stick with the soft drinks.

⇨ 172

Our department head puts people down. In a meeting, one of us will make an observation or a suggestion, and he often responds by saying, "Yes, but even more important. . . . " I wonder if he's even aware of it.

He's probably aware that he says it, but he may be surprised, even chagrined, to learn that others feel put down by it. Make him aware of it. After his initial embarrassment, he'll probably appreciate what you've done. Say to him something such as,

"I'm sure you say it without thinking, and the fact is, your ideas are sometimes better or more important. But every time you say it, someone in the room gets needlessly hurt. I thought you'd want to know about it."

Unless he's an ogre, he'll try to stop it. You may have to remind him again, but laugh as you do. He'll probably take it good-naturedly.

➪ 173

I've done my job well for a long time, under two other bosses. Now I have a new one who keeps looking over my shoulder. It upsets me, because I think I've proved I can be trusted.

Apparently you have not—at least not to the new man. I suspect that, since you want to be left alone, you don't maintain close contact with your boss. If he doesn't know you and your work well enough to feel he can trust you, he's not getting a chance to feel otherwise. You're going to have to bridge the gap. I judge that your autonomy is a matter of pride, but you'll probably pay a high price to maintain it. If your boss distrusts you and, in your eyes, meddles, you're not going to be happy.

Bite the bullet; the agony may only be temporary. Schedule periodic meetings with your new boss, during which you can discuss what you do, how you do it, and how what you do fits in with his plans.

In all likelihood, the man wants reassurance that you are willing to travel in the same direction as he. Once he gets that reassurance, and when your performance backs it up, you'll probably find yourself enjoying the old autonomy.

Give the new man a chance to know and trust you.

⇕ 174
I'm angry that my boss took credit for something I created.

Bosses have been known for such perfidy. If you want to press it, and thereby give indication of the kind of loyalty to you that you'd like to see in the future, talk to him privately: "I'm glad you liked my innovation. In fact, I'm hearing through the grapevine how much you liked it, and that pleases me. However, I wish I could hear that in some way I was connected with it."

Bosses have also been known to feel shame and to offer redress in the form of a memo to higher management emphasizing their subordinate's role in the innovation.

⇕ 175
Lately my boss has begun to leave the office early in the afternoon for a couple of drinks before going home. He seems to want my company, because he asks me nearly every day to join him. I've gone with him a few times, but I'm getting nervous about leaving early, and my wife raises hell because I come home half in the bag.

Worry about your job as well as your liver. Your boss may not have enough to do, and that may be by management's design. Clearly he is not on the fast track, and he may even have been shelved as a has-been. If that's true, management probably will put up with the early departures so long as he does not create problems.

You, however, are more vulnerable. Higher management expects you to put in a full day's work. They may even have more interesting plans for you, now that your boss is out of the traffic pattern.

If your boss is not a shelf-sitter but is coasting, then he is vulnerable and may drag down anyone too closely associated with him.

So, you see, in either case, you have much to lose besides your health and sobriety in those hours at the pub, no matter how jolly. Of course you want to stay on the good side of your boss. If you feel you must occasionally join him, make it as rarely as possible. For the remainder of his invitations, be specific about the work you have to do. Tell him what you're working on. Don't just say, "I'm too busy." He may feel less rejected if you are doing so for specific reasons.

Boss's Ineffectiveness

◊ 176
My boss makes fast decisions that are often awful.

There's a difference between being decisive and being a good decision-maker. Often the decisive manager operates from biases, preconceptions, and confidence—sometimes excessive—in the source of the information on which the decision is based. The good decision-maker recognizes his or her biases and preconceptions, but rises above them to look at all the options that can be generated within a reasonable time. The effective decision-maker also favors certain sources of information as more credible than others, but doesn't lose sight of the fact that those favored sources may also be biased. Thus, he or she seeks out other sources to confirm or deny the information received from the favored sources.

Finally, the good decision-maker takes time and trouble to try to anticipate the consequences of the decision, a step that many decisive managers don't take, to their and everyone else's regret.

▷ 177

I work for a person who doesn't take charge and lead. She waits for others to tell her what she should do. How can I get her to be a leader?

Leaders can lead from the rear, too. If you're looking for someone to charge up the hill, I don't think you'll ever find that person in your boss. But reactive people can be very useful to their subordinates, and very much agents of change. If she listens to you, welcomes your suggestions, agrees that they ought to be considered, and takes action on some of them, what more are you asking? Apply your influencing skills. If she wants input, give as much as you can. With a truly responsive boss, you could be a crucial—and influential—subordinate.

▷ 178

I'm a vice-president of a family-owned company. The founder and chairman is a strong personality. He hired me. But he also made his son the president. The son, I'm convinced, is a pathological liar. He lies when he doesn't have to. I'm under a lot of stress because I have to deal with the son in almost everything, and I can't trust him.

I empathize and sympathize. I've seen too many similar situations, and they're usually the result of a strong father-weak son relationship. In one case, the son, who must have felt in his early life that he couldn't cope with his father's demands on him, retreated into another world. He became schizophrenic, passing in and out of the safer world he had created for himself. Coworkers couldn't trust him because they were never sure which side of the looking glass he was on.

That case may parallel yours. Father probably knows, but denies his son's infirmity. Your best course of action may be to form an alliance with the other officers and managers of the company, who are undoubtedly suffering as you are. At some point, probably after some egregious behavior by the president, you're going to have to confront the father. It will be useless to have a showdown with the son, who will only lie about the lie. If the managerial staff stays united, the chairman will have to take some action. He can ill afford to ignore the complaints of everyone.

At the risk of sounding pessimistic, I doubt whether the father will take the drastic action that is called for. He'll probably continue to nurse his illusions about his son. Until the father recognizes that his son desperately needs professional help, you may not see a long-term solution to the problem.

◊ 179

How do you get a boss to listen? Sometimes I think I've gotten agreement or permission, only to find out later he hadn't remembered it.

With this person, you need to give the punch line first to get his attention. Don't give a preamble. Say, "I want to attend the such and such conference in Seattle next month." After you've gotten his attention, give the details and supporting arguments. If you try to build up to your main point by giving the explanation, you may lose his attention.

Get response as you talk. Don't give your data in nonstop fashion. If you do, you won't know whether you're sweeping him along or you've left him behind in some backwater. Throw in a question: "When I first thought about the project, I wondered whether I should postpone it until May until after the sales meeting. I'm leaning toward not putting it off. What are your thoughts?" Avoid questions that call for just a yes or a no. You want some involvement, or at least you want to assure yourself that the boss is still awake.

Get action. Tell the boss what you want and try to get it before leaving. Once you've gotten it, send him a follow-up memo explaining to him what he has agreed to.

▷ 180
I'm stuck behind a shelf-sitter. He's gone as far as he will go. I feel really dead-ended.

Your frustration is understandable, but don't let it blind you to taking advantage of the opportunity you may have to develop your skills and knowledge as a manager. Shelf-sitters are often superb teachers. Since they are not preoccupied with their own ambitions, they have the time and the willingness to share their experiences. Your boss may be willing to delegate to you, and give you room for experimentation and innovation. The boss who is on dead center may offer you a protected environment where your mistakes can lead to learning instead of disaster.

⋄ 181

My boss is very cautious and takes forever to make decisions. How can I hurry the process?

Before you present your next proposal to your boss, think through the following recommendations:

- Make it valuable to the boss.
- Make it interesting.
- Make it easy.

Give your boss a reason why your idea will benefit him and the operation. Explain it clearly up front, so he doesn't lose interest or become confused while you are getting to your key point. Finally, show him how the idea can be made a reality in simple ways: "First, I'll get a memo around explaining the new procedure, then I'll train the supervisors to train their people. We should have the whole thing in place by the end of the month. If you'll okay this, I'll get started on the memo today."

Try not to leave his office without his approval. Keep selling the benefits and how easy it will be if he leaves it to you.

⋄ 182

When I go to my department head for a decision on important matters, he'll almost always say to me, "Let me get back to you on this." He usually doesn't. How do I get a decision from him right then?

Do what salespeople do. They're forever in danger of getting stalled by their prospects.

First, make sure that the boss really understands the issue. He may be putting you off because he hasn't really grasped the issue.

Second, give him a reason to buy now. Come up with a benefit for an immediate decision: saving time or money, preventing a mistake, keeping employees happy, and so on.

Third, if he still doesn't move on the decision, ask him what has to happen for him to decide. He may not be able to come up with a good answer, and may agree to decide then and there. On the other hand, if he says, for example, he wants to talk with someone else, suggest that the three of you schedule the meeting now, or that he pick up the phone and get the matter off his desk.

Fourth, find a way to make the decision-making an easier task. You might say, "If you just give me the okay, I'll get my people to sketch out how we can do this in a short time, and then I'll get back to you with the plan." The more details you can remove from his shoulders, the more likely you'll get a decision.

Five, do more selling. Don't be in a hurry to leave just because he wants to stall. Find another benefit to sell and then close again. After the additional selling, ask him for the decision.

If everything you do fails to get a decision, try to pin him down on a time and date when he will make the decision. Let him know that you'll check back with him then.

⇨ 183

I have a boss who describes himself as a laissez-faire manager, but it sounds like a cop-out to me. He isn't very effective. Are there times when it is justified?

Some work teams are so experienced and expert that they can run themselves. Indeed, their semiautonomy is a reward for their good performance. They'd probably resent much monitoring by the manager, and he or she would no doubt be wasting time by closely supervising. In laissez-faire situations, the manager stays out of the everyday operation except to deal with problems and threats to the work group. The manager, in such a case, spends time doing what managers should do: planning and designing for the future, training to upgrade individual and group effectiveness, and maintaining liaisons with upper management and outsiders.

In my experience, such a style of management isn't justified in most situations. Granted, many managers practice it, but if the work group is not highly developed as a team, the results can be low morale and productivity—and much resentment by employees who dislike working in a vacuum.

▷ 184
My boss has a problem with listening. I'm looking for ways to hold his attention.

Make sure you get his attention from the beginning. I advise following these three recommendations: Whatever you have to say, make it (1) interesting, (2) valuable, and (3) easy.

For your boss, make it interesting in two ways. First, start off with your key point. Don't preface your comments, as so many do, with a here's-why-I'm-telling-you-what-I'm-about-to-tell-you statement. You can explain later, after you've gotten him involved. The second way you make your remarks interesting is to keep them short. A concise explanation following your key point is essential with a boss who doesn't listen well. Break up your supporting statements with questions such as, "Am I making myself clear?" or, "Do you have questions about what I'm saying?"

Involvement of your boss is necessary. Too much uninterrupted talk and he is off in his own world.

Make what you say valuable by immediately giving your boss a reason to listen. What you're about to say will save money, time, help a failing employee, make the boss look good, streamline operations, and so on. The boss is sitting there saying to himself, "Why should I listen?" Supply a good reason and you'll get attention.

Make it easy for him to listen and to do what you want. For example, "Here's a simple solution to the problem we've been worried about. Step one, step two, step three." The easier you can make it for the boss to say yes, the more attention and earlier action you'll get.

Friction and Conflict

⇩ 185

I don't understand my boss. About two weeks ago, he mentioned a project that he has long wanted to initiate but hasn't had the time. I had some time and took it on without telling him. It took a lot of work, but when I showed him what I had been doing, he raised the roof about my neglecting my regular work.

When the boss offers a wish list, it may not carry a priority with it. However, the fact that the boss has spoken it seems automatically to make it a priority item to subordinates. You assumed it was something the boss wanted done now after waiting so long, but in fact the boss may have been thinking aloud. "Someday, I hope. . . . " If, in the process of helping him to realize the dream, you failed to keep your own work going, you were vulnerable to criticism.

Do I need to suggest that next time, before you start to work on your boss's wish list, you make sure it is really something he'd like to see actualized?

⇨ 186

I have been with my company close to 30 years. I've just acquired a new, very young boss, who seems very defensive and on guard. I want to have a close working relationship with him, but I think he worries about my being trouble for him.

He's probably suffering from the stereotype of the old-timer who is automatically resistant to change, suspicious of youngsters, and generally a know-it-all.

Surprise him. When you've gotten more comfortable with him, and he with you, suggest changes yourself. He'll probably want to put his stamp on the operation, so give him some hints as to how he could improve things.

Be open and accepting of him. That's not what he expects. Give him the respect you would any boss. He's worried that you'd only respect a man your age. And there is probably much in him to respect: his technical knowledge, drive, and ambition.

Of course, you do know the operation much better than he, but you don't have to push your knowledge. Let him know that it is there if he wants to tap it. Be especially careful not to make comparisons of him with past managers, or to talk about the way things used to be done, or always have been. When he comes up with ideas, talk about them as positively as you can. At least present a balanced analysis. He probably expects you to begin every response with, "The trouble with that is. . . . " It's a statement to drop from your repertory.

◊ 187
I'm a lot smarter than the man I work for, and I know he feels threatened. I don't want or expect to be his second-in-command forever, but I don't want him to cause me trouble.

You are sufficiently smart to realize that you can make your boss feel and look good, and that your concern for him will ease some of his stress. Be comfortable with your intelligence; he may never be. But you can make him comfortable with your managerial talents by investing them in making a successful operation for both of you. Keep him informed. Show him deference as boss. Be open in your relationship with him. Don't give him cause to worry about your strategizing behind his back. The more relaxed you are in your dealings with him, the less he will worry about your superiority.

◊ 188
Our boss wants to install a Management By Objectives (MBO) program. I'm against it because I've heard it doesn't work.

It's true that MBO hasn't worked in a number of organizations that have tried it. There are at least three reasons why it has been disappointing for so many managers who experimented with it. First, the installers grew impatient with it. I've heard estimates that it takes a good five years for the MBO system to take root. Many managements have discarded it long before. A second reason why MBO does not have a good record is that it must be practiced at all levels of management, top to bottom, without fail. It often isn't uniformly applied. Finally, there is too much slippage in many systems, too much forgiveness of goals not accomplished.

The MBO approach can work, chiefly because it goes with the human grain. Human behavior is directed toward goals. People always have reasons for doing as they do. When you formalize the goals, you are taking steps to enhance the motivating forces in people. But MBO takes persistence and patience, and American managers are not known for either one.

▷ **189**
My manager is about to promote a woman named Sally to supervisor, but I think her promotion would be a big mistake. The boss knows that I've never been one of this woman's fans, but I do feel that I should warn him.

Acknowledge your bias at the outset. For example, you might say, "John, you know that my opinions of Sally are not the highest, but that doesn't mean I can't have a somewhat objective view of her. I'd like to tell you what I think are some of the minuses in giving her more responsibility. You can take what I say and mull it over, but I want to be up front about my bias. I'm not blind to it. May I tell you what's on my mind?"

Your openness about how you feel toward Sally should impress your boss and persuade him that it is in his best interest to listen to you, at least. I wouldn't advise you to press your case. State how you feel and think, and conclude simply: "Take it for what it's worth. I wanted you to have my thoughts on the subject."

⇨ 190

It's hard for me to deal with my boss. When I suggest a new way of doing things, he bucks. Sometimes he wears me down with his objections.

Don't wear yourself out by trying to answer his objections. He may be telling you that he hasn't been sold by your presentation. Also, if you are debating with him, you may be using the yes-but approach: "Yes, I hear what you say, but you're wrong." When you rebut, no matter how tactful you believe you are, you may sound as if you are discounting his thinking.

Use the yes-and tactic. When he voices an objection, say, "Yes, I can see that is a consideration in your mind, and here's something else you might want to think about." Sell, or resell, another benefit to his going along with you. When you've finished your sell, ask for his okay. If he continues to voice the same objection, then you must eventually confront it. Qualify it, however, as a salesperson does. To illustrate: "If I could remove the time lag that you're concerned about, would you be willing to give this a try?" If he says yes, then show him how you'll take care of the time problem, and get his okay to go ahead.

⇨ 191

I want to promote Al because I think he'd make an excellent supervisor, but my boss cautions me against it. He says his gut tells him otherwise. I have a feeling if I do it and am wrong, my boss will hold it against me.

It sounds as if it is your intuition against your boss's. Surely you have more to go on than gut feeling. Al must have proved that he has initiative, that he can work well with people, and that he really wants to take on this responsibility.

Nevertheless, you should seek the boss's opinion. Get as much information as you can. If the boss has only intuition to offer, make your judgment based on what you know as well as what you feel. You can't afford to keep a good man down simply because you worry that your boss might hold a mistake against you.

⬦ 192

A few months ago, I took over a department that had been well managed by my predecessor. The trouble is, my boss keeps comparing the way I do things with the way the previous manager did. He'll say, "Jim used to handle that by doing. . . . " My ways are different. I don't want to be compared with Jim, no matter how good he was.

You're probably going to be compared with good old Jim until you begin to make a record on your own. Your boss is no doubt expressing his concern over how you will fare. As abrasive as the comparisons may be, you don't want to shut out the possibility that Jim may have had a trick or two that you might emulate and from which you might benefit. So listen patiently. Then make your own judgments. As you become confident and successful, the comparisons will, in all likelihood, stop.

If at any time your boss seems to be advising you to follow in Jim's footsteps, you should be prepared to explain, calmly and in detail, why you want to follow your own counsel instead. It might be useful for you to be more forthcoming with your boss in general, showing him how you operate and why you do as you do. The concern he expresses may derive from a lack of communication on your part. Fill him in and feed his confidence in you.

⇦ 193

I work for an authoritarian manager who doesn't think people can be trusted. How do I get him to understand that most people really want to do a good job and don't have to be pushed or threatened?

It's taken a lifetime for him to get where he is now in terms of how he views employees, so you can hardly expect him to change for you in a short time. In fact, he won't change substantially and on a broad front even over an extended period of time. You'll have to concentrate on small changes. From time to time, tell him specifically how an employee has taken the initiative on something and carried it through on his or her own. Relay to the boss suggestions employees have made to you. After a task has been done successfully, describe how you let the employees involved work out their own schedules and methods. He can't quarrel with that success, although you may have to show him that the success would not have been greater had you exercised tight control. If there are examples of employees voluntarily taking on extra work, let him know of those cases.

The process is one of slow softening. You won't get vast or rapid changes in his perspective. After all, you're trying to unfreeze a lifetime of conditioning.

⇦ 194

I don't like the man I report to, and I think it's mutual. We're both serious and intelligent, and we get our work done. But it creates a lot of tension.

If you're both serious, intelligent, and effective, you have a lot more going for you than you'll find in many boss-subordinate relationships. There are many likable bosses who just aren't very competent, and that creates a strain, believe me. It sounds to me as if you have the basis for mutual respect, if not friendship. You don't mention trust, which is another essential building block in a good working relationship. If you're not sure of the trust, start working on it. Each of you has to know that the other will not consciously work to deceive him. One way to build trust is to maintain frequent contact, something that admittedly is more difficult to do when you don't much like each other. Another way is to keep the boss informed of what you're doing, something that subordinates don't always like to do even when they like the boss. In summary, frequent contact and full communication are the keys to a trusting relationship, and both trust and respect will carry you a long way, even without affection. You may have much to learn from this boss. Take advantage of the opportunity. If the lack of warmth between you becomes too burdensome, then leave. But it's not likely to if the two of you work well together otherwise. An effective working relationship makes up for a lot.

The longer you stay, the greater the chance that you will score points with others in the organization, who will see that you're the kind of person who works well even under less-than-perfect conditions.

▷ 195

Our manager brought in an outside consultant to give us some management training. I think the guy is terrible. I know the boss is paying a lot of money for this person, and I'd like to keep him from wasting it on future programs conducted by this man. How do I get the message across tactfully and without appearing to be negative?

Much depends on the relationship you have with your boss. If he highly regards your judgment, then your feedback will be welcomed. After all, the boss doesn't want to look foolish by bringing in an incompetent to train his managers. If you worry about coming off negative, suggest areas or subjects that were not covered that could or should be, or show how what was covered could be improved. Once you've presented the positive, you might continue with a negative evaluation of the consultant. But don't commit overkill; you'll make the boss feel foolish. Pick a few of the most glaring examples of ineptitude and let it go at that. Bear in mind that the more specific you can be in making suggestions or criticism, the more acceptable your opinions will be. You will not be seen as conducting a vendetta against the consultant, who is, after all, the boss's choice.

If you do not have the kind of credibility that will enable you to make an impact on your boss, gather evidence among your colleagues. If they share your negative feelings, ask for a meeting with your boss as a group. The boss can't overlook mass disapproval, and he can't single out an individual to punish.

◊ 196

I'm in hot water with my boss because I won't send any more of my supervisors to the company supervisory training programs. Those trainers fill their minds with a lot of garbage that doesn't work. It's a waste of time and money.

One way you can get out of the hot water and get more relevant training for your supervisors is to sit down with the corporate training department and tell them what you need. Training departments often provide standardized, sometimes packaged programs because the line managers they deal with don't specify their departmental or divisional needs. If you're working with professional trainers, you'll find that they'll collaborate with you in customizing a program for you. They'd like to have you as a client. It does not reflect well on them that you don't send your people. You may have to pay a bit more for your own program, but if it provides the kind of training that your supervisors can apply, it will pay for itself.

Of course, this advice assumes that you are regarded in the company as an effective manager. If you're seen by higher management as a maverick or a stubborn holdout, you could be making a lot of trouble for yourself. You may have to make some compromises so as not to be labeled countercultural.

⇨ 197

I'm often asked to draft letters, memos, and reports for my boss, but no matter how much time I spend on them, he always heavily edits what I write. It ticks me off.

Some people are compulsively heavy-handed in their editing. If they don't reconstruct what you've written, they think they haven't done their job. They'll continue to do so for that reason, regardless of whether you write as well as Graham Greene.

However, consider the possibility that you, like perhaps 98 percent of the population, do not really write well (not that your boss writes any better). The boss is trying to tell you that through his extensive alterations.

Take some edited copy to your boss and say, "I really want to do a better job for you the first time, so that you don't have to spend a lot of time rewriting me. How can I do that? Give me some guidelines so I can write the way you'd like." With that, you've given the boss some sense of how you feel about the reworking he does, and you've shown him you're open to writing more closely to his style. If he doesn't have any guidelines, he may let up in the future, knowing now how you feel. If he does, he'll give them to you and save you some wear and tear next time.

Still, double-space your drafts. He won't stop the practice at once.

⏵ **198**

I work for an old-fashioned manager who has been with the company for 35 years. I have an MBA. He's authoritarian and I'm democratic in my style. We don't communicate too much, but I know he's suspicious of me. I think he believes I'm going to give away the company, to let the employees walk all over me.

There are at least three fairly easy steps you can take to ease his suspicion. First, although you say you do not communicate well, keep close. Because of the awkwardness, you may feel more comfortable with the gap between you, but try to close it. The more he sees you, the less he worries about what objectionable things you might be doing behind his back. The second step in allaying suspicion is to talk with him about your plans and problems. He's an old-timer who probably feels he has forgotten more than you'll ever know. Encourage him to talk. You don't have to accept every suggestion or bit of advice, but you might learn something from him, and you'll compliment him enormously. Third, reassure him that your department works well by letting him know of the achievements of your employees. When their performance is praiseworthy, do the praising publicly to him. Your employees will be gratified, and the boss's tensions will be eased.

Many old-time bosses are scornful of the young breed of MBAs because they suspect that the juniors really don't respect their seniors. If this suspicion lingers in your boss, your increased contacts will dilute it.

⇨ 199
I've become very active in my professional association, and I'm due for a vice-presidency in it. Although I'm very careful not to take time off for association work and keep up a good performance on the job, I'm getting some flak from my boss about how much time I'm devoting outside. What do I do?

The first thing to do is find at least one reason why it will benefit your company for you to be active in your professional association. At the moment, your boss probably suspects that you are neglecting your work, or that you are making contacts that will help you to make a job change. Some of the advantages you might cite are: good publicity for the organization, relevant experience that will be useful on the job and make you a more skillful subordinate, a source of industry or professional information that could create a competitive edge, and so on.

Once you have your arguments in place, sit down with your boss and negotiate. You want his support, and he, as well as the organization, can benefit from your involvement. Don't forget to reassure the boss that you are continuing to perform effectively on the job, and that your job is your first priority.

If your professional association has interesting meetings and social events, invite your boss as your guest from time to time. As he becomes more familiar with the extent and the value of your involvement, he's likely to give you the support you seek.

⬦ 200

My boss has made a decision that I think will lead to a big mistake. He's not an easy man to deal with if he thinks he's being criticized. How do I approach him?

You might say, "I was thinking about that decision, and I was wondering about the construction costs being high. I know you anticipated the extra cost, and I wondered how you factored it in." The idea is to suggest a problem or drawback that you worry about, but for which you figure he has already planned. You just want to know what steps he took to resolve that problem. Of course, you may suspect he has not, and this is a tactful way to alert him to a reality for which he may not have planned.

Another approach is to ask him to review his decision-making with you so that you can understand how he arrived at the conclusion he did. Whenever he mentions a potential problem, you can ask, "Do you see that as a red flag?" He may not, and he may ask you whether you do. Or if he does see a threat to the decision in the problem, you can ask him to tell you how he reduced the threat in his mind.

Open up the chance for a discussion. He may still reject your concerns, but you will have expressed them to a fairly open mind, whereas had you criticized, you might have found the thinking doors shut.

⬦ 201

My boss gave me a directive that I don't like. I know it's going to upset the employees. How do I enforce a policy to which I object?

Unless the policy is unethical, illegal, or immoral, you should promulgate and enforce it. Give it to your employees straight.

Let them know where the policy originated, but don't say anything that would constitute editorializing. If they appeal to your sympathy, simply respond that your obligation is to announce and back the policy. If they complain, tell them you will relay their opinions to your boss. The only stand you need or should take is that you must do what the boss expects you to do. It's your choice whether you reveal to your employees that you objected to it. But if you say that much, resist the temptation to give the details. You have been overridden, and that's what is important.

Your employees will understand. If, however, they test you on the new policy, you must respond as you've promised to do.

▷ 202

I'm a female assistant with an MBA. My boss's wife apparently believes I'm a secretary, because she called me to give me a message for her husband, my boss. Today, she asked me to run an errand. I said that wasn't my job. I was probably very brusque. What do I say to her next time?

There shouldn't be a next time, and you shouldn't complain to her. Go to your boss and tell him what's been happening. Treat it with humor, because he'll probably be embarrassed.

If he thinks that it's his wife's prerogative to ask female employees to run errands, you can tell him any way you wish that that sort of thing went out at least 20 years ago. You can smile when you say it. If he's so completely ignorant of where the world has gone since then, you may hint that you regard that attitude of his to be risky for the company.

Dissatisfaction with the Boss

⇨ **203**

There's one thing my boss can't seem to handle: when I compliment her on some decision or action that I think is especially shrewd or effective. I guess she think's I'm polishing the apple, but I really mean it.

Some people cannot handle compliments. How many times have you heard a variation on this theme? "That's a pretty dress"; "Oh, this old thing?"

There's no point in continuing to make her uncomfortable when you want to give her a bit of praise. Try a more subtle approach. Ask her what went into a particular decision. What factors did she consider? Why did she choose that option over others? She'll have your recognition of her competence without feeling embarrassed. And she'll undoubtedly be gratified by your interest and the chance to talk about what led her to do what she did. At the same time, you have a chance to benefit from some expert mentoring.

⇨ **204**

The top guy in my department believes that he is plugged into every circuit in the company. When I go to him with a rumor or a bit of gossip he hasn't heard, he asks, "Where'd you hear that?" He's offended. And I wind up naming my sources, which makes me uncomfortable.

No wonder you feel uncomfortable. Not only are you threatening your boss, but you break your confidences. I can understand your wanting to check out the validity of the rumor with your boss, but it sounds as if it is Russian roulette you play when you do. On the other hand, if there is a possibility that you may, deep down, really want to one-up the boss, you should examine your actions. The game may not be worth it.

In the future, when you want to check something out, you might use this approach: "Putting some pieces together, I wonder whether John is being told he's going to step into Mark's slot," or, "I've been doing some speculating. Do you suppose it's possible that. . . ?"

Your seeming speculation will constitute less of a threat.

◊ 205

Although I have a very quiet style, I get things done. But my boss seems to like more flashy people who, I believe, usually have more show than substance. She promoted one of my peers the other day, a woman for whom I've never had much respect. I don't know what to do, because I'm not good at doing PR for me.

You don't have to be flashy to mount a public relations effort for yourself. You may be too quiet. Find ways to talk with your boss about what you are accomplishing. Invite her to tell you what you could do better. For example, "I feel good about what I've been able to do."(List some of your chief accomplishments). "But I know there's always room for improvement. I'd welcome any suggestions."

Accept your boss's suggestions. You don't have to act on all of them, and you shouldn't argue about any of them. Resistance suggests that you don't really want the boss to recommend improvements. Act on those suggestions that you can. When you have, thank your boss specifically for having recommended your course of action. By doing so, you're making the boss feel good, and you're calling attention to your achievements.

⟩ 206
I had a great relationship with my previous manager. He liked my work. But my new boss seems cold and standoffish, even though I'm doing the same kind of work I did before. I sometimes think that he knows about how I stood with his predecessor, and he doesn't want me to take things for granted.

It's possible that you have made a risky assumption: that what stood well with your previous boss should work fine with this one. And if the new boss worries that you will try to take things for granted and perpetuate the old ways of working, your assumption will only reinforce those worries.

Every new boss wonders whether the loyalties of his or her new employees will remain with the previous boss. Dispel the uncertainty. Schedule a discussion with your new manager, during which you can get clear on what his or her goals and standards are. That kind of query and opening yourself up will probably go a long way to thaw out the new boss. You'll be saying, in effect, "You're in charge now, and I want to do what you expect of me." When you actually work within the new boss's expectations, the transfer of loyalty will be explicit.

You should also consider the possibility that your boss does not warm up to you as a person. You can't easily change your personality, but you can concentrate on building the boss's respect for you. The above steps should help you make progress in that direction.

⇗ 207

My boss plays favorites. When I complained about the preferential treatment a coworker gets—time off, for example—my boss said, "Work like he works, and you'll enjoy the same." It's unfair.

I agree that favoritism is unfair when it is based on anything but performance. When people perform well, they deserve to get rewards and considerations that lesser performers don't get.

However, your boss's advice to you was ambiguous. No two people can work just alike. Employees should not be compared. A more appropriate response to you would have been, "Work up to my standards and achieve your goals, and you'll enjoy the perks, too."

⇗ 208

I have a manager who is so ambitious that he looks up most of the time, not down.

He has to do some looking down, because he needs you to help him look good in the eyes of the people above him. Do just that. Report to him from time to time on the successful and outstanding accomplishments of your work group. Written reports are better than verbal ones because he can pass them along. If you can slip in some good words about him, so much the better. For example, you might indicate that you value this advice and guidance in certain matters, and that such advice has paid off in such and such a way.

When you talk with him, and after you have given him the positive, talk about your problems and concerns. He'll undoubtedly understand that this is the price he must pay. And, of course, he's not anxious to have any unresolved problems lying around that might detract from his image, to which you have generously contributed. You're probably better off if you suggest solutions to your problems or requests for approval for whatever projects you would like to undertake. Make it easy for him to say yes by being specific and providing the direction.

Later, when the problem has been solved or the project has been launched successfully, give him credit for having known a good thing when he heard it—from you.

◊ 209
From time to time, I invite my boss to sit in on my departmental meetings. He's a strong personality and sometimes dominates. I'd like to be able to have him there without his playing leader.

Define his role for him. For example, you see him as a limited visitor. That is, you believe he'll be interested in part of the agenda. Tell him when to come for that part of the discussion. Or if the item of interest leads off, announce that he wanted to sit in for that segment, and then say to him, "Charles, after that, you're welcome to stay for the rest of the meeting, but if you want to get back to your work, we'll certainly understand."

Tell him how you see his participation in the discussion. "Charles, feel free to contribute, if you like." If he begins to contribute more than you'd like, say something such as, "I'm glad you're here, Charles, so that we could hear your thoughts. Let me go around the table and get some reactions."

Sit in a seat of authority, whether it's in the middle or at the end of the table. Never invite the boss to sit in a chair that would suggest you are yielding your leadership role to him.

There may be times when you want him to give a report, say, on a new corporate project. Make his time limit clear. "Charles, will fifteen minutes be sufficient?" After he's finished, say, "Thanks, Charles. We'll move on now to. . . . You're welcome to remain, if you like. Otherwise, we understand and appreciate your taking time out of your busy schedule."

◊ **210**

I have a new manager who seems to want me to do everything the way he'd do it. When I get an assignment, I also get detailed instructions. When I finish the job, I'm asked how I did it. I guess he's checking up to see whether I followed orders.

When you're given the job, ask how important it is that you do the job his way as opposed to your way. You'll probably hear that what is important is that the job is done right. You may, of course, also hear that he knows how to do it right, which is why you should follow orders.

Try to establish a contract. If you get the results he wants, will you be permitted to follow your own experience and instincts? If he responds that he wants to be sure the job is done right, ask the same question again: If you get the results he wants. . . .

You'll probably get a grudging, wary consent. But, of course, you must be sure to get the results he wants. The next time it'll be easier.

In the rather unlikely case that he persists in telling you to follow his way, don't respond if you are convinced there's no need. If he asks you whether you understand, say that you do. If he further asks that you promise to do so, say that you can't, that you will promise to do it the best way you determine how.

At this point, he will probably consent, although he will warn you that you are taking a risk. But taking a risk is the only way you are going to achieve some independence.

◊ 211

I sometimes think my boss doesn't know what I do or how I do it. I need to mount a public relations campaign to get some attention. How do I begin?

One easy way to begin is to send your boss copies of memos you send to people in your department, if they are complimentary or discuss an unusual task or project. Also relay to your boss suggestions that have been offered to you by your employees on how to improve the work. Have the employee write the suggestion down so you can pass it along.

Occasionally, when you plan a meeting that you believe will impress the boss, invite him or her to attend to see your people in action.

Whether you have MBO or not, develop some personal goals for your growth and progress, and discuss them with your boss. If you go to a seminar or conference, attend a lecture, or take a field trip, write a short report on the experience for your boss.

Try to meet with your boss every week or two, on an informal basis, to talk about your progress and the results you believe are significant.

The above are a few of the ways you can bring your operation—and you—to your boss's attention.

◊ 212

I always hear from my boss when I've made a mistake, but he hardly ever tells me when I've done things right.

Like most managers, he forgets to tell you, or he doesn't know how to give a pat on the back. Help him. When you believe you have done well, schedule some time with your boss and tell him you'd like his candid evaluation of how you've done. Explain that you need the feedback to be sure that you continue to do the right things well. Granted, he should be initiating such sessions, but doesn't. So you'll have to. You'll probably get some negative feedback at the same time, since he appears more comfortable giving that. But you'll also get some grudging positive reinforcement, and even grudgingly, that's more than you get now.

⇨ 213

My division manager is a thousand miles away. I think I have little influence over him, and he doesn't have much interest in me.

He may be giving you a compliment: You don't need his attention. It may not occur to him that you'd like a little of his time.

Send him letters containing your thoughts on improvement. Call him up to chat from time to time. Invite him to come for a visit now and then.

Tell him you have a need to touch base with him from time to time. Gaps can be filled from either end.

⇨ 214

I lost out on a promotion I wanted very much. When I got the news, I asked the boss to tell me why I didn't get it instead of the man who did, but he refused to tell me. He kept saying, "It's no use worrying about the past. You've got to think about the future." But I need to know what sank me in order to prepare for the future.

It could be that your boss was reluctant to tell you why you lost out because the reason may have little to do with your abilities. Sometimes choices are made on bases other than qualifications. It could also be that your boss felt you were not in a calm, objective state in which you were ready to hear about the shortcomings that lost you the promotion.

Now that time has passed, schedule an appointment with your boss and tell him essentially what you said above: It would be helpful for you, in looking to the future, to know what the people making the decision regarded as your strengths and weaknesses. By this time the boss knows you have accepted the reality, and he may be comfortable in leveling with you.

Take advantage of the time with him to ask what he sees as your opportunities in the future. He might be able to suggest some forthcoming developments and openings that could spell advancement for you. Then ask his advice on how you can best prepare yourself for consideration.

Your Boss and Your Subordinates

⟡ 215

A subordinate has gone over my head to complain about the way I've been managing him. Now the boss has suggested that the three of us sit down together to work it all out. My instinct tells me this is wrong.

Your instinct is right. If you consent to your boss's idea, it means that every time your subordinate has a complaint against you, he can run to your boss for a three-way peace parley.

Explain to your boss that you are convinced the problem must be worked out between your subordinate and you. Otherwise your hold on the employee will be weakened, and the boss will find that he or she has literally opened the door to all sorts of grievances about you that should have been voiced to you—or perhaps not at all.

◊ 216

My department head occasionally bypasses me to give instructions and jobs to my subordinates. It upsets me, and I'd like to put a stop to it, but I don't want to get on his bad side.

You're going to have to show him the consequences of what he is doing. For one thing, you can't very well schedule and assign work if some of your employees, unknown to you, are already doing your boss's assignments. Second, his bypassing creates conflicts for your employees, since they don't know which of the two of you gets priority.

Those are two good reasons why he shouldn't do what he is doing. But if you want to throw in a clincher, explain that you can't be as effective a manager as you would both like for you to be if you are not in charge of work flow. Thus, he's hurting not only you with his bypassing, but himself, too.

You probably won't have to show that you're upset to get his consent to stop his self-defeating practice.

◊ 217

I gave one of my senior employees a poor appraisal because of his performance. My manager and the employee are old friends, and my boss has asked me to change the appraisal to make it better. He asked, but I got the idea I'm expected to do it.

It's easy enough to do. Just lie. But then you have to live with yourself, as well as the other employees who have now been shortchanged by your bogus appraisal of their poorly performing colleague. You've also deprived yourself of any drastic recourse you may want to have in case the man continues to perform the same way. In short, you have no hold over this employee once you start to forgive his poor performance. Certainly, your impact on other employees will be lessened. In all, you're in for a miserable time either way you choose.

I suggest that your best bet is to try to shame your boss into realizing the heavy price he has asked you to pay. You might give him a speech such as the following: "If I do as you ask, the positive side of the ledger is that I stay in your favor. The negative side is that I lose control over the man who is cheating us all with his bad performance, I lose the respect of my employees who see me winking at the cheating, and finally I lose my self-esteem because I lie. It could be that I'll lose my job if that lie becomes known. My problem is that I don't want to offend you. I want to be an effective manager for you, but if I do this, I'm undermining my effectiveness. If you were in my shoes right now, what would you do?"

Your boss may not like your standing up to him, but he has to respect your integrity. Your choice may cause you to be uncomfortable, but you'll be less miserable than if you lied for him.

⇗ **218**

One of my subordinates is my boss's old-time friend. From time to time, the boss will stop by to chat with this man, and maybe they'll have lunch. I have no complaints. I am under no pressure from my boss to

favor this man in any way. But other employees grumble about this relationship. Should I tell the boss that he ought to make his friendship less obvious?

Possibly you ought to ask yourself what your motive is for wanting to deliver the above message to your boss. Are you feeling uneasy? Envious? It seems to me that the boss is behaving in quite an acceptable manner, keeping the relationship open for everyone to see. If he became more covert, people would worry more, I suspect.

If the boss is not asking for favors from you, and if the subordinate is not receiving favors from the boss and does not complain that he is being ill-treated by his coworkers, what is the problem you want to correct? So long as there is no evidence of discriminatory treatment, your other subordinates' envy of the man's friendship with your boss seems understandable and proportionate—but not threatening.

◊ 219

One of my old-time employees, a man in his 60s, does lousy work. Yet, when I complain to my boss about him, I somehow become the villain for complaining.

I'm puzzled by why you complain to your boss about your employee. If I were your boss, I'd wonder why, too. The old-timer is your responsibility, not your boss's. It's possible that your boss likes the man. Perhaps they've been associated for years. But you give no indication that the boss prevents you from doing what you will probably have to do: Give warnings, criticize, and set a time limit for improvement.

It's also possible that your boss, in making you feel as if you're wrong to complain, is saying that you should be handling the problem employee without asking the boss for help.

Special Problems

⬦ 220

Lately I've had some compliments from top management about the way I handled some special projects. In fact, the chairman personally stopped by my office. My boss is feeling threatened, and I want to stay on his good side.

The praise you are getting from higher up makes a sufficiently loud noise; you don't need more from your boss. It might be discreet not to discuss your accomplishments with him unless he brings them up. If he does, respond with what he wants to know. If you regard his questions or comments as an invitation to do a bit of boasting, however justified, you will only increase his threatened feelings.

This is a time when you want to discuss more routine matters with him, to allay any fears that your priorities have changed or that you don't need to have frequent contacts with him— and your contacts should be frequent. Bring everything between you and your boss back to normal to show him that you are a loyal, responsive, and responsible subordinate who reports to him, not to higher management.

If you want to boast without being threatening, and come out looking like a nice guy, talk about the contributions and achievements of your employees that relate to the success of the projects. Be as specific as possible about the achievements and the people. Statements such as, "Without my people, I couldn't have done it," don't count for much.

⬦ 221

The boss and I were recently on a business trip. One night he got drunk and told me of some very

confidential political things involving top management, as well as some personal information about a couple of executives. It could be embarrassing for him if it got out. Now he's a bit wary around me. I think he's worried that he was indiscreet, and that I might be also.

He may not be sure of how much he told you, and he may test you to find out. If he does, by bringing up any of the gossip he confided to you that night, pretend you don't remember because you had a lot to drink yourself that night and the evening is very fuzzy. That, and your protecting his confidences, will ease his worries.

If you were not drinking that night, you may have to be straightforward: "Henry, I realized that night that you wanted to talk, and that you were telling me some confidential stuff. But I wouldn't do anything to hurt you, so I've just blocked it out. It's not my business, so there's no way I would talk about it." It may take a while for him to completely trust you, but if you act as if the conversation had never taken place, he may actually develop more trust and respect for you than he had before the incident.

⇨ 222

I made a decision that has proved to be a bad one and it's going to cost us some money. How do I break the news to my manager?

Quickly, quietly, and honestly. Don't postpone scheduling a conversation with the boss. You want an appointment when you have sufficient time to explain what has happened, and you want the time to be uninterrupted. Ask for that in advance. Come right to the point: the consequences of your decision. Many people adopt the Agatha Christie approach: explaining the sequence of the decision-making and getting to the culmination or consequences later. Ironically the "mystery" approach only raises suspicion and anger, as the boss is trying to figure out what you are getting around to. Do your explaining or justifying after making your point.

If your boss gets upset, give him or her time to vent feelings. It might soothe the boss's anger if you are prepared to suggest ways in which the mistake can be softened or corrected. Unless the boss is abusive, don't try to debate the issue or rationalize. You made a mistake, a costly one. The less talking you do while the boss expresses his or her bad feelings, the sooner the unpleasant episode will be over.

◊ 223
I've taken on a job I can't handle. But if I go to my manager and tell the truth, it'll be a black mark.

How long do you believe you can keep the secret? Even if your subordinates can carry you, eventually the word will get out: He's a lemon. Go to your boss and level with him. You'll probably earn his or her gratitude. It's doubtful that you will get a black mark, because the people who erred in letting you have the job are not eager to broadcast their mistake.

Suggest that the job be restructured, if possible, to more closely fit your talents, or that you be given training to upgrade your skills.

If you hesitate, you're going to undergo punishment to body and soul from the stress.

◊ 224

There are two of us in the division competing for a promotion that is going to be made soon. I think the boss, who will make the decision, favors the other man. How can I find out how I stand?

If you have a good working relationship with your boss, you might try the direct approach: "John, I'm really interested in that job, and I'm asking you to seriously consider me for it. Candidly, my instinct tells me that, in your mind, Phil has an edge, and I'd like to talk with you about what I can bring to the job."

He may indeed favor Phil, but it may also be something he won't admit to himself, let alone you. If he does admit it, press on. Find out what qualities Phil has that put him ahead.

Whether the boss talks about Phil or not, be prepared with a sales presentation on the strengths and resources you have to offer. When you're finished, ask your boss what other criteria he has for selecting a candidate for the promotion.

At least you've put your boss on notice that you suspect he favors Phil, and that revelation may cause him to take a more objective look at your candidacy.

◊ 225

I have a boss who is sitting out time till his retirement. I can't move up until he goes. Another manager has given me some hints that I could transfer to her department. I've never worked for a woman, and I don't know whether I could be comfortable reporting to her. Also, people who work for her tell me she is tough and demanding. They don't much like her, but they respect her.

There are times when a lateral transfer can be as important as being promoted. This may be one of those times for you. Most men I've talked with who were initially uncomfortable about working for a woman have eventually gotten over their hesitation, especially when the boss offers advantages such as a challenging job and an opportunity to learn and advance.

Reading between the lines, I'd say you have the choice between going stale or being shaken up by a tough and demanding boss. Outside of not being bored, what are the other benefits? You have to consider those. What will you get out of the move? Money? Growth? A new career path? A good feeling about coming to work in the morning? More responsibility?

Don't overlook the advantages of working for a boss you respect, because you've probably lost much of that for the shelf-sitter you are now stuck behind.

⇗ 226
I want to get involved in a professional engineering group, but management has never liked us to get involved outside. How do I sell my manager on it?

Put together a brief, informal sales presentation that explains what you'd like to do and why you want to do it. Explain what is involved in time and effort—yours and the organization's— and show how the organization will benefit: prestige, visibility, increase in competitive information, broader recruiting opportunities, and so on. Add to the list the benefits that will accrue to the organization indirectly through your experience as an official, for example, your sharpened abilities as a manager and decision-maker.

You are selling a product—your involvement. But bear in mind as you try to persuade your boss that you must translate what you want into benefits to your boss and the organization. The boss won't buy simply because you believe your product is good, but rather because your product meets some needs or wants that the boss and the organization have.

◊ 227
I have a new department head coming in. How can I get a head start in looking good in his eyes?

Don't come on too strong immediately. Let another manager make that mistake. There's bound to be an introductory period during which he must learn about the people and the operation. It's a stressful time; respect that fact. Let him know that you are ready and willing to fill him in on the details of your operation when he is better able to absorb the information.

Invite him to lunch. He may be reluctant to single out any one of you with an invitation, so take a little heat off him by asking first. If you sense he is uncomfortable with the idea of lunching alone with you so early, arrange a group luncheon. You'll come off looking like a leader. One advantage of talking with the boss in an informal setting is that you can more freely ask him about his background and priorities. The more you know about where he is coming from, the better you can speculate about how he will decide and act in his new setting.

Look for personal help you can offer, especially if the boss is new to the geographical area. What's a good bank? Where should his family shop? Who are good doctors? And so on.

Don't be hasty about referring to operational problems. He may not be ready to deal in detail with the problems in your department. Prepare a written rundown on the people and the projects you're involved with, so he can study it at his leisure. Your new boss may have been oriented by his predecessor or his boss, but you can fill in some important gaps.

Ask key employees to contribute to your memo, describing the important work in progress: who does what, why, and how far along the work is. This may be an appropriate time to forward suggestions and grievances from the people who report to you. It is a legitimate time to call attention to you and your operation, but sell softly. Write down what you want him to know, but expect that he will want to defer discussion.

Timing is everything. You'll have to be alert and judge when your new boss is ready for more extensive contacts with you. Meanwhile, brief written reports and summaries can keep your name before him.

FOUR

YOU AND YOUR PEERS
228–276

Conflict

▷ **228**

Today I was walking down the corridor and without warning another manager began to chew me out for something I had said to him in a meeting. I was so startled that I just stood there with my mouth open. Later I was mad as hell. How do you deal with a sudden attack like that?

Your first concern is to stop the tirade. Interrupt to say, calmly, "Let's go in my (your) office and talk this over. This is no place for this kind of thing." Then start walking in the direction of the office. If your attacker refuses, say, "I'm not going to stand here and have an argument with you. Let's go to a more private place." If he still refuses, tell him, "I'm going to walk away. When you want to talk, I'll be in my office."

In the privacy of the office, listen to what he has to say. Don't rush to explain or defend yourself. When you speak, take your time and stay cool. Eventually the anger will subside and the two of you will be able to talk.

Never, under any circumstances, try to respond to your attacker in public—and certainly not in kind. Always keep your voice low and calm.

◊ 229
I'm trying to sell another manager on adopting some new procedures for our two departments to follow in working together. But despite my showing him how this will help the company and even add to the bottom line, he resists.

It sounds to me as if you are appealing to his patriotism by running your ideas up the flag and telling him he ought to salute them. Your product makes a lot of sense to you. But apparently it does not yet look beneficial to him. You need to know more about your prospect, his needs and wants. Then you must hook your benefits to his needs. For example, if he is conscious of his image in the eyes of higher management, how will this new change make him look good? Will the procedures ultimately make the job easier for his employees, thereby increasing their productivity? In short, what is this man's hot button, and how will your suggestions press it? That's what you have to find out before you can sell your product.

◊ 230
Another manager called me this morning on the phone and told me rather offhandedly that an important project I'm waiting for will be late. The lateness is bad enough, but her manner infuriates me. I'd like to tell her off.

I usually assume that unless I've had a history of problems with a person, the offensive behavior is an accident, that the other person may not even be aware of his or her impact on me. If I don't work out my anger, I'll suppress it, and later, in some dealing with that person, the anger will come boiling out over some trivial incident and I'll be embarrassed and the other will be mystified.

Go to her and tell her how you feel about the way she gave you the news. Don't label her behavior, for example, "You were so offhanded and unconcerned." Express what happened in terms of your perception: "I felt you were offhanded and unconcerned." If you label what she did, she can argue that the label is false and unfair. But she cannot argue with your perception. You are an expert in how you feel.

Chances are she'll be chagrined to find that she upset you so. The next step is to work out a solution for the inconvenience. After you've squared away the misunderstanding and the anger, say, "Okay, now how can we fix this problem we have with getting out the project?"

⇨ 231

I bawled out another manager for a clear case of stupidity that caused my department a lot of trouble. But we fixed it, and now I think I overreacted. I was harder on him than I really needed to be. Should I just let the matter lie?

Your behavior was out of proportion to the offense, and if you feel a bit uneasy about it, you should act on that. Go to your colleague, tell him that your people fixed it up, and then say, "In my anger, I was rougher on you than I think you deserved. I want you to know I'm sorry, and I want us to be able to work together well in the future." Then shake hands and let it go at that.

⬦ 232

Today another manager came to me with a complaint about how some of my people have dealt with his. He got hot under the collar, and so did I. I think we're worse off now than we were before.

He probably came to your office primed for a fight, and that's exactly what he got. There's a relatively easy way to handle conflict without necessarily agreeing with the charges. When the other manager complains, answer, "I can see there's a problem." You're not legitimizing the specifics; you're simply allowing that there is a problem, even if it is largely in the other person's mind.

Once you've accepted that there is trouble, say, "Now what do you think we ought to do about it?"

⬦ 233

I've got to straighten out a problem with another manager, and I'm certain I'm going to be angry, and that's going to cause more trouble.

Usually anger causes trouble for us when the other person doesn't know it's coming. So when you feel yourself getting angry during the conversation, give warning. A simple statement such as, "This is starting to irritate me," or, "I'm feeling very angry," can help. What isn't helpful is maintaining a facade of rationality while your voice and gestures give away your real feelings.

Be specific in describing what has been wrong, but don't drag in a laundry list of past complaints. You want the other person to change an irritating behavior, and he or she can't do that when buried under an avalanche of grievances.

Stick to talking about actions and behaviors. Don't judge attitudes or motivations; you can't see them. You can only guess what they really are, and if you try, you can get mired in a long, irrelevant debate.

Listen. When you've had your say, you must let the other person have his or her say. If the other person gets angry, he or she may find it hard to articulate. So you're going to have to be patient and empathetic. After all, you got angry first.

Look for solutions, not who did what. You don't like the situation now. How can the two of you fix it?

⇨ 234

My department has been having continuous friction with another with which we must work. The other manager has suggested that the two of us sit down with a few of our key people and work out the problem. I don't know how you run a meeting like that.

Allow for a thorough discussion. This meeting should not be rushed. For one thing, each of you should describe the problem as you see it. And don't be surprised if the versions or perceptions are different. Also, you need sufficient time to develop openness with one another. Try to avoid accusations. What's more important is that you generate alternative ways of working together that will help you avoid the difficulties you've been having.

Keep in mind that the other people have their own view of the situation, and that they believe their view is as valid as yours. But also remember that they are as interested in arriving at a solution as you are. Such attitudes will help you keep your objective in mind: to develop a constructive working relationship.

⟡ 235
I've been assigned to work with another person in a collaboration, but it's gone poorly. She just does not work as I do, and I get impatient. I'd like to get us back on track.

Having written a book with a coauthor, I'm very sympathetic. People enter into collaborative arrangements without realizing their methods are different, and those differences will cause misunderstanding and tension.

The two of you need to talk openly about your different ways of working. Stay away from judgmental talk that implies your methods are actually more efficient, even if you're convinced they are. Also don't talk about the blame for the awkward and strained situation you find yourself in. Focus on the future. Ask each other, "How can we get this project moving?" Make tentative suggestions: "Suppose we try this? What do you think?" You can hardly expect instant agreement. For one thing, you need time to develop mutual trust and respect. Each of you will have to try ideas and methods and be prepared to back off when they don't work, or when one of you finds he or she can't work with them.

Go slowly for a time. It will be a while before you can build up to the desired speed. You'll have to be prepared to talk out your difficulties, something you probably haven't been doing. Any suppressed feelings of tension and frustration will get in the way of doing the work, as you've already seen.

Give feedback to each other. If your partner's work is good, don't assume she knows you value it. Tell her. If it isn't up to snuff, be tactful but forthright in making suggestions.

Be prepared to give a hand. You may believe the work should be performed equally, but if you find she's having difficulties staying with you, offer to lend a hand. That's better than fuming about her not doing her share.

Collaboration is extremely hard sometimes, but the rewards are many: the excitement of bouncing ideas off one another, a successful project that may be better than what either of you could have brought off alone, and a working friendship that has deepened because of the problems you've worked through.

⇨ 236

My senior supervisor has to work closely with a counterpart in another department. Lately he has complained about the lack of cooperation, the mistakes, and the generally negative attitude of the other man. My relationship with the other manager has been good, and I want to help my man, but I don't want to upset my long-term relationship with the other manager.

Get as many facts as possible from your supervisor. But before you discuss them with the other manager, ask your colleague whether his supervisor has complained to him. It's possible that the blame goes both ways. Listen to whatever problems he recounts. Then talk about what you've gathered from your supervisor. Avoid any fingerpointing, and if the other manager starts to assign blame to your man, respond that you're much more interested in working out solutions. Your theme—and you may have to repeat it—is: "We don't like what's going on now. What can we do to change it? What would be a better way to operate?" Keep everyone's eyes on a solution.

It may be that the two of you will want to sit down in a four-way discussion with your supervisors. Or perhaps they can work it out themselves. Even though it was your man who made the first noises, it's probable that no one is comfortable about the existing situation, and everyone is open to change.

⟡ 237
I went to another manager I've had some difficulties working with and said, "We have a problem, and I'd like to see us work it out." He said, "I don't have a problem. You do." I got so defensive, and I tried to show how wrong he was. I just made everything worse. What would have been a better approach?

You might try something such as this: "I'm not happy with the way I'm working with you. I suspect you're not altogether happy, either. What I'd like is to discuss how you and I can be more effective, working together. How do you feel about that?" It's hard to imagine anyone of good will turning down an earnest suggestion like that, especially when it contains no hints of "you're to blame."

⟡ 238
I've been interviewing to fill a position in my department. One candidate seems to be right for the job, but the personnel director doesn't agree. Frankly, I think the personnel director is a fuddy-duddy, and I'm inclined to disregard him.

Try to forget for a moment that the personnel director is a fuddy-duddy. Your perception of him is affecting your hearing what he says. After all, even fuddy-duddies can have sound ideas. Encourage him to tell you his objections to your candidate. See how reasonable they might be. On the other hand, if his explanation of his objections sounds like a package of prejudice, you can feel freer to ignore them.

Under the circumstances, it would be a good idea to have your candidate interviewed by one or two other people whose judgment you respect. If their conclusions about the candidate reinforce yours, you can then be a bit more confident about overriding the objections of the personnel director.

⬦ 239

I like to kid around. I'm known for my sense of humor. But the other day, I was kidding a woman who works with me and she started to cry. Now she won't talk to me. What should I do?

A lot of people use humor as a weapon; they conceal their hostility and anger behind it. People who have been wounded by such a weapon may suspect any teasing as being malicious in intent. Accept the possibility that, while you believed you were innocent, you were not seen as being so.

Because humor is very subjective, and because it may be tainted by hostility, use it sparingly. There will be people who respond well to it, and who will kid you back. Save your funny remarks for these people. For others who may be suspicious or take everything literally, play it straight.

Also, remember my rule of thumb: Half the people who hear your funny comments either will not understand the humor, or will not think them funny. Why be only 50-percent effective? Target your audience and be 100-percent effective.

◇ 240

The other day I wrote a humorous memo to another manager about a project we're both involved in. I was sort of poking fun at both us and the project. He was furious. I kept telling him I meant it as a joke, but he wouldn't buy it. He said I was being underhanded, and that hurt.

There are two points I make with managers about using humor in memos or letters. The first is that, since it takes a lot of skill to write humorously, the memo probably isn't as clever as the writer thinks it is. The second point is that whenever you use humor, you can almost be guaranteed that you will lose 50 percent of your audience. Half the people who read your writing or hear you either will not understand your point or will understand it and see nothing funny in it. In your case, you lost 100 percent of your audience.

Furthermore, most of us who have had extensive careers in organizations know that some people use humor to express their anger or hostility. If you have ever had humor used as a weapon against you, you can't help being at least a bit suspicious when someone pokes fun at you—as you did your colleague.

What is indicated short term is an apology from you and a reassurance that you meant no harm. Long term, stay away from humor. It takes much more confidence to appreciate humor, especially when it is directed at oneself, than most people have.

◇ 241

Another manager and I have been rivals for a long time, and it hasn't been friendly. He was promoted the other

day, and now I report to him. It's an armed truce. Would it be better if I quit?

Quitting is an option you will always have. Let's look at one you may not be thinking of at the moment, probably because you're feeling the pain, the embarrassment, even the humiliation of having lost out. The first positive thing you should tell yourself is that you are not necessarily inferior because he was chosen and you were not. There may have been factors involved in the decision that didn't pertain to your inherent worth. The second positive thing is that, having been with your organization for a long time, you must have a lot to offer in knowledge, experience, and skill. With that in mind, go to your erstwhile rival and make the following points:

1. You acknowledge that competition has existed but you'd like to see it come to an end.
2. You tell him you have much to offer and would like to work together.
3. You ask how the two of you can begin to collaborate instead of competing.

He may be very touched and gratified. And the two of you may develop a fine working relationship, one that both of you can take pride in. If that doesn't happen, you know that you can always transfer or quit.

▷ 242

I got mad at another manager because of some things I'd heard he had done that caused me some embarrassment. He didn't deny anything. He just sat

there while I told him off. Now I find he wasn't to blame at all, and I feel stupid. I have a fence to mend.

Why don't you tell him that you feel stupid? Then tell him that you believe you wronged him, and you'd like to know how to repair the damage you may have done to the relationship.

For my money, being straightforward and eating a slice of humble pie is the only way to go. I wouldn't try to justify my behavior by saying that I got erroneous information. It was, after all, your responsibility to check its veracity. You didn't do it. You wronged a coworker. Now you must be prepared to take a bit of punishment, at least in your embarrassment.

But if you are honest and sincere, you'll probably get the pain over with fast, and your colleague will probably respect and admire you for the way you handled it.

⇨ 243
Somewhere in the consideration of an idea I had circulated, someone succeeded in getting it killed. Rumor has it that it was a manager I've always regarded as a friend. I'd like to confront him on it.

Talking to him is certainly all right and probably desirable for your sake and the sake of the friendship. But it sounds as if you've nearly convicted him. I'd tell him that I was sorry the idea died, and that I was interested in what happened for my learning purposes. What could he tell me? He might say that this was a problem, and that was a difficulty, and so on. Each time he speaks in the objective or as a third party, ask him, "Is that the way you felt?" As his real negative feelings emerge, you can say, "So you were pretty much against it." If he answers yes, you can respond, "I wish you had felt you could tell me that before. If it happens again that you disagree so strongly with an idea of mine, would you please tell me that before the fact?"

There's no real advantage to you in being vindictive. The best you can hope for is a more honest relationship in the future.

▷ 244
Another manager has been trying to lure away my assistant. I'm angry about it, and I want him to stop it.

The other manager can't lure the assistant away unless the assistant consents to be lured. I'd start with the assistant. Is your assistant restless? If so, what could you do to still that restlessness? Different job duties? More challenge? Perks? Perhaps your assistant feels unchallenged or unrewarded or unappreciated.

It's worth finding out and doing some negotiating.

Politics

▷ 245
I've been directed by our v-p to get a task force together to look at some marketing issues. I've managed to get representatives from every department involved except one. The manager of that department is, I suspect, playing games with me. She's not sure she can spare anyone. "Everyone is so busy." I'm thinking about letting the v-p know about my difficulty.

If you complain to the v-p, you might indeed solve one problem and create two more: One, you won't score points with the v-p, who sees now that you have to be bailed out; and two, you now have an unfriendly, embarrassed colleague. You'll have to watch your back.

She may indeed be playing games. That's your interpretation, and you are about to act on that interpretation. In your mind you are dealing with an adversary, and if she is not one, in fact, you will render her so by the way you act with her.

Try negotiation rather than intimidation. Say to her, "For the most effective task force, I need someone from your group. You have a problem of sparing someone. Let's put our heads together and see what kind of solution we can come up with that will take care of both our problems." Perhaps you can schedule your task force meetings to make them more convenient for her representative, for example. Give her a chance to suggest a way out of your problem—and hers. Remember that if your task force is about to tackle a significant job, she won't want to be left out. She'll want to offer input and share in the glory.

⧫ 246
Two of my managerial colleagues are locked in heavy combat. They aren't talking to each other, but they talk to me. I seem to have been elected go-between. Am I going to regret this role?

Any communication going through a second party is going to be suspect. Each may wonder whether you are relaying the substance of your conversation accurately and without bias. It's just too easy for one or both to begin to believe that perhaps you are taking sides.

Agree to play the role of mediator only if (1) both managers want you to, and (2) both are willing to sit down with you for a face-to-face session. Then you can mediate more safely, and possibly bring this unpleasant situation to an end.

◊ 247

**Two factions in my company are vying for power. I
don't know which will be the winner. Both want me to
join them, and I don't want to. How can I stay out of it,
and not make everyone angry?**

You may not be able to stay out of the arena indefinitely. However,
you don't have to be forced into it before you're ready to choose.
In the meantime, be open to both sides. You can listen to them,
even discuss the issues with them, without seeming partisan.
Remaining neutral doesn't mean staying ignorant. Know the
issues so that when the time comes you can decide.

Maintain contact with both sides. Don't, however, play an
active role such as conveying information or gossip from one
side to the other. You could wind up being suspected by both
sides. Balance your contacts so that both sides will see that you
are not spending more time with one than the other.

Respect both sides. This is no time for a plague-on-both-your-
houses game. One side will survive the plague and return your
scorn.

You want to be seen by everyone as thoughtful, objective,
and fair. It's possible that, without taking sides but by discussing
issues openly, you may make an impact on the partisans. You
may show them that they are out of line or excessive. You may
actually encourage change by your nonemotional examination
of the facts and issues.

◊ 248

**Today a friend of mine who is having a big argument
with another manager suggested that I advise the
manager that if he took certain steps, it would ease the
conflict. I'd be a go-between, but the other manager**

wouldn't realize it. It would look as if I were acting in everyone's interest.

In fact you'd be acting on your friend's behalf and in his interest. Once the other manager found out about your true role as emissary and not go-between, he's bound to resent your action. He would probably see it as manipulative. Tell your friend that you would be glad to set up a meeting at which he could deliver his message in person.

⇨ 249

We have a management club in our company that meets for dinner once a month. I think it's a waste of time. It's a boozy bull session. I'd like to stop going, but since all the other managers go, I worry that it won't be a good political move.

If you stop going, you are sure to convey the message to others that you disapprove of their activities at the club meetings. No one wants to be censured, even in an indirect manner. Since you feel stuck, why not explore ways in which you can take a more positive role in making these meetings more worthwhile? Think of activities that would be meaningful, such as bringing in outside speakers, or asking managers from different operations in the company to talk about their solutions and innovations. Suggest yourself as program chair. You'll probably discover that other managers feel much as you do, but are hesitant to voice their frustrations.

If you assume a leadership role, not only will you make the management club more interesting and valuable to all members, including yourself, you'll get recognized throughout the company as a mover and shaker. As they say, don't sit there with lemons—make lemonade.

⇨ 250
After a recent meeting in which I took a strong stand, one of the older managers spoke to me privately and advised me not to flaunt my intelligence. He said it was a threat to the males. I resent the fact that I have to hide my intelligence just because I'm a woman.

There's a difference between not flaunting your intelligence and hiding it. Anyone, male or female, who is very intelligent and who flaunts it in an organizational setting risks threatening and alienating people who may not be so intelligent. Remember that, according to most managerial protocol, you are expected to be a team player rather than a virtuoso. It's true, some people believe that as a woman you are to be somewhat deferential to men and definitely not to display any superiority to them.

You have a choice. You can work subtly with your intelligence to get what you want, or you can continue to threaten your colleagues. Why don't you accept their estimate—unspoken— that you are indeed intelligent? They'll probably not tell you, but you've already had confirmation of the fact from the older manager who gave you advice. Confident of that recognition, put your mental faculties to work to devise ways of influencing people in less formidable ways. Speak not so much to impress but rather to gain allies and sponsors. Work tactfully with others, in meetings and out. A loud intellect is suitable for a platform, but in most organizations things get done in a more quiet, indirect manner. If you do not make them feel obviously inferior, you'll find that your colleagues will be complimented by your wanting them to work with you, especially if they believe you are an intelligent person who knows how to get things done.

◊ 251

I know I'm brighter than the men I work with, but I think it's dishonest for me as a woman to play up to them and make them think they're so much smarter and more clever than I am.

I'm wondering why this is such an issue that you are arguing that you don't think you should play games. Perhaps you're feeling that you haven't been as effective in working with these men as you wish.

Very smart people in corporate life almost always have a problem having to work, by and large, with people who are not as intelligent. After a while the intelligent person's patience with the sloppy thinking, the inability to think creatively, the lurching from unanticipated situation to situation, and the disdain for intellectuality that others display grows thin. Intelligent people who are frustrated and feel outnumbered begin to push, to show disapproval and impatience, and to broadcast that they should be listened to because they are brainy. They choose words and show body language that turns off less-gifted people.

Have you been guilty of this? It's understandable. Any very intelligent person would sympathize, but if you have fallen for the temptation to assert your intellectual superiority, recognize that you thereby have impeded your effectiveness.

Redevelop your listening skills. Find your tactical patience again. Sharpen your persuasive rather than your debating skills. Discover qualities in less intelligent and creative people for which you can show respect. In time, they will come to accept your intellectuality without being so terribly threatened by it. They'll even regard it as an asset to the management group.

⟡ 252

Almost all of the other managers in my division seem to pride themselves on the long hours they work. They take work home. I manage to get my work finished during the day, but when I walk out of the office without a briefcase, I get nasty remarks.

I can appreciate the pride you feel in your superiority—and it is indeed that—but why should you want to continue to rub the noses of your associates in that superiority? Besides which, someone in charge will decide that you don't have enough to do, and from that point on, your distinction will lie in the fact that you have a heavier work load than anyone else.

Carry your briefcase home with you, even though it may contain a paperback at night and your lunch in the morning. Everyone will breathe a sigh of relief.

Embarrassments

⟡ 253

I wrote a confidential memo to another manager, criticizing an executive in the company, and the executive told my boss he has a copy of that memo. The manager swears he is not responsible for passing it along. My boss is mad at me. God only knows how angry the executive I mentioned is.

Someone saw that memo as an aid to accomplishing at least one of three ends: getting back at you or the executive, or scoring points with the target of your criticism. You violated the first commandment of business writing: Thou shalt not say anything negative in print about another.

Hope you like the taste of crow. Take your knife and fork and napkin to your boss and ask him or her to act as peacemaker. You should also suggest that the three of you meet so you can apologize for having embarrassed the executive through your memo.

Then promise your boss that you'll be more discreet in the future.

⇨ 254

I worked late the other night, and I realized I needed a report that I had passed on to another manager. I figured he had it in his in-box, so I went to his office. When I opened the door, I saw him on the couch, seminude, with one of our male secretaries. I was so shocked and embarrassed. I closed the door quickly and went home. What should I say to him? I never knew he was gay. He must be very worried that I will talk.

Probably the best reassurance you can give him is to treat him just as you did before your discovery. If you bring up the subject, he will be even more embarrassed—and fearful that you will let it slip. Don't say anything. If he wants to talk to you, listen to him, then say that you have no intention of talking to others about a matter that is his business.

⇨ 255

A few days ago, another manager invited me out for a drink after work. We talked pretty openly about people in the company, but I didn't worry about it until I started hearing some of my opinions going around later.

He had blabbed some of the things I would never have said if I thought he couldn't be trusted. He was indiscreet that night, too. Should I counter with some of the things he said? I'm boiling.

There's an old executive commandment that constitutes good advice for you: Don't complain, and don't explain. In fact, don't even acknowledge. The damage is done. You can't undo it or repair it. The best thing you can do is to let it die. And it will die if you don't feed it with your denials or retractions or explanations. Practice being nondefensive when people check the rumors out with you. You don't have to lie. Just say something such as, "Where'd you hear that?" And if the person tells you, add, "I can't figure out why he's saying those things." Say it without rancor, more with surprise or sadness.

At least now you know with whom not to drink.

⇨ 256

At a cocktail party for one of our executives, I had too much to drink and told off another manager. I'd been having some problems working with him, and I got carried away. Do I just hope he doesn't remember clearly or that he understands I'd had too much booze?

He probably won't forget and he may subscribe to the *in vino veritas* theory: truth in wine. Therefore he may take what you said very seriously. If relations between the two of you haven't been good, they certainly won't be better now.

Apologize for having discussed a serious and real issue with him while under the influence. Acknowledge that your taking him on under such circumstances hardly promotes cooperation between you. Tell him that you'd like to see the two of you work together more effectively. Don't suggest that the two of you have a problem. He may respond, "I don't. You do." Wind up your short speech with the question, "How can we work better together?"

If the other man wants to review the problems between you, listen, but continue to emphasize that you'd like to develop ways to work better from now on.

⇨ 257

During a meeting on a controversial project, I spoke up against it, and I quoted another manager who had told me privately before the meeting that he was against it, too. But he told the group that I had misunderstood him, then seemed to retract what I know he told me. He made me look like a fool, but now he's the one who won't talk to me.

He may have pulled the trigger, but you put the gun to your head. You embarrassed him, obviously. If you didn't get his permission to quote him, you were in the wrong. He spoke to you privately, and he had every right to expect you to respect his confidence. You didn't. And since he apparently didn't want to be on record as opposing the project, he disassociated himself from you. Perhaps, as you believe, he wasn't quite truthful before the group, assuming he told you his real opinion. But he felt a need to defend himself, a situation that you created. Now he is angry with you, most likely because you took away from him his choice to speak up or not.

My advice to you is to go to your colleague, acknowledge that you put him on the spot, apologize, and express the hope that this will not permanently harm your relationship. Next time, remember: Don't quote anyone without getting permission, unless, of course, the person has already gone public with what you're quoting.

Objectionable Behavior

◊ **258**
Another manager, who's a friend, has begun to drink heavily, on the job as well as off. I'm sure he doesn't believe anyone notices, but they do. Should I tell him?

It's true that heavy drinkers often think no one knows they are tippling. Chances are not good that you will persuade him to stop the drinking. Something is working on him that you'll probably not be able to touch. But you can alert him to the need to be more circumspect—or to cut back where he can.

Don't tell him that everyone knows he is drinking more. He may argue that he is not. There's just no point to getting mired in that question. Simply say that you want him to know, as your friend, that there's a lot of talk going around, and it's not doing him any good. Describe the talk, but don't take a position. If he retorts that he isn't drinking, that the gossipers are wrong, stick to your story: People are talking, and this is what they say.

◊ **259**
A colleague is always threatening to quit if he doesn't get his way. He's very noisy and irritating, but he gets a lot of attention from management. It seems to work.

The grand desperate gesture: If I don't get this, I'll quit. It's appropriate, in my judgment, if you don't have any other tactic left in your repertory and you are prepared to follow through. If they call your bluff, you can't expect to use the threat again and be believed.

As far as your colleague goes, I suspect that he has cried wolf so many times that no one really believes he'll quit. I knew a man who behaved similarly. Management gave in because they were intimidated by him. He really was a bully. And he had built up his credibility to the point that no one really wanted to test him on his threat, although they were fairly confident he wouldn't go through with it.

Your man sounds like another bully. It's an unpleasant role to play, and I doubt whether you'd want to understudy it. But it does succeed sometimes, distasteful as it is.

◇ 260

I have an associate who imagines himself to be very intellectual. In fact, he is pompous as hell. It's difficult to have a conversation with him. He loves to hear the sound of his voice. It's dull and excruciating.

You left out something: Why do you have to put up with it? Why can't you simply excuse yourself as being under pressure and walk away?

If you must converse, break into his monologues with questions that interest you. Or say, "Henry, I'm not sure I see how what you're saying relates to what I said. Could you tie it up for me?" You can't change his image of himself, but you can force him to be relevant.

◇ 261
One man in my management group is a real put-down artist. I'd like to know how to handle him effectively.

If he puts you down in a group, respond immediately. Don't join in the laughter. Don't raise your voice or show your anger. Say something such as, "I have the feeling I've been put down, and I don't know why." Or pretend to be uncomprehending: "I missed something there. There was a message for me. What was it?"

You're the victim. He knows it. Everyone knows it. You're signaling that you will not willingly play the role. You may cause the put-downer to back off, even to apologize, and you may enlist an ally or two among the others, who, presumably, have also been victims.

If the practice continues, you may wish to have a private talk with him. Tell him that you feel quite negative toward him when he puts you down. He may try to deny that that is what he does, but you can respond with, "I'm telling you what it looks like to me. I'm asking you not to do it, in the interest of our working together."

◇ 262
I've joined a management group where there's a lot of kidding around. I think some of the jabs must hurt, but everyone laughs good-naturedly. I'm uncomfortable because I know that eventually the jokes will be on me.

A group that insists on joking relationships is usually much less cohesive when it appears superficially. Often the humor conceals unresolved issues and conflicts. Sometimes the humor camouflages hostile expressions.

Understandably, you don't want to be a part of anything that appears to be as sinister as this situation does. Don't participate. You don't want to be a sourpuss; just don't laugh or retaliate in kind. Ask people to clarify the humorous messages for you. You can appear to be a bit dense when it comes to translating humor. It will be uncomfortable for you to seem not to understand the private jokes, but you'll force the jokers to communicate with you in a more natural way.

When you see someone being made the dunce, stop the game simply by changing the subject. Don't remonstrate with anyone, because even the victim may turn on you.

Eventually you'll be able to spot what everyone is trying to avoid with their funny remarks, and when you do, you can gradually get it on the table where it can be dealt with. Your colleagues may be angry with you at first for forcing them to do something they have been avoiding for a long time, but your reward will be a healthier group.

⇨ 263
One coworker has a habit of groaning loudly in a meeting when she hears something she disagrees with. I've told her that I think it's rude. She says she has a right to express her opinion.

She has a right to groan, if that's her way of expressing dis-agreement, after the speaker has finished. If she does it while the person is talking, her groan could be a shutting-off device. People take note of the groan and stop listening carefully to what is being said. Or the speaker gets distracted and is less effective because of her interference. Intervene by saying, "I'd like to hear the rest of the comment before you respond."

▷ 264

Sometimes when I come back from a field trip or from a professional convention, I bring ideas that might be useful to another department. But the manager of that department always says the ideas won't work in his operation. It's very frustrating.

Save yourself frustration. It seems obvious that your coworker will not accept outside ideas or ideas that come from you. Don't keep butting your head against the wall, and don't waste time wondering about his psychological deficiencies, of which he probably has a few.

When you return, write a concise report of the ideas that you think are applicable to your boss, with the suggestion that he might wish to pass it along to his counterpart. He can do so without putting himself at risk or in an embarrassing position. He simply does what you suggest. The other manager can decide whether he will pass your report along. But if that manager does, the report will carry a bit more weight and influence than if it came directly from you.

Furthermore, all parties involved have a chance to see how well you are looking out for the organization.

▷ 265

A colleague has a habit of constantly interrupting me when I'm talking to her. I'd like to break her of it.

You have at least two ways of giving her feedback: the patient or the impatient technique. The patient option goes like this: You wait until she has finished her statement before resuming your line of conversation that was interrupted. Unless she is grossly insensitive, she will soon understand that she interrupted you.

The other approach involves your holding up your hand as a traffic policeman would, and when she stops out of puzzlement, you say, quietly, "I haven't finished. May I continue?"

If she still doesn't correct her behavior, you always have a third option: Tell her. For example, "Often, when I'm in the middle of saying something to you, you break in as if I weren't talking. That's very frustrating."

◇ 266
A fellow I work with is very sarcastic. I'm never sure whether he's putting me down.

A key question is whether he is sarcastic to others as well. That doesn't mean that he's not putting you down, but it's less personal when he spreads it around.

It sounds as if you don't know whether or not you are offended. You could always ask him what he means, but you do so at the risk of sounding defensive. Perhaps he enjoys that. Many sarcastic people see themselves as clever and funny. If you don't feed that perception—don't laugh or otherwise show appreciation—you may become less of a target. But there's no guarantee.

In short, if you're just one of the many victims, you might find it less stressful in the long run not to react and not to reinforce. Just ignore the sarcasm. However, if the manager focuses on you, then you'll have to confront the behavior: "I'm not able to work with you as I'd like to, because I wonder why you are sarcastic with me. If there is something between us, I think we ought to talk about it. Otherwise the situation will only get worse."

⊅ 267

Another manager has a couch in front of his desk that is lower than his desk. It's the only place in his office to sit. When you sit there, he's looking down at you. I think it's a cheap power play.

It may be. It's a common tactic of people who want to put others at a disadvantage. When you go to his office, stand in the doorway. Or if you want to put him at a disadvantage, stand over his desk. People are uneasy only when they have to sit on the couch, and you don't have to.

⊅ 268

One of the managers I have to deal with makes frequent anti-Semitic and anti-black comments or jokes. It offends me, but I've never said anything to him. I'm getting to feel a little guilty because I haven't.

Many people simply try ignoring offensive comments, but their silence is often interpreted as consent. If you are uncomfortable, if you find the remarks offensive, you have a right to express yourself. Don't say, "That's wrong." Instead, express your reactions in terms of your feelings: "I'm very uncomfortable when you talk like that." Or even stronger: "I'm upset when you use that kind of language." If you have to work with the man, you can say, "When you talk like that, I get so upset that I can't hear anything else you say. It affects my being able to work with you."

Most people who are offensive in ethnic ways usually believe that other people agree with them. Or they've just never thought about the remarks as being offensive. For example, a group of businessmen were sitting around in a bar, and one man told a joke about rape. Several men laughed, but one man said quietly, "Rape isn't funny when your daughter gets raped." His remark had a profound effect. On another occasion, a man told an acquaintance an offensive joke about Jews. He was shocked when the other man replied, "I'm sorry you said that. It affects my opinion of you. My wife is Jewish."

As I have said so many times, people do what they feel rewarded for doing. When others express shock or disgust, there's little way the offenders can feel rewarded, unless they are pathological.

▷ 269
Our publicity director gets smashed every day at lunch. She's impossible to deal with in the afternoon. She's dropped the ball on some of my projects. I want to complain to higher management without being labeled a whistle-blower.

You probably don't have to complain to anyone. There aren't many secrets in corporate life, and her intoxication is undoubtedly well-known. For some reason, however, no one wants to ac-knowledge or deal with it. Therefore you will not be a hero for raising even a quiet fuss about it.

You are better advised to work with her mornings only—and do a lot of following up.

▷ 270
Another manager is forever saying at meetings, after someone else has talked, "What Tom (or Jane) is trying

**to say is. . . . "When he does it, I can't stand it,
especially when he follows me up.**

Next time he tries to interpret for you, stop him. You might say, "Wait a second, Jerry, I thought I made my point clearly, but maybe I didn't." Then turn to the other members of the group and repeat the essence of your idea. Follow that up with, "Is that what all of you understood?" If you get a yes say, "Fine. When Jerry started to translate for me, I was worried that maybe I hadn't been understood."

Two or three times of that and Jerry should get the point, especially if other members of the group begin to adopt your tactics.

◊ 271

I'm in charge of an offsite meeting of the management group. After the day's events, we'll have an open bar and dinner. But one particular manager always drinks too much. I hate to shut down the bar and deprive others of drinks just because of him. Should I talk with him ahead of time?

Not unless you're very good friends and are willing to put a strain on the friendship. Most people who have drinking problems deny the fact, even though deep inside they worry about it. Granted, you are saving him from himself, but he probably won't thank you for it. Limit the time of the open bar. For example, have the bar serve for one hour before dinner. Close it down while people are eating. Unless your corporate culture encourages heavy drinking, you'll find that most people won't mind. The only critic you may have is your drinking colleague. After dinner, you may want to open the bar for another hour so that people can have nightcaps.

Since your colleague probably can't resist temptation, restrict that temptation. For other people, one or two drinks will be just fine.

Special Problems

◊ **272**

I'm the first woman manager in my division. My peers are nice to me, but they seem to have a tight little group that doesn't include me. They go out to lunch together, and occasionally have a drink after work. I'm the odd person out. How can I persuade them to make me a member of their club?

They're probably not being intentionally rude. And they're probably not even aware of your feelings. In fact, if any of them has thought about the situation at all, he's concluded that as a woman you don't have an interest in joining an all-male group.

Nibble at the edges. Pick one of your colleagues and suggest that the two of you have lunch together. If that works, wait a few days and repeat the invitation with another. If you overhear them making lunch plans, ask, "Is this exclusively for men, or may a woman join you?"

If, as you say, your male colleagues are nice to you and are not being intentionally rude, at least one of them will experience a light bulb going on in his head. First thing you know, you'll get your invitation without having to suggest it.

◊ **273**

A newly promoted young manager is making a number of mistakes in dealing with his boss, whom I've known

for many years. I'd like to give him some advice, but I don't know how he'd take it.

You might arrange to have lunch with him. It's good to get away from the office for this kind of mission. You might open like this: "This is strictly from the Department of Unasked-For Suggestions." (Avoid the word "advice.") "I've known Tom for many years, and I want to recommend some ways in which you can be more effective and influential with him." If he resists, and he probably won't, talk about something else for the rest of the lunch. If he argues with your recommendations, simply say, "Look, Peter, you don't have to accept anything I say. I just felt that I wanted to say these things to you." Don't argue or defend your points. When he sees that you don't want to debate, he'll let up.

In offering your recommendations, don't seem to imply that he's been doing things wrong. Keep to your theme: You want to help him be more effective and influential with his boss.

▷ 274

One of my colleagues is very confrontational. Whenever he has a problem with another person, he goes on the offensive. He tells the other person what he or she has been doing wrong and how he, the confronter, feels about it. This manager claims it clears the air and surprises others so much that they don't have time to make excuses or defend themselves. Is this a good style?

I believe in confronting issues, but not people. From your description, it sounds as if the man is accusatory: "Here's what you're doing that's wrong." An approach such as that is a good way to polarize a conflict immediately, because every person has his or her own way of looking at the situation. It may be quite different from how you see it. Furthermore, the other person in a conflict probably believes that his or her perception is just as valid as yours is. What you hope is that your disputant will be as uncomfortable about the conflict as you are, and will be agreeable to working out a solution that is acceptable to both of you. Your confrontational friend seems to be saying, "Change." In fact, it might be useful for both parties in a conflict to change.

In short, I advocate approaching an antagonist with the words, "I'd like to have a good working relationship with you, and I don't think we have that now. How can we achieve such a relationship?" Such a message is free of fingerpointing and accusations. It looks toward finding a solution rather than causing guilt.

◊ 275

We have a new and very young manager in our group who is full of energy and not much wisdom. He makes a lot of mistakes in dealing with subordinates and peers. I like him, but I'm not sure whether I should let him learn on his own and occasionally fall on his face.

He probably won't learn from you unless he wants to. Why don't you test him to see whether he would appreciate your taking a mentor role with him? Have lunch or a chat with him in his office. Encourage him to talk about what he is doing. As he describes decisions or actions he is taking, ask him what he considered in making his choice. He may eventually ask you how you would judge what he did. That's an opening. If he doesn't open the door, let him know that you're available to him anytime he wants a friendly ear.

If he takes you up on it, your mentor relationship has been born. Otherwise, don't push your wisdom on him, unless, of course, he is about to inflict grave harm on the organization. Even then, present your opinions as biases. He may find them more acceptable than if you give him advice for his own good.

⬦ 276
I think he's a boor, and not very smart, but he knows how to get management to okay his projects. I guess intelligence doesn't pay off that much in corporate life.

He may not be smart, but it sounds as if he is shrewd—not necessarily the same thing. He also must have good selling skills. He knows how to read management's interests and come up with projects that coincide with those interests. He seems to be a successful boor.

FIVE

YOU AND YOUR SUBORDINATES
277–386

Criticism/Feedback

⇨ **277**

Some of my people have poor work attitudes, but I'm not sure how I should phrase my criticism of them.

Well, you shouldn't criticize them for having poor work attitudes, whatever they are. You can't see attitudes or motivations, and what you can't see, you shouldn't criticize. In fact, you can't criticize, because neither you nor the employees know for sure what you are criticizing.

Focus on behavior you can observe and describe to the employee. You can then describe the behavior you want. You want letters that are free of typos, deadlines that are met, telephone calls answered courteously. People can visualize behavior, and you can know when they change it.

◊ 278
What kind of documentation should I keep on an employee's performance that would help me to avoid trouble with the antidiscrimination laws?

You should certainly keep appraisals that show the employee's shortcoming or shortfall in performance. You'll want evidence that you discussed goals and standards with the employee, and that the employee knew clearly what you expected of him or her. Your file should contain dates of criticism of the employee's performance, and a review of what you said during those interviews. There should be a record of your having had a counseling session with the problem performer, at which you tried to develop a plan of action or improvement. At some point, either during the session or after, you gave an unmistakable warning that if the employee didn't meet standards, you would have to put the employee on probation, suspend, or terminate him or her. The date of such warning should be noted as well as the time frame involved in the probation or suspension. Of course, all of the above assume that the standards you imposed are reasonable and that you provide resources such as training or coaching to help the employee to be effective.

◊ 279
How do I get employees to give me feedback on my performance? I almost never hear anything.

You have to send the message to employees that you want feedback. And when they begin to feel free to talk *about* you *to* you, you must be careful not to look disapproving, be defensive, or do a lot of explaining. If you want feedback, your role is to listen. And you must listen to everyone, not just the people who will tell you favorable things about yourself. Seek out people who might be less than approving of everything you do. You don't have to ask them to tell you what they think about your managerial performance. The fact that you have opened communications with them will lead them, in time, to give you some feedback. First they have to get comfortable with the idea of talking to you about anything.

When you hear something from one source, check it out with another. For example: "I heard a rumor the other day that people were concerned that the new procedures on checking work might slow everything down. Have you run into that sort of concern?"

When one employee gives you an opinion, ask, "Do you think that others share this?" Don't follow up a yes with, "How do you know this?" or, "Are you sure?" The main thing is to avoid any statement that might seem to put an employee on the defensive.

Eventually you'll reach the point where you can confidently ask employees, after an action you've taken, "What's your reaction to that?" knowing that you'll get a candid answer.

⇨ 280

I've heard you say that you shouldn't mix positive and negative when you criticize employees. But I think it's good to start off criticism by complimenting the employee on some aspect of his work. It relaxes him and makes him more receptive to the bad stuff.

Not if he's been through the process once. Now he knows what to expect, but he doesn't know when it's coming. Thus, he's probably so worried about when the other shoe will drop that he's not hearing the good things you say about him.

Some managers have developed to an art the mix of positive and negative. It's called the Sandwich Technique: a slab of criticism between two slices of praise. The problem is twofold: The praise dilutes the criticism, and the criticism contaminates the praise. Sometimes employees walk out of such a session not quite sure what has been done to them. But sometime later, when they do realize, they usually resent the manipulation.

◇ 281

I agree that it's best not to muddy up a criticism session with praise for the employee, if you can help it. But I'm about to sit down with an employee who is heading up an important project, and I've got to give her a periodic report. I'll have good and bad. How do I do it?

Start with the negative, not the positive. When you've finished, go on to the positive part of the session and don't return to the negative. Let her know the proportion of one to the other. For example, "I wanted to cover the bad side first, even though most of what I have for you is good," or, "That's the negative part. There is a bright spot, although I have to tell you that the negative far outweighs the positive."

◇ 282

One of my salespeople is so sharp that it's a pleasure for me to make calls with her. The last time I went with her, she asked me at the end of the day what suggestions I could give her to improve. I said, "Whatever you're doing is right. Just keep up the good

work." I heard later that she was disappointed with my visit. What should I have done?

If she is the pro you describe, she knows that she can always improve, and it's very important to her that she does. She looked to you for help, and you gave her nothing on which she could really work.

Next time, as you watch her work, think of something you can offer her, no matter how small. If you can't think of any area for improvement, take note of anything she does exceptionally well. Then reinforce these in your discussion with her at the end of the day. It's a way that you can say, in effect, "You are doing superbly in these areas. Congratulations."

⬦ 283
How often should I sit down with my people to give them some counseling on their future and careers?

Each year, certainly every two years. People change, readjust their sights, and develop new interests and perspectives. The organization changes emphasis, grows, and shrinks. All of these factors influence an individual's planning for the future.

⬦ 284
I hired a very promising young employee who needs a lot of coaching and attention, which I've given. But now I'm getting some stuff from the grapevine that says the other employees think I give too much attention to this man. How can I show them the potential I see in him?

Measuring potential in a person is very subjective. I doubt whether you could make a convincing case with the other employees, especially if they believe you are neglecting your other boss-subordinate relationships. And, of course, as a manager, you have to worry about the halo effect, exaggerating some quality in this person so that your overall assessment of his ability to skewed. Certainly some employees may think you are already a victim of the halo effect.

At any rate, temper your interest, for the time, in this person. If he needs coaching, assign your subordinates to help you with that job. You can probably benefit from some objective evaluation of the new employee's talents and potential. By letting go, you'll relieve much of the tension quickly. Resume your contacts with and interest in your other subordinates.

◊ 285
I suppose I should give criticism more often, but I hate to hurt people.

It isn't possible to take all the pain and embarrassment out of giving people criticism when they don't perform as you think they should. But if you try to spare them hurt by not telling them what they do wrong or deficiently, you virtually condemn them to continue their ineffective behavior. People don't like to fumble or fail. When they need correcting, most people would choose the pain over silence. After all, their self-esteem is involved.

Help them to do the kind of work they really want to. Show them how to be more effective. Show them what they are doing that is less than effective.

Stick to behavior. Criticize as soon as you've observed the deficient performance, and be specific about what you want.

Appraisals

⟡ 286
I hate to do appraisals. I feel like a judge or a teacher.

Think of yourself rather as a coach. You're helping the employee to be more effective. To do that, you must know more about the employee—his or her talents, skills, knowledge, and preferences. Appraisal time should be an occasion of dialogue and planning. You ask the employee, "Let's talk about where you are and where you'd like to be." At the same time, you say, "I want to tell you what kinds of tasks and responsibilities I have available." Both of you are increasing what you know about each other. Both of you are exploring how that employee can be more of an asset, and how you can be more of a resource for the employee.

My point is that the actual recording, judging, and evaluating need occupy only a portion of the appraisal session. The rest is dialogue that the employee recognizes as helpful in planning how his or her energies are best invested—for both the employee and you—over the next 6 to 12 months.

If you establish the planning, helping, and guiding context that I've described, you'll find that the threat and discomfort that you both feel will be reduced. Yes, the recording must be made. You're obliged to go with the system. To cheat is to deny your managerial responsibility, and the system is probably far from perfect. Many appraisal instruments are not fair, balanced, or informative.

But you can create fairness and balance and information.

⇨ 287
Everyone dreads appraisal time. How can I reduce the stress?

I've always said that appraisal time should not be stressful because if employees have been getting the right feedback all along, they know what to expect. There shouldn't be surprises. If an employee has performed well, he or she should know that from the manager. If the employee has done poorly, that also should be known. I know that in many organizations appraisal time is just about the only time when employees find out how they have done or what the manager thinks of them. No wonder the annual appraisal is so stressful.

Reduce the stress for both of you by setting measurable goals and tying evaluations to the achievement of those goals. That way, if an employee achieves or does not achieve them, he or she knows. Add to the self-knowledge your own periodic feedback to the employee: "You're doing well in such and such an area," or, "You need to improve on such and such."

⇨ 288
I like to announce appraisal sessions with little or no warning, because I think the short time doesn't permit tension to build as much as in the case of longer notice.

I'm idealistic enough to believe that if employees get feedback regularly on their performance, they won't find any surprises in their evaluations. Thus, there shouldn't be much tension.

I also believe that appraisals should be a joint effort. Employees need to think about their part of the interview, just as you need to think about yours. If you don't give them any time, your sessions are bound to be predominantly one-way.

◊ 289

My employees get miffed with me because I give honest appraisals—certainly as honest as I can—whereas they say that other supervisors cheat by giving all employees top ratings, or average so that no one looks bad.

It sounds very much as if your employees don't understand what appraisals are supposed to accomplish, and that you may have done a less-than-great job in explaining to them what appraisals are about. An appraisal is a developmental tool. People are evaluated on their relative effectiveness, and from the evaluation session each employee is supposed to receive guidance on how to become more effective and to get better results more often from his or her work.

Employees sometimes view the appraisal system as punitive. "I'm giving you a bad rating because you didn't do what I wanted," is what they hear the appraiser saying to them. Other employees see the whole process as essentially valueless, and that's apparently how your employees feel. Otherwise they wouldn't be asking you to follow the examples of the other supervisors.

Show your employees that you want the appraisal system to work for them, not against them. Spend a lot of time during your sessions with them giving them feedback and inviting theirs.

◊ 290

I worry when I see how my subordinate managers appraise their people. The evaluations are all over the place and seem quite subjective. Frankly, I think many of the appraisals are useless.

It's strange that so many organizations simply hand appraisals to their managers as if appraising were as natural as eating; one doesn't have to learn how to do it. Left on their own, many managers will be very subjective, using their own criteria. Or they will average their ratings so that no one gets hurt or helped much. Or they'll rate on the curve.

Your managers obviously need your help. If your organization does not have an appraisal training program, start one in your own department. Bring in a trainer, or conduct a session yourself. Help your managers to develop criteria that are common among them, so that all of them are evaluating on similar scales. Show them what you expect from appraisals, that they are a tool to help employees become more effective. They are not instruments of punishment. You might explain to them how you evaluate them. They need to understand what they are doing and why. And when their appraisals of their employees seem unbalanced, call the managers in to explain them.

Above all, emphasize the positive aspects and purposes of appraisals. Perhaps then your managers will become more comfortable with them.

⇨ 291
Is it fair to refer to past appraisals?

Sure it is, if there has been a lot of improvement during successive appraisal periods. That evidence ought to make everyone happy.

You may also feel free to refer to past appraisals if an undesirable behavior or low performance has continued without improvement.

Other than those cases, it seems to me that past performance is just that. Unless what went into those evaluations is significant to what happens today, it's best to let it lie. It may be tempting to resurrect old appraisals to build a laundry list against a troublesome employee, but that's not a good idea. It won't accomplish anything constructive.

◊ 292

Our performance appraisals concentrate on traits and characteristics. For example, I have to judge maturity, confidence, and intelligence. I'm miserable when appraisal time rolls around because I can't judge these things.

Try to translate traits and characteristics into behavior. For example, someone who is mature may work through a conflict with another person, or develop skills that enable him or her to work effectively with a difficult employee. Someone who is confident may take initiative in rescuing a project in trouble. Someone who is intelligent will come to you with suggestions and solutions. Develop lists of helpful and productive behaviors, and see how many might flow from the traits you are asked to measure. Then evaluate accordingly. If your appraisal has space for you to explain your evaluation, use that space to describe the appropriate behavior.

Your evaluations, when based on behavior that you've observed, will be rooted in reality, will be measurable with some objectivity, and will constitute guidelines for the appraised employees. They will know what behavior you believe is constructive and should be continued, and what you think is obstructive and should not be repeated.

◊ 293

Occasionally employees pass along critical remarks about other employees: This one sneaks out of the office during the day; another smokes a joint in the rest room; a third fudged some figures in a report rather than do the job he was supposed to do. How much of

what I hear from employees am I permitted to put down on appraisal forms?

Hearsay is no more admissible on appraisals than in the courtroom. It's just not fair to evaluate one employee on what another has reported about that employee. Generally you are restricted to observed behavior or firsthand collection of data on an appraisal. If you didn't see the behavior or the evidence of performance deficiency, you shouldn't write or talk about it.

If an employee tips you off to a performance problem or a problem employee, you can follow it up. If your monitoring results in your seeing it for yourself, that is acceptable.

◊ 294
I've just taken over a department. My predecessor sat down with me before he left and gave me a rundown on each employee, strengths and weaknesses, successes and failures. How much of my predecessor's reports may I use on appraisals?

I would be hesitant to use any of it. Undoubtedly, when you arrived, some of the employees may have hoped to start out with a clean slate. It's demoralizing, maybe even demotivating, for them to feel they must carry the brand that your predecessor put on them.

Set your own goals and standards. Evaluate your employees on what you see and measure.

It would be nice for you to let employees know that you will be depending on firsthand observation for the appraisals. Employees will surely appreciate that you are not going to incorporate the possible biases of your predecessor.

Motivation/Rewards

▷ 295
Why should I reward my employees for doing what they're paid to do?

If you are satisfied with simply continuing the level of performance you have now, you may be right. However, if you'd like to see your people give you more than they have in the past, give them some goals to achieve. And when they've reached them, reward them.

I can't prove it, but I doubt whether there really is such a thing as maintaining one level of performance. Without rewards, some kind of recognition, I suspect that people slack off. Rewards give people a reminder of what they are supposed to do and an incentive to continue to do it.

Finally, I think the issue is also one of common courtesy. When people have done well for you, they deserve a thank you. Those two words can, in themselves, constitute a nice reward.

▷ 296
I have a potential fast-track employee whom I want to encourage. I think there's going to be plenty of opportunities for her here. I don't want her to get restless and leave. At the same time I don't want to look as if I'm promising her anything.

When you're holding up the promising vista of the future to your high-potential employee, don't speculate on dates, facts, or figures. They may come together for someone in the organization, but you can't be sure it will be her. As you talk, think about how your words would look on paper, and try to hear what you're saying from the subordinate's point of view. For example, what is the most favorable construction she could put on your words?

Translate the future into a challenge: "This is a growing organization. There will be more than enough tough jobs for the people who show they can handle them."

Schedule periodic follow-up sessions with her when you can be a bit more specific about the organization's plans and needs. Such sessions also keep you updated about her objectives.

⇨ 297
My employees belong to a union. I can't give raises. How can I reward them when they do good work?

How about a "Thank you," a pat on the back, or, "Hey, that was a nice piece of work you did"?

An expression of your gratitude or specific praise for work well done means a lot to your employees. A more subtle but very important form of positive reinforcement is the trust you show that your employees will perform well without constant monitoring. In work situations where this trust does not exist, you'll hear employees complain about supervisors timing and limiting bathroom breaks. The message is clearly conveyed that management does not believe employees will put in a fair day's work unless they are compelled. When you broadcast otherwise, your employees—most of them, anyway—will respond positively. They will feel complimented and praised.

Thus, you don't need money to make an employee feel that his or her performance is recognized. Every day you have opportunities to say that you appreciate the work your people do. You have simple ways to add to their feelings of dignity and self-esteem.

Regrettably, many managers overlook those opportunities and wonder why their employees don't commit themselves enthusiastically to their manager's goals.

⇩ 298
I have one section that is so sharp and productive that I'd like to point to it as a model for everyone else in the department. Is this a good way to motivate the others?

It may be a good way to frustrate some of the other employees who will never be able to perform as well as those in your sharp section. You set the standards of performance for your employees. Your message to all should be: "Do as I expect. Observe my standards. Reach my goals." The word must not be, "Do as they do"; that sets up a competitive environment. Some people thrive on competition. Others shy away from it. Still others become resentful of the success of the people who are capable of producing more. Such competition as you contemplate could give you a fragmented, hostile department. And the productivity may be disappointing, since some of the less-successful achievers will invest time and energy rationalizing their failures and the others' successes.

⇩ 299
There are goals and there are goals. The good ones are those to which employees commit themselves. But how do you know in advance which are good goals?

I usually apply the test of the 3Rs. First, a good goal is realistic. It is, in the eyes of the employee, achievable without undue risk or superhuman effort. Most people will simply not perform extraordinarily, except in exceptional cases. Second, the goal should be relevant. The employees must be able to see that the goal has a relevance to the health of the organization, in which, of course, they have an interest. Goals that are seen as arbitrary and of interest only to the manager will not receive much enthusiasm. And finally, goals must relate to the personal objectives of the employee. The employee can accomplish those ends that are of importance to him or her by committing to the achievement of the organizational goal.

⬦ 300
I think you have to be very careful about giving praise to employees. Otherwise they'll want more money.

There's no essential cause-and-effect relationship between praise and money. Managers who reinforce their employees with praise don't report that they are barraged with requests for raises. In fact, it may work the other way: Employees who are reinforced with nonmonetary rewards may, in fact, exert less pressure on their bosses for more pay.

There's no evidence that managers should think of only one or the other, praise or money. Both should be granted in proportion.

But in most organizations, I suspect you'd find majorities of employees telling you that they don't feel they get enough of either.

⬦ 301
As a manager, I believe in treating all my employees equally, but I don't get equal performance from them. Some do well, some don't.

Try a bit of favoritism. People who perform well for you get preference on rewards, privileges, perks, and your good will. People who don't work well for you should know that if they do well they'll enjoy the same kind of treatment your better performers get now. Just make sure they understand that the only basis for your favoritism is performance.

⇨ 302

I was hoping to give raises of from 6 to 10 percent this year because my people have worked extra hard on some demanding projects, but now I'm told I will be restricted to 4 percent. It's hard for me to see how I can prevent my people from being demotivated.

Employees may be disappointed when raises are lower than they'd like, but they aren't necessarily demotivated. The fact is that most people work for reasons other than just money, and they are realistic enough to know that, these days, the money doesn't come down to them as it had in the past. Organizations everywhere are squeezing.

Let your subordinates know you are disappointed, that you want to recognize special performance this year. Spend time with each employee, describing what you most appreciate about that person's performance. Be specific. The time with you, and your explicit and detailed recognition, constitute a reward.

In the coming months, resolve to give frequent positive feedback when employees perform well. Be consistent and specific in your praise. Granted, your people can't buy groceries with it, but you'll feed their self-esteem, a powerful motivator.

◊ 303

You say it's important for employees to be able to achieve their personal goals on the job, and managers should know what these personal interests are in order to assign the appropriate work. But I'm new and I don't feel I know my employees well enough to ask them to tell me their personal goals.

Ask your employees to define their personal goals for themselves, then to suggest to you the kinds of work that they feel would help them achieve their personal needs and wants. They don't have to confide anything personal to you, but they can help you to make assignments and distribute responsibilities.

◊ 304

One of my key people is showing signs of entrepreneurial tendencies. I suspect I'm going to lose him eventually, but how can I keep him for the foreseeable future?

The key is to provide this achiever with autonomy and excitement. Perhaps the ideal situation is one that involves a start-up project in which he can be in on the planning from the outset. Once the project becomes operational and is absorbed into the bureaucracy, he will probably lose interest. If you want to keep him, have another new project ready. Entrepreneurial people love to solve difficult problems, create innovations, and work outside the regular chain of command. Give him a department or a task force, or let him work by himself. Let him pioneer something.

It's good that you are resigned to losing him some day. Corporations don't usually tolerate the independence an employee may crave.

⟡ 305

When I took over the shipping room, one of the older employees took me aside and said they'd deliver for me if I didn't come down too hard on them about work rules. Now when the bell rings indicating break is over, the men sometimes sit around for an extra five minutes. But they've increased daily shipping by more than 20 percent. Today my supervisor came through after the break, saw them sitting there, and chewed me out, even though I could show him the results I'd been getting.

Now you can understand why many managers grow cynical as they grow older. Your supervisor has told you that you will be rewarded not for increases in productivity but for adherence to rules. Let your men know the truth about the incident, and explain further that you cannot be effective as a manager if your boss sees you as an antagonist. Chances are they will understand the corporate reality. As your employees, they won't benefit if you are isolated as a rebellious maverick.

Perhaps you can find less conspicuous ways to reward them for increased productivity: extra smoking time away from the department, an occasional personal call on your phone, or time to run a short errand. Such bargains are contingent on continued productivity.

Even in the absence of such bargains, let them know you expect good performance. Reinforce them positively with praise when they work well for you. Be prepared, however, for a fallback to the old level, and accept it. They will be telling you how they feel about management policies. You can all hope for a more enlightened boss, in time.

� 306
My subordinates are not very well paid, and I never have much to give in the way of raises. How can I make them feel rewarded?

There are three principal classifications of rewards you should look at. One is more interesting, challenging work. People who do well can feel rewarded if given more responsible work. At least vary their assignments; some people thrive on variety. Job rotation may add value to the work, since it gives employees a sense of being multiskilled.

Another classification of reward is access to you. Spend time talking with and listening to your good workers. Consult with them on departmental problems. Counsel them on their careers. Chat with them. Your presence and accessibility will help to make them believe they are valued members of a team.

Finally, provide training, if you can. Most people like to feel that they can grow and advance on the job, that they are more skilled and knowledgeable this year than they were last. People are gratified when their potentials are recognized and actualized. Whenever you can increase a person's self-worth, you are rewarding him or her hugely.

Of course, you can look for little perks: extra time off, a piece of new furniture or equipment, a more desirable work location, and so on. Don't forget your praise, perhaps the least utilized reward managers have. And you have an inexhaustible supply of it.

◊ 307

I believe in setting objectives high, because people will try harder than if I made them too achievable. But lately, my people aren't even doing what I consider average work. What's happening?

What's happening is that people have become demotivated. They're giving up. Generally, employees will not commit themselves to goals that they believe are beyond their ability to reach. People tend not to want to take immoderate risks. They are probably saying to themselves, "There's no chance we'll be able to do it. There'll be no reward, anyway, so what's the use of trying?"

Sit down with your people on a regular basis and ask them to help you to set goals. You'll find that most of your people want to achieve as much as you want them to. In fact, you may have to scale down some of the goals they want to set because they may exaggerate their abilities. Helping you to set goals will increase their motivation.

◊ 308

I worry that my salespeople are making all the money they want and need, maybe more than they need. How can I keep them motivated?

You have a happy problem, and you're right to worry about it. Find ways, in addition to money, to recognize your salespeople's superior performance. Public praise for exceptional accomplishment increases the competitive urge in some salespeople. Provide advanced training for your sales representatives. They won't turn down opportunities to learn how to be even more professional. In fact, if the training is sufficiently sophisticated, they will respond favorably to the growth opportunity. Consult with them on selling and marketing issues. Let them advise you on what they believe will sell. Find perks to give them: nonmonetary prizes, new equipment, gadgets, and so on. Set up a high performers' round-table for the top people, and arrange for them to meet each year in an exotic location.

In short, many of your salespeople want growth, opportunities for achievement, increase in self-esteem (and that of others), and higher status. The question you ask yourself is how you can translate these individual needs into reality.

⇨ 309

At a recent meeting of my managers, I brought in, as speaker, one of the big sports names to give a motivational talk. But after I spent a lot of money, I don't see any results in increased productivity.

Inspiration is not necessarily motivation. Usually an inspirational talk will get people charged up for a few hours, perhaps even a few days. But it wears off. Besides which, it's often difficult for most people who are average achievers to identify with a celebrity who is an exceptional achiever.

In the future, when you have a well-known inspirational speaker, accept the fact that you're paying to give people a thrill out of being in the same room with a celebrity. They'll like you for having provided the opportunity, but they won't necessarily work harder.

⇨**310**

I've heard you say that giving a good worker more work to do is a reward for the person's previous performance. Isn't this a contradiction? Won't the employee feel taken advantage of?

The employee must see the additional work as a reward for good performance. But it should be an assignment that the employee wants to do, not just more of the same. Frederick Herzberg, who pioneered job enrichment, advocates giving the employee responsibility from a level higher than the employee's. You might consider delegating a task or a function that you like to do, but which you believe the employee could be capable—or helped to be capable—of doing.

Make sure that the employee is a willing recipient of the delegated responsibility before you assign it. The fact that the employee is part of the delegating process will provide an additional sense of being rewarded.

A word of caution: You must be alert to the possibility that the additional responsibility could cause an overload. If it looks as if it might, discuss with the employee how the responsibility might be reduced or altered. It should not, however, cease to be a source of work satisfaction for the employee.

⇨**311**

I buy the fact that employees work best when they can achieve their personal goals on the job. But how do I find out what their personal goals are?

Unless an employee's goal is to replace you, he or she is likely to tell you what is important about the job if there is trust between you. Employees open up about what they want from the job if they believe you will honor their confidences, make a reasonable effort to give them the kinds of work that will help them get what they want, and treat what they say in a caring manner.

If you hesitate to ask for their confidences, you can suggest instead that they tell you how they see their personal goals being met through the work. That is, what kinds of responsibilities, tasks, assignments, training, and so on will advance their interests. What they say to you can help you in developing the effectiveness of your work group as a whole.

◊ 312

I'm never comfortable when I have to discipline and punish an employee. I just don't think that fear is a good motivator.

First, let's get clear that you are talking about two different things. When you punish, you do so to make the person stop a certain behavior you don't want. So when an employee is tardy, careless, disruptive, or insubordinate, you must apply discipline to convince the employee that such behavior is inappropriate and must cease.

Motivation is more concerned with starting rather than stopping. People are motivated to do something. When you, as a manager, enhance the motivation of subordinates, you are appealing to their motivational forces to work with you in the achievement of organizational goals.

People don't generally learn to do something through fear. They are more likely to learn not to do something. So you're right; fear is a poor motivator. But it may be useful in correcting behavior that you don't want.

⇨ 313
I've heard that money is not a motivator, yet many of my people are always screaming for more. Can you explain?

Frederick Herzberg's famous research that led to his two-factor theory of motivation suggests that salary is not a motivator. That is, what a person earns does not motivate him or her toward better performance on the job. But money can be a motivator before it is part of the salary. To illustrate, if you promise an employee in October that if he does a good job in the last quarter you will give him a nice raise in January, that potential raise can be a motivator. Once the employee receives it, however, it ceases to have a motivational value. It can, however, be a dissatisfier: If employees don't have as much money as they think they deserve, they will be discontented. In most organizations, most people, it's safe to say, never have as much money as they would like, so they clamor for more. Ironically, the amount of noise may not have any essential relationship to motivation.

⇨ 314
How do you restore the work ethic? These days all you hear from employees is, "What's in it for me?"

When people want to know what their reward is, they're being human and natural. The fact is that all human behavior is directed toward goals that people believe are valuable to them. Motivation theory states that human behavior is a function of (1) the reward that a person anticipates as a result of doing a certain task or choosing a course of action, and (2) the expectation of getting the reward. So people select a certain action, task, job, career, or food over another because they believe their choice will have a greater value to them, in pleasure, satisfaction, or taste, than another choice. However, the chooser must believe that the reward he or she expects is attainable without taking much risk.

So when people ask you, the manager, "What's in it for me?" they want to know whether the reward of doing what you want them to do is valuable enough for them to commit themselves to the work. If you can make the work rewarding, you'll find that you don't need to worry about the work ethic. You'll have plenty of hardworking, motivated people.

▷ 315

Turnover in my department is heavy, chiefly because the work is monotonous and, frankly, dull. How can we better attract people to do this kind of work and cut down on the turnover?

The first thing you should do is to stop projecting your values: The work may be monotonous and dull to you, but not to everyone. There are people who have a high tolerance for the work you dislike. There are also people who prefer routine work that doesn't require thinking; their interests are elsewhere.

Thus, there is a work force for you, but I judge that your recruiting methods haven't uncovered it. It may even be that because of management's self-consciousness over the nature of the work, your advertising or information to employment agencies portrays the work as more interesting and fulfilling than it is. Once hired, people whose expectations were higher soon grow disillusioned and leave. Tailor the description of the work more closely to what it really is, to attract a more suitable, tolerant work force.

◊ **316**

It's hunting season, and before that, it was boating and fishing, and after that it will be skiing. I have some people working for me whose interests are not at work. How do you get people like that to get more involved in the job?

You may not ever get the avid fisherman or hunter that seriously interested in what you think is important. These people work to support a particular life-style. As a manager, you have to make sure that even though their primary interests lie elsewhere, they work up to your standards. Many of these employees will work satisfactorily so as to pay for the good life outside. If they don't, let them support it elsewhere. But don't frustrate yourself trying to change their priorities. And be cautious about loading responsibilities on them that will detract from their ability to enjoy their lives outside of work. They may disappoint you.

Control

◊ **317**

No matter how strictly we apply security measures, employee pilferage gets worse.

I've always suspected that when security is tight, employees become challenged to prove it can't work. And management, of course, broadcasts the message to employees, "We expect that you will steal."

Security measures must exist, if only to establish the behavioral norm: We can't tolerate stealing. But the real cure is systemic.

When employees identify with the organization, and indeed when they feel a part of it, they will tend to be less tolerant of pilferage. That isn't to say that the problem will disappear. It won't. But when employees believe that management looks at them as partners and not as potential adversaries, stealing and dishonesty often decline. You can't hire enough security people to equal the effectiveness of employees who frown upon stealing by other employees.

⬦ 318
Why don't today's employees have the discipline that their parents had? That's why we have the drop in productivity.

Don't confuse discipline with motivation. When people have to do jobs that they aren't terribly interested in doing, or that are unpleasant or unsatisfying for them, they call upon discipline. The word has a negative connotation. Very often the parents and the grandparents of the young workers called upon discipline to do jobs they didn't much enjoy, because jobs might have been hard to get and disastrous to lose. Most of those employees would not have dignified their jobs by considering them careers.

Today's employees want to commit themselves to a career. Employees want a job that will give them not only a living but satisfaction as well. They see work as a means of accomplishment, status, and self-esteem. When they see that a certain kind of work has a value to them, and when they see that they can successfully perform that kind of work, they commit themselves to it voluntarily.

I doubt whether there are any studies or statistics that show that the employee of today is less productive or less willing to produce than his parents or grandparents.

Sadly, I long ago decided that managers today complain about the low productivity of their employees because those managers understand so little about what it takes to turn people on to the work.

⇩ 319
I have to limit the time I'm available to employees because of the pressures of my work. What's the best time of the day to have the door open for employees?

Unless there are constraints in the scheduling of their work, I suggest that the decision be based on when it is best for you. You might take a hint from the way I schedule accessibility. When I'm under work pressure, I limit my contacts during my peak energy hours. I'm more efficient and effective in producing in the morning hours. Therefore I like to make my telephone calls and receive visitors between the hours of noon and three o'clock. After that, my energy curve goes up again, and I can once more be at peak efficiency.

Using my example, you have to determine when you can most afford to take time away from your work.

⇩ 320
Sometimes I can't get my own work done because employees are in and out of my office all day. I know I have to be accessible, but when I can't get my own job done, I get very uptight.

When you're in a bind because of your own work pressure, you don't have to be always accessible. Set up will-see times. Perhaps you can establish periods first thing in the morning and last thing in the afternoon, at which time you're free for consultation. When people come to see you or stop by to talk, remain standing. Don't invite the other person to sit down. Those who have brief business will get out of your way soon. Those whose business is more complicated justify more of your attention. You can then suggest they sit down.

See people outside of your office, at their desks, workstations, or in their offices. That way you can easily control the length of the interview.

◊ 321
One way I cut down on employees who try to dump their problems on me to solve for them is to make them bring me a solution to every problem.

Suppose they have problems for which they can't come up with solutions? What do they do then—simply keep the problems to themselves until they become catastrophic? What do you say then—"Why didn't you tell me sooner?" They'll reply, "Because you said not to bring you problems without solutions, and we didn't have any."

If people bring you problems, coach them through the problem-solving process. Make them do the bulk of the creative work; you don't have to accept the burden. Besides, by making them work the problem through, you're giving them valuable training.

◊ 322
I don't believe in discipline. Unfortunately my boss does. I've been warned that if I don't discipline my

people who don't perform well, I might find myself looking for another job.

If you have employees who do not perform up to standards, then you have to take some action. The first steps involve giving the employee feedback through criticism and counseling. The second step is to develop a performance improvement plan to which the employee commits himself or herself. But if the employee does not improve, and if you are convinced that the employee *can* improve, then you may have to apply the threat of punishment: suspension, probation, no pay increase, or even termination.

Not only does your threat signal the erring employee, it conveys a message to other employees who are performing well: Good performance is expected; poor performance is not tolerated. People who have committed themselves to helping you achieve organizational goals need to know that they do not have to carry people who won't make such a commitment. No one likes to see laggards get away with it.

◊ 323

Some of my employees make inspection trips locally— we call it going into the field. I like them to phone their supervisors after each inspection so we can update the files and maintain some kind of control over the inspectors. But most of them don't make the calls. They say they can't get to a telephone or don't want to wait in line at a public phone. To me, those sound like excuses.

To me, it sounds like rebellion. Your inspectors are telling you they resent the close monitoring. So long as they feel this way, they will continue to be unable to find telephones and unwilling to wait in lines.

The bottom line, if I understand you, is the number of files that are updated each day. Let that be your control. You may have to give up the idea of being able to track your inspectors hour by hour. The remaining question is, How can you get the files updated? Can it be done in late morning or at the end of the day? Updated files will be the record of their achievement. How can you and they get it done?

They'll tell you. And don't be surprised if you begin to get more files done than before, when you tried to monitor them closely.

⬦ 324
I have an open-door policy, but the chief result so far has been that a lot of people come into my office and take up my time with trivia. Sometimes I don't even know what they want. I'm falling behind in my own work. What am I doing wrong?

An open door doesn't mean open season on the boss. And you shouldn't be people's excuse to take a break. Establish some rules to protect yourself. First, consider limiting your open-door time. You don't really have to sit there from nine to five with your open door flashing an invitation to anyone passing by. The rule is, when my door is open, feel free to knock. Or, when my door is open between one and three o'clock, I'll be happy to see you. At other times, check with my secretary. Another rule is that you may have to limit visits to 10 minutes when your work load is heavy or you're working against a deadline. That gives you more control, since you are the judge of your work load or time pressure.

You may have to be somewhat directive in helping people get to the point of their visits. If, after a minute or two, you aren't sure where the conversation is going, let the employee know you still are a bit uncertain as to the purpose of his or her call. You certainly aren't required to sit there for 10 minutes wondering what it's all about. Actually, some employees will welcome the help, especially if they are a bit embarrassed or timid about the business that has brought them to you.

⇩ 325

I've just come back to my department after having been ill for some weeks. The department has been pretty much running itself, although not always to my satisfaction. How do I reestablish control in a short time?

Your highest priority is to avoid taking steps that would discount what people have been doing successfully in your absence. It's easy for a returning manager to say, in effect, "All right, forget what you've been doing, and do it my way from now on." People who have exercised initiative will feel put-down and demotivated.

Move slowly to reassert yourself. Compliment those who were responsible for carrying on in your absence. Next, look at the procedures and techniques your people preserved (from your management) or developed on their own that have done the job. Single out these procedures and techniques for notice. You'll want to signal, thereby, that you want that sort of effort continued. If your people have developed methods that work as well as your own, let them continue to use them. They have ownership of those methods.

In the case of methodology that isn't what you want, discuss with your people how that methodology can be improved. It's better to have them work with you than for you to simply impose your own recommendations. The latter may be faster but not necessarily more effective in the long run.

Keep a record of the managers and leaders who emerged in your absence. You may find you have an enviable management reservoir.

Finally, take pleasure and satisfaction in the fact that you did a good job of leading before your illness. Otherwise your department would not have run itself.

◊ 326
Subordinates bring their work problems to me, and I wind up being stuck with them. How can I break them of this habit?

It's called reverse delegation. If you want to break them of the habit of letting you do their work, you'll have to change your own behavior first. When an employee brings you a work problem, say at the outset of the discussion, "I'll be glad to talk with you about this, but I want you to know that when you leave, you take the problem with you to work out." Or if that approach is too straightforward and undiplomatic, after you've talked through the problem, ask the employee, "Now how do you see yourself tackling this?"

Adamantly refuse to let them leave anything with you other than your responsibility for the task.

◊ 327
My home office generates a lot of paper for our managers in the field, and I'm sure some of them put

much of it aside for reading later. The trouble is that occasionally I send out letters that require immediate attention, and I don't get it. I have to call people up to remind them, and then I hear that they don't remember seeing my requests. How can I get responses from them without going through this expensive, time-consuming process?

Distinguish your requests for action from all the other paperwork that goes out only to land in somebody's to-be-looked-at-later-but-maybe-never pile. Requests for attention should be marked ACTION in large letters, with the deadline equally clear. Or have your action request printed in different colored paper, or with a red border around it. You'll find your field managers appreciative. They won't have to read through the papers to find the one to which they should respond. You'll make it easy for them, and people usually act on what is made easy for them.

⇨ 328

One of my better employees likes to come in and chat from time to time. I often feel pressure because I'm right in the middle of something important. Still, I hate to sound rude.

What means the most to your good producer, I suspect, is accessibility to you. Chances are he or she regards those chats as a reward—your recognition that the employee is important enough to spend time with.

   If you feel pressured, say so. Ask when the employee might be available to talk at a later time, after you've finished. I doubt whether the employee will feel that you've been rude. Remember that the employee is asking for a perk—talking to you informally. The time is secondary.

◊ 329

I've been trying to explain to my employees that we have to institute some new procedures because the old ones don't work anymore. It's so simple, yet I'm getting a hostile response.

Why don't you switch your emphasis to how the changes will make their work easier and improve the quality of their work life? Right now you're knocking the status quo, and that means you're criticizing the way they've been doing things. They may interpret that as criticism of themselves.

It seems subtle, but it is significant to explain change as something that will result in savings of time and effort, and that will make everyone more effective, rather than as a correction.

Management Style

◊ 330

I once had a boss who was very manipulative. He was always praising people and patting them on the back, even when they didn't deserve it. I'm hesitant to praise people because I don't want to appear as a bull artist or a manipulator like him.

Most employees aren't fooled. They know when they deserve praise, and when they don't. And they won't respect a manager who trowels it out indiscriminately.

If you make it a practice to regularly praise good performance and abstain from patting poor performers on the back, your message will be clear and strong: You appreciate good performance and recognize it. People will know you are genuine and respect you for it. You must, however, be consistent. Keep this recommendation in mind: Reward the performance you want; don't reward the performance you don't want. In time, people will realize that your compliments are something to seek.

⇨ 331
When there's an emergency, I tend to freeze. My people want to know what they should do, and I can't get my act together.

Why don't you let your employees tell you what they think they ought to do? There's no law that says the manager is the only person who is permitted to come up with solutions and action plans. Next time there is an emergency, call your employees together (or at least some of them), describe what is going on, and ask them to put their heads together to come up with recommendations. They'll probably jump at the chance to show you what they can do in a pinch.

⇨ 332
On any important job, I have to step in to make sure the work gets finished. You would think my employees would want to have a sense of accomplishment.

Your employees probably believe it is important for you to have a sense of accomplishment—of everything. No doubt they've gotten the message: You will be there at the finish line. They suspect that you want to be there, and that you want to cross the line by yourself.

Don't be a rescuer. And—you'll forgive my candor—don't seem to be a hog. Yes, your people would relish achievement. Give them a chance.

⋄ 333

I want to have a more participative management style, but I haven't been successful. For example, in my meetings I try to leave the agenda as loose as possible and let my subordinates put it together to suit themselves. But it seems like we just go around and around and nothing really gets done. Other times we sit around and hardly anybody says anything. Does participation really work, or is it just propaganda?

You're trying to build a team, and yes, it can work. But usually in the early stages of a team, the people who will eventually become its members are still individuals and depend on you to give them guidance. Give them the outline of an agenda; help them to get started on the discussion; encourage and reinforce them as they do speak up and take initiative; and, as they take over more, let up on your active role. When they have participated in making a decision, they'll have the knowledge and experience to make another one. Gradually their dependence on you will fade.

⋄ 334

I'm tough as a boss, but I consider myself fair. Lately, I've been hearing through the grapevine that a lot of employees are complaining about me. They say I'm not a good boss for whom to work. I don't believe in coddling people, and I think that's what they want.

How you consider yourself needs to be tempered with how your employees feel about your management. They may not see you as fair as you see yourself. In fact, I confess a prejudice: When managers insist they are fair, I usually wonder why they feel a need to do so. The managers whom I have considered the fairest never referred to themselves that way.

You might want to have some private conversations with a few key trusted subordinates to ask them what are their perceptions of your management style. Such conversations are threatening, however, to you as well as to them. You may not get the critical information you need.

Examine your practices. Does everyone in the department know clearly what performance you expect? When people need help, do you make it available—for everyone? Do you regularly give both positive and negative feedback—to everyone? And when people perform well, do you reward that performance? Fairness is not necessarily treating everyone the same way, but rather in giving everyone the same chances.

I used to know a manager who chewed out her employees in public. She described herself as fair because everyone who worked for her was vulnerable to the same public humiliation. Despite her nondiscrimination, her employees did not regard her as fair.

⬦335

I admit I ride my salespeople hard. I help them make a lot more money that way, but I've lost three already this year. I'm afraid I'm going to be criticized for the turnover.

Not every employee responds well to the same style. Some of your salespeople will react to your hard-driving manner by selling even more. Others, perhaps the three who have left, will be turned off. You have at least two options: One, you can try to recruit just those who like to be ridden, or don't mind it; or two, you can vary your style of managing according to the salesperson. Trying to recruit one type of follower takes time and probably trial and error. It seems much simpler to me to drive those who respond to driving, and use a gentler touch with those who don't. In managing, treating everyone equally usually doesn't work. You have to be flexible. As I've said often, the practice of management is one to one. So, if you've driven someone who doesn't respond with greater productivity, try being supportive and understanding. That doesn't mean that you yield on your standards. You should continue to insist on those. But you may have to occasionally present yourself as a friendly resource rather than a fierce driver.

Employee Attitudes

⊅ 336
Whatever happened to old-fashioned loyalty? Employees just don't seem to have it anymore.

Sure they do. They may not display it for you or for the organization because they're too realistic to do that these days. Working people don't see the old-fashioned commitment of managers and organizations to them, either.

Employees today are loyal to their goals or to their professions. They enter into psychological contracts: I'll commit myself to this person or to this organization if by doing so I can achieve what I want. Such contracts can be powerful and binding. But few people are fooled into believing that such contracts are irrevocable and unending.

Look for ways in which your subordinates can achieve their personal goals by committing themselves to helping you achieve yours and the organization's goals, and you'll enjoy today's equivalent of employee loyalty.

⇨ 337
I've just taken over a thoroughly demoralized department. It's obvious that people are confused, unhappy, and no longer committed to doing the work. How can I get their morale up?

Don't start by trying to raise morale. Managers often concern themselves unduly with morale, even though morale may have little to do with getting the work done. There is a myth that happy people work harder. Yet all we know for sure about happy people is that they are happy. In fact, I've seen examples of happy work groups where the productivity is astonishingly low. People come in late, take long coffee breaks and lunches, and go home early—smiling all the time.

Concentrate on motivation. Take care of their confusion by telling them exactly what you expect of them. Give them feedback: If they do well, praise them; if they continue to do poorly, criticize them and let them know you will not tolerate a continuation of such performance. When they succeed, find ways to reward them.

Most employees don't want to be confused. They don't want to flounder. They do want to do a good job. Help them to do just that, and you'll see the morale go up rapidly. You'll have helped them to regain their feelings of self-worth and achievement.

⇨ 338

Morale in my company is terrible. Employees really don't have much confidence in management, and vice versa. Most employees don't care anymore. I want my employees to produce. How can I manage this when things are so terrible?

It's tough to manage well when your own morale is low, but it's even tougher to go through the motions without results. You can manage well under the adverse conditions you describe, and your satisfaction will be great, knowing that you have succeeded where others have given up.

First, set reasonably high standards and attainable goals. Others in departments around you may suffer from malaise, but you must let your employees know that you will not tolerate that. Most, probably all, will respond to you because they want to do meaningful work.

Second, stay close to your employees. Other disheartened managers will tend to reduce contact. Instead, increase contact. Give employees frequent feedback, chat a lot, and share what news you have. Be open with them about conditions. No one will be fooled by your putting on a happy face.

Third, when employees do well for you, recognize that performance. Your praise, private and public, will do much to encourage people to continue to work hard and well.

In short, create an atmosphere in which people can feel good about themselves and their work. Regardless of what happens outside your department, you are likely to have a productive, if not happy, group.

⇨ 339

I've recently become manager of a department that had the reputation in the company of being the greatest

place to work. But now that I'm inside, I'm appalled at the lackadaisical attitudes people have toward their work. They're very happy but not good workers.

What you're seeing is another demonstration of the fallacy of the human relations approach to management: Make your employees happy, and they'll work hard for you. In fact, all we know for sure about happy employees is that they're happy. The link between morale and motivation has not been clearly established.

Concentrate on their motivation, which sounds as if it has been somewhat neglected. Set goals and standards. Make sure people understand what you expect them to do. Give them both positive and negative feedback as they try to do what you expect. Reward those who actually meet your standards and goals. Insist that the others alter their ways to do the same.

It will take time before you have employees who are both happy and productive. And indeed some of your happiest people may become unhappy enough to go looking for another boss who places high priority on their happiness. Those who stay will have no doubt about what you require, as long as you give a consistent message: I shall reward the performance I want; I shall not reward or tolerate performance I don't want.

◊ 340

I'm taking over a department that has been a mess. Morale and productivity are rock bottom. Should I be a new broom or make changes slowly?

Let your new employees give you a clue. If morale is indeed low and employees seem disoriented, you might want to consider some sweeping measures. Talk to them. If they want change, they'll tell you about all the things that need to be corrected. That could be your sign to start making corrections.

If, however, your discussions with them are inconclusive and wary on their part, make changes slowly. Be sure to explain the reasons for each change, and give employees time to adjust to the new conditions.

In each case, the ideal thing for you to do is bring employees into the change process. Let them help you design a new operation.

Under no circumstances criticize what existed before. You don't know how many of them may have played a part in creating the old conditions, and there's no point in starting your new association by telling them that what they've been doing is ineffective and dumb.

Resistance

⇨ **341**
How can you anticipate resistance to making a change—and overcome it?

People resist anything that seems to threaten them. That's easily understandable. So if you want to head off the opposition, answer the questions that people are asking in the face of the change. For example, What does this change mean for the operation? Is it growing or cutting back? What does the change mean to my job now? To my future? Does the change mean that management believes I have not been effective? What will I lose or gain from the change—independence, authority, money, prestige, status, . . . ?

If you allay the fears people have that they will be worse off for the change, you can lower their resistance.

◊ 342

I've come into the division as a manager hired from the outside. I detect some resentment from subordinates because the man they hoped would get the position didn't.

Some managers in your position would make a big mistake. They'd curry the favor of the people who have been disappointed. That would be a high priority.

My advice would be to demonstrate your competence and ability to run an effective operation. Explain what you want, enlist employees' participation in setting goals and planning for their achievement, be fair and consistent in giving feedback, and show how much you value good performance by always recognizing it.

Competence is what you will be judged on most. People will hardly be able to say, "Well, management made a mistake in bringing him in because he doesn't know what he is doing." The favor of your disappointed employees will come your way in time.

Employees want most to feel good about themselves and what they do. An effective manager enhances both.

◊ 343

I'm a new manager and I'd like to institute some changes in the department I've taken over. How do I reduce the resistance that people have to change?

The first step in lessening opposition is to explain why you think the changes are a good idea. But that is not enough. Give your change a trial period, and label it as such. If people think you are not yet totally committed, that your mind is still open to suggestions, they will be more likely to level with you about how they view the change. "Let's see if this works," is a better approach than a flat edict.

During the trial period, check back with people at reasonable intervals. Let employees know clearly that you want their feedback on the change. Don't ask people if they like the change. Yes or no doesn't tell you much. Instead, ask people specifically how it has affected their work.

⇗ 344

I've been in my management position about six months, and I'm thinking about reorganizing the department to make it more efficient. But I worry about the resistance I might get from my employees. Someone suggested to me that I plant a rumor about the change and see what kind of response I get from my people.

Suppose you don't get any response. Taking that as a sign of assent by your people, you make the change and run into all sorts of opposition. That's a scenario you'd like to avoid.

On the other hand, you might get vocal resistance from one or two people who don't really represent the rest of the employees. So you decide not to reorganize the department, even though most of the employees might have welcomed it.

If you have a small department, bring your people together, tell them what you'd like to achieve, and ask them to suggest ways the department can be organized to effectively achieve those ends. They probably know the workings of the department better than you do, and they might come up with a better plan. Certainly some of their suggestions might be useful to you, and the fact that you brought them in to the decision-making process may increase your employees' feelings of ownership in the reorganization. That ownership usually results in a greater commitment to making the change work.

If your department is too big to bring all your employees together in a group, choose a task force of five to seven people to represent the rest of the work group. They can tap the thinking of other employees, add it to their own, and come up with recommendations.

Assigning/Delegating

⋄ 345

I assigned a project to a key assistant, but I'm convinced that it isn't going to fly. But it's only partly his fault; the project is too complicated for us now. How can I shut it down without hurting the employee?

Give him the news, but leave out the part concerning his responsibility, unless it's feedback you think he must get. Explain your more recent analysis of the feasibility of the project. It might comfort him to know that you don't plan to include this failure in his evaluation, since it's something he didn't have control over. It might also help if you have another, more realistic assignment to offer him. He needs to have something with which to redeem himself.

⋄ 346

I have a fairly risky project I want to assign to one of my ablest people. I want the project to succeed, but if

it fails, I don't want the employee to be devastated. Still, I don't want to be giving permission to fail.

Be up front about the degree of risk. If the employee underestimates how much risk is involved and takes it on, he or she might give up in desperation. It's important for the employee to measure whether the risk is acceptable before the project begins.

Emphasize that, because of the risk, there'll be much glory and recognition following the successful completion of the project. But if it doesn't work, you can explain, we'll turn the page and go on. It'll be forgotten quickly. There'll be no repercussions.

I think you must have more faith in your employee not to be casual about failing. Chances are he or she won't interpret your statements as permission to fail.

⬦ 347
I have a very bright, talented subordinate whom I depend on greatly. In fact, I worry about overloading him.

It's natural to depend on people who are dependable. What a joy they are. But you could be piling it on without hearing a protest. After all, you are the boss, and he doesn't want to seem lacking in your eyes. Perhaps you ought to start checking with him when you give him a new task as to his ability to deliver what you want and when you want it. Let him know that it's important to you that you not be unfair to him. Also, when you have tasks that are not as important as others, give him that information so he knows how to schedule the work.

Bear in mind that when you favor delegating to him, you may be depriving others in your department of the chance to do your important work. For optimal effectiveness, you need to develop all of your people, not just an outstanding one. And delegating more responsible and interesting work is often seen as a reward for good performance by employees. They won't be appreciative if you save the rewards for one person.

▷ **348**

My Indianapolis office is in desperate need of a good manager to go in there and clean up the mess. The man who could do it doesn't want to move. How can I persuade him?

You might ask him what it would take. He might have a price that you could afford to pay.

If he resists, sweeten the pot if you can. What can you give him as a reward for cleaning up the mess? Put a time limit on his stay there, if he worries about being far from home. If you make the job valuable enough, he might be challenged.

Would you be able to place him on temporary service there, rather than asking him to move? The prospect of a few months, with periodic visits home, might tempt him, especially if he believed he'd be a hero after a success.

If, after offering him whatever value you can extend, he still says no, try asking him to do it as a favor to you. If he likes and respects you, he may not wish to turn you down. But remember that you will have incurred an I.O.U. that you'll be expected to pay eventually. Can you afford it?

▷ **349**

I'd like to delegate, but my employees are just too busy.

Have you tested your assumption? You could be observing Parkinson's Law, you know: Work expands to fill time available.

You can test by experimentally adding interesting work to their present work loads. Of course, you should tell them that they perform so well that you want to add to their challenge. They'll then regard the additional work as your recognition that they are good performers, and they'll accept it as a compliment. If they take to the idea, delegate some more. Incidentally, delegate first the work that you like to do, not what you'd like to get rid of. That makes the additional assignments even more complimentary.

You may be surprised and gratified to find what many other managers have found: Few employees are overburdened with interesting work.

⇨ 350

How do you know when you've overloaded someone? I have a tendency to load a lot of work on my best assistant. But she might not tell me when it's too much.

I judge that, in your mind, you are paying her a compliment. She deserves more challenge because she handles it so well. Make it clear to her that that's why you give her the heavy work load. With that understanding she may find it a bit easier to let you know when the compliment has become an excessive burden. The point is that she knows you are not asking her to do the work because you have no one else to whom you can assign it.

Watch her schedules. If she flags, begins to cut corners or turn work in late, check the load.

⇨ 351

I recently assigned the same task to two different subordinates without telling them. I wanted to see how

they performed under similar circumstances. When they'd done the work, I told them, and they both surprised me by being upset.

They may have reacted to what they thought was manipulation on your part. Each undoubtedly had taken on the job looking for a chance to do it well and enjoy a sense of achievement. But then your announcement probably conveyed to them that you may have been less interested in the work itself than in what it showed you about them. You took at least some of the joy of achievement away from them, and you concealed the real reason why you wanted them to take on the task, which can be interpreted as manipulation.

⇨ 352

A key supervisor may be out for several weeks because of illness. Should I replace her myself or delegate her work to one or more of her subordinates?

It's an opportunity for you to identify and develop the skills of potential supervisors in your department. If your absent supervisor is not threatened by your delegating, I would suggest that you seize the opportunity. You can direct and monitor the work. It will be easier than if you tried to take over her duties, and it would serve a developmental purpose.

Training

⇨ 353

My managers come back from our company management development programs with all sorts of

techniques that I think are impractical, given the employees we have. If they can't learn something they can use here, why should I send them? It's a waste of money and time.

I can only guess as to why you believe the learning your managers have been exposed to is impractical. One reason may be that much classroom training can be divorced from the realities of the work scene. Another is that the manager, in this case you, may disagree with the management approaches advocated by the corporate trainer. In either case, I agree that money is wasted. You should ask your corporate director of training to supply you with a training specialist who can serve both as a consultant and as a designer of programs that will serve the needs of your managers. In the consultant role, the trainer will see what is effective in the management of your operation and thus what needs reinforcement. He or she can also recommend changes that will improve the effectiveness of your team, changes that will be incorporated into a new training program for your managers. You and the trainer should jointly prepare the program and schedule. The effort will take time and money, but at least you will get training for your people that will help them to do a better job for you.

◊ 354

As department head, I occasionally have to do training or coach employees through problem situations. I just don't have the patience for this kind of work. I'm sure I do more harm than good.

Some people don't make trainers or coaches. Look for an employee in your department—or employees—who can provide training and coaching. Peer mentoring is a perfectly acceptable way to get the job done. Actually, trainees may prefer to work with their own kind rather than with you, even if you did have the patience. You'll still have responsibility for all the training and coaching, and you may have to train the trainers initially.

Chances are that your trainers will see their new responsibilities as enrichment of their jobs, a sign of the esteem you have for them. Reinforce that idea.

⬦ 355
I know that I should provide my subordinates with training and development, but I worry that they are going to train and develop right out of my department. I'd be developing assets for somebody else.

You have a choice, but regardless of which route you take, you'll probably wind up in the same place. If you keep a lid on your subordinates with high potential, you'll probably lose them eventually because they'll go elsewhere for the opportunities you've denied them. On the other hand, if you help your good people to develop their talents and skills, you also risk losing them. But one way you create resentment, and the other, good will and perhaps an enviable reputation. Good performers will want to work well for you, because you are helping their careers along. Higher management looks at you as a developer of assets. That's a nice credit, but don't forget to trade it in on something nice for yourself, such as a promotion.

Communicating

⇨ **356**

I've heard you say that managers ought to sit down with their employees periodically to tell the employees what is expected of them. I don't think I've ever done that on a regular basis, and in some cases not for years. How do I start after all this time?

Start by admitting that you have not held these discussions in the past on a regular basis, but that you think such interviews will be helpful to everyone in the future. All of your employees will be operating on the same information, and that's more fair.

Your employees will appreciate the fairness of it. They'll welcome your openness about goals and standards. It won't take you long to get over any awkward feelings.

⇨ **357**

I don't like gossip. I think there's far too much in my department, and I'd like to discourage it.

You can take a positive step that might cut down on the gossip: Be a source for more information. Often, gossip exists in inverse proportion to the information provided by management. When the formal channels close up, the informal conduits become busy in compensation.

If you don't like hearing the gossip, make that plain to the employees who try to pass it along. Bear in mind, however, that you won't stop their gossiping. That's a natural part of any society. You will, however, discourage them from letting you in on the news. And there's a danger there: You may not hear some information that could be useful to you.

◊ 358

I've had an extensive lateness problem in my department. The other day I sent out a memo clarifying starting-time policy. I expected that just the violators would be unhappy, but now I find out that almost everyone is. I thought the "on-timers" would be glad I took a firm position.

They would have been happy had you taken a firm position with the offenders, but instead your memo was all-inclusive. The conscientious employees received the reprimand just as the violators did. The good people got tarred as well as the bad ones.

Next time you want a certain behavior corrected, deal only with the people who need correcting. Departmental memos don't distinguish.

◊ 359

My departmental goals are spelled out for me by higher management. It's a bore to sit down with employees and present them with a fait accompli. How can I jazz up things?

Even the dictated goals can create excitement if employees have some freedom in achieving them. Can you extend discretion in the methods used by employees to get the results management has decreed?

In addition, there are other goals that you can set with employees and in which they can have ownership. For example, there are problem-solving goals. No doubt in your department there are problems that, if solved, would make the operation more efficient. Let employees suggest problems for which they'd like to take responsibility. Another kind of goal is innovative. What new procedures or techniques could produce better results? Some of your employees may want to take on the responsibility to come up with new ways to do things, or new products or programs. Finally, there are personal goals: What will the employee do to increase his or her worth? What skills, knowledge, or talents can the employee acquire in the months ahead? How shall they be acquired? Have employees accept responsibility for the growth.

⬦ 360
For weeks there have been rumors of a big cutback in personnel. I can't get confirmation, but the rumor mills still grind away. How can you keep people's minds on their jobs?

The first thing you do is to remind your employees that you expect them to meet your standards and achieve your goals. Then follow up to make sure they do. Share with your employees any real information you have. If they come to you with the rumors, simply respond that you have no information that those rumors are true. There will be much anxiety and talk. There's little you can do about that; it's natural in such circumstances. But even though morale may fall, you have a right to expect people to work up to your standards. If you are firm about that, you increase your chances that people will perform as you wish.

People will usually respond to a manager's insistence on good performance. They have no wish to dissipate their energies and to feel useless. Don't be surprised if morale climbs again as people devote themselves to the work that is important to them.

◊ 361

One of my best people is very restless and has already told me he's looking around. I know of a new secret development in the company that could be a terrific opportunity for him. Would I be justified in confiding that to him?

It's a risk, especially if you can't promise that this new development will be an opportunity for him. If you leak the secret, and if it got around, it's doubtful that anyone in management would be sympathetic with your reason.

You might say to your restless employee, "Look, I know you want more challenge. It might be that soon the company will have something in which you might be interested. But there's no promise. All I can ask is that you hang on for a time."

Of course, I wouldn't even go that far if I thought he might be able to guess the secret from that hint. Your obligation to higher management, in this case, takes precedence.

◊ 362

What do I say to an employee who asks me questions about information that is still classified by higher management?

You can always say such things as, "I can't comment on that." But the employee will consider that at least a partial validation of what's rumored.

Ask the employee, "What have you heard about that?" Not only will the question divert attention from you for the moment, it will tell you what's making the rounds—and how accurate it is. If the information is grossly distorted, you may want to send the word up the line. After the employee has finished, say, "I'll look into that, and get back to you." And you will, as soon as you have permission to talk.

Some managers don't like this route, because they believe it makes them look foolish, as if they aren't in on the information. But your first obligation is to protect confidentiality. You can look good later when you reveal to employees what you knew and why you couldn't tell them.

⇩ 363
When things are bad, I try to shelter my people. I think a manager should be positive.

I think a manager should also assume that employees are sensitive and knowledgeable enough to know when conditions are bad in the organization. I certainly don't believe that managers should be grim throughout a downturn or a crisis, but I have to wonder how a smiling, positive, things-will-work-out manager appears to employees who wonder what there is to be positive about.

If I were one of your employees, I'd vote for candor and naturalness. "Please don't try to shelter me," I would say. "On the other hand, don't cry doom, either. Just give me a fair assessment of what is going on and how we can plan to work ourselves out of the difficulty."

Any other stance would make me suspect authenticity. Optimistic behavior that doesn't seem real not only won't work, it could also undermine my overall confidence in you.

◊ 364

Each six months I sit down with my employees and tell them what new goals have come down. But I get a polite, almost ho-hum response.

You might get more involvement if you let the employees suggest how the goals might be achieved. I assume you are explaining the output goals—what will happen as a result of their efforts. Have them prescribe what the input goals are—the means that will achieve the output.

Furthermore, insist that each employee come up with a personal goal he or she wants to reach, something to do with personal development: a skill, an area of expertise, training, education, and so on.

Promoting

◊ 365

I'm looking for a new manager, and the man I have in mind is superb in dealing with people. He has integrity, he works well with others, and he communicates clearly but is tactful and sensitive. The only problem seems to be his reluctance to step up to the responsibility. I think I can persuade him, but I have this doubt deep down that I should.

I suspect that it would be a mistake to sell the job to him. I've always felt that being responsible for the work and well-being of others was a prospect that either turned you on or turned you off. That is, if you were a good prospect and were offered managerial responsibility, your reaction would be, in all likelihood, excitement. To carry the theme further, the best managers, in my experience, were people who wanted to manage.

When you're talking about significant responsibility, a reluctant candidate is probably telling you that he or she knows the job isn't suitable.

◊ 366
I have an opening for a supervisor. The best candidate I have is ambitious and hard-driving. She has always done top-quality work because her standards are higher than mine. I think she'd be a real spark in the department.

Be careful that the qualities that have made her a top performer for you will not work against her as a supervisor of others. She sounds very competitive and task-oriented, but the standards that she imposes on herself may be unrealistically high for many others. Like most hard drivers, her people skills may be primitive. Furthermore, her loyalty is probably strongly directed to herself, not to you, the organization, or the people she'd be managing.

From the brief description you provide, and what I know of others like her, this high performer would not be successful as a manager who has to depend on others to get results.

◊ 367
I'm promoting a very unpopular person. Her technical skills are superb, and her knowledge of the company and the industry are way above average. But a number

of her colleagues don't care for her because she's very results-oriented. Her new employees have already complained to me about my choice. I'm wondering how to stop this apparent revolution.

You say nothing about her people skills, her ability to persuade employees to do what she wants them to do.

You need to make it absolutely clear to her that you will evaluate her on results. If she sets reasonable standards—and watch this, because she can't expect everyone to work at her level of performance if she is indeed as superior as you describe—and provides herself as a resource to help her people meet those standards, she'll be a winner. The exception, of course, would be if her department's absentee rate and turnover go through the ceiling.

Support her toughness but insist that she practice good management skills. You may have to provide some training and coaching—and mentoring.

As far as the complaining employees are concerned, tell them to show good faith and commit themselves as they did for you or her predecessor. You need to make them understand you are supporting her unqualifiedly. Without that support, she'll have a rough time.

⇨ 368

Two of my subordinates have been considered for a prestigious new job. The decision has been made by top management, and I know which one of the two has been chosen, but I'm not at liberty to reveal the choice at this time. I know that the woman who has not been chosen is expecting the job, and she's going to be

devastated. How can I prepare her for the disappointment without betraying a confidence?

Call in each of the candidates and give him or her the same speech, namely that the decision is being made, that one of them will necessarily be disappointed. Suggest that each candidate start thinking about what he or she will do to counteract the bad news. If you can persuade each to start developing options at this stage, you may be instrumental in helping the loser maintain some equilibrium. It might also be useful if you offer yourself as a planning resource to the loser: "When the decision has been made, we'll talk about optional career paths."

Let each candidate know that you are saying the same thing to both, and that you believe it is unwise for each to expect to receive the new job. You won't be able to eliminate the pain, but you can lessen it.

⇗ 369

I have two candidates for a management position. Both are reasonably qualified, although one has the edge on knowledge of the work and of the department. The problem is that the one who is superior is not popular with employees. He doesn't have warm working relationships with employees. The other candidate is less knowledgeable but has better rapport with people.

Good managers don't have to be liked by their subordinates, but they must be respected and trusted. Employees need to know that their managers will, to the extent possible, provide them with meaningful work that will help those employees have a sense of dignity, pride, and achievement. Further, employees depend on their manager not to knowingly betray their interests and loyalty.

If your superior candidate understands the importance of people in getting the job done and can build a foundation of trust and respect, then employees will respond to him even if they don't feel warm toward him. You also have to consider the possibility that the candidate who has close working relationships with employees may not be able to utilize those relationships as a manager. He may still want to act as one of the guys.

One other consideration needs to be factored in: An effective manager looks up as well as down. Your candidates need to have a good working relationship with you as well as with employees. Which candidate do you believe you could work better with?

◊ 370
One of my field managers has retired, and I am thinking about replacing him with a young salesman who has been a leader for the past three years. My problem is that I hate to lose a good salesman in the process.

You may have more than the problem of losing a good salesman. You may wind up with an unsuccessful, unhappy manager. The very qualities that have contributed to his being a leading salesman will work against him as a manager. He has been competitive and responsible for himself. Now you are asking him to be responsible for others and to achieve his satisfaction through their work. The candidate for the management position should want it, and should manifest a desire to work through others. Look for salespeople who have given a high priority to the company as a whole; have contributed suggestions that would benefit everyone; and have worked well with others on the sales force, perhaps in training. Is the candidate a sharing person, considerate of and sensitive to other salespeople on your force?

You'll probably find that your less-than-leading salespeople may offer more promising candidacy. They know how to sell but they don't have the strong individualistic drive that militates against managerial performance.

At any rate, don't consider any salesperson for promotion before you satisfy yourself that he or she wants to move into management.

⬦ 371

The woman I want to promote to manager is bright, impatient, and demanding. I worry about her ability to get along with her employees, to get them to do what she wants, but if I don't promote her, I'll lose her. I have mixed feelings.

The primary question is not whether you will lose her but rather whether you want to promote her. Otherwise you are yielding to at least imagined blackmail. And there are other ways to take advantage of her ability and to keep her challenged: working on an innovative project or heading a task force. Either situation allows you to delegate authority and responsibility without risking a management debacle.

If you do want to promote her, you need to prepare both sides: your manager-candidate and her future employees. To the employees you might say that you are providing them with the chance to excel, perhaps to work harder than ever before, but at the same time to achieve more results, satisfaction, and gratification than they've had before. Frederick Herzberg, you'll recall, insists that growth is an important motivator. People like to feel that what they can do tomorrow is more and better than what they can do today, that what they will know is more than what they know today. By promoting this woman, you are giving employees opportunities for growth and advancement in their work.

Your new manager must understand that you will be evaluating her not only on the high standards she sets, but on her success in persuading her employees to meet them. Up to now, she has had only herself to worry about; now she has to concern herself with others. You'll have to be firm on that.

Special Problems

⇨ 372
One of my employees is gay. Some others in the department don't want to work with him because they're afraid they'll catch AIDS.

It's hard to be patient with ignorance. You have to maintain a firm position, which I'm sure is difficult because you have some fine employees who otherwise work well for you. But there's no ethical justification for backing down on this. If they want to continue to work for you, they must work with their gay coworker. Explain to them that there is, as of now, no evidence that people get AIDS in casual, nonsexual dealings.

If you have some influentials in your department who seem to show more savvy, you may want to quietly take them aside and ask them to calm down their coworkers.

Once your employees realize that you are prepared to replace those who refuse to work, they'll settle down—most of them, anyway. They may never be friendly with your gay employee, but that's not what you ask.

◊ 373
Won't there always be some employees who don't do a good job? Someone has to be on the bottom.

If you rate or evaluate your employees on a curve, you're right. But why use a curve? What's unfair about using the curve is that performance standards are set by the person at the top of the curve, and not everyone can keep up with that person.

Standards should be set by you. People should be compared not with one another but with the standards you've established. The bottom should be the minimally acceptable performance level. Below that is intolerable. In a well-run department, everyone must produce at least at a minimally acceptable rate.

◊ 374
I want to put together a committee to explore a project that I've been thinking about for a long time. How do you spot people who work better in a group than others?

Look for people who have the following characteristics: They are analytical, judgmental, and/or creative. It's improbable that you will find all three traits in the same person.

Analytical people have the ability to diagnose the causes of a problem, to pull pieces of a situation apart so that they can be examined more easily. These are the "why" people.

Judgmental types evaluate, test, and measure the practicality of an idea and are able to foresee the direct and indirect consequences of its application.

Creative people think associatively. They see links and connections that others simply don't see.

▷ 375

Two departments in the division I head up are having a bitter conflict that keeps them from working together. The conflict starts with the managers and travels down. I need a good technique for resolving this situation once and for all.

Suggest that the two managers, or two teams representing the departments, sit down separately and answer the questions: What should the other department do to improve cooperation between us? What should we be doing?

Then get them together and have them work on four lists:

1. According to George's department, Susan's group should. . . .

2. According to Susan's department, George's group should. . . .

3. According to George's department, his group should. . . .

4. According to Susan's department, her group should. . . .

Edit out complaints so that you have positive solutions left. Change, "They should stop doing. . . ." to, "They should start doing. . . ."

Define common goals. Rank them by priority. Then decide who will do what by when.

⇨ 376
A key subordinate won't take a vacation. I think it's unhealthy, but he shrugs and says he's not interested.

Some people don't value vacations. You can insist that he take off for the prescribed period, but if he doesn't want to, all you accomplish is doing without him.

The primary consideration is whether his reluctance to take off affects the quality of his work. If you can't see that it does, ease up.

⇨ 377
My best performer asked me for an extension on his vacation. But I found out he doesn't have those days left to his credit. I'm ambivalent as to whether I should quietly let him have the time off.

If you think he won't abuse the privilege greatly, I'd wink at those few days. Of course, I'd also let him know why: his good performance.

I remember having a boss who let me know she would not count my vacation days, and I knew it was because of my productivity. I doubt whether I ever did take extra days, but I know that I felt rewarded. So should your best performer.

⇨ 378
This morning, in my staff meeting, one of my assistants flared up at a colleague without warning, and then got up and left the room. Should I say anything to him?

The cause of the disturbance might have been a problem with the other person that he brought into the conference room. Or it might have been stress-related and unconnected to anything that was going on. Whatever the reason, if this kind of behavior is unusual in him, why embarrass him further? He's aware of what he did and the disruption he caused.

Be available to listen should he want to clarify his behavior—and he probably will. Otherwise, let it pass, unless, of course, something similar happens again. Then you'll have to ask for an explanation.

⇩ 379
I've just hired an exceptionally sharp man. However, he's so much a cut above the others in my department that I'm worried they'll try to freeze him out.

Build up the esteem of everyone, the new man and the veterans. Emphasize that he has a good record and you think he'll measure up to the department he's joining. Ask the group to bring him quickly up to their high standards by showing him the ropes. Suggest that the reason you got this fine person is because he wanted to join a first-class group.

⇩ 380
My department is an old and close group. I'm bringing a new man aboard, and I worry that he'll feel isolated.

Be an advance man for your new employee. Describe the person and why you believe he will bring strengths and resources to the group. Be careful not to sell hard. That could create resistance.

When he comes aboard, have one of your veterans take charge of him and his orientation. The veteran can do the introductions, arrange for whatever training you want the new man to have, and be a temporary mentor.

Choose some employees who have been around for a while and are influential with others, and ask them to welcome the new man, fill him in informally about the organization, and explain how things are done.

When the influentials shake his hand, the others will follow.

⋄ 381

The other day a very important client visited my office. I asked my secretary to get him a cup of coffee. She did, but later told me that she would appreciate it if I did not ask her to do that again. I think that what I asked her was part of client service.

The client didn't ask her for a cup of coffee; you did, so she probably saw it as servicing you. Many female employees today do not regard getting coffee for the boss as part of their job description. If your secretary is one of them, do you really want to make an issue of this? Do you want to alienate her over a cup of coffee? Good secretaries are hard to find, so if she does her other work well, this doesn't seem to be worth your repeating the request.

I always found that visitors to my office appreciated my personal offers to get them coffee. The fact that I was concerned enough about their comfort to fetch the coffee myself scored points, I'm sure.

⟡ 382

I have one salesman with whom I hate to spend time. He's vulgar, brash, and dumb—but dumb like a fox. He sells. But the way he sells is foreign to me. Maybe he'd also be happier if I didn't work with him.

Don't bet on it. If he's good, he wants you to recognize that fact. And one of the ways you recognize his performance is to give him attention. You don't need to spend a lot of time with him. If you average, say, two days at a time with the others on your sales force, you can probably afford to cut your visit to his territory to one day. You may not like his means, but you have to like his ends. Praise him highly on his results. If you can make specific recommendations from time to time for improvement, do so. He'll undoubtedly like the fact that you take the time to suggest ways in which he can better himself. Keep your suggestions to small points. He isn't about to make vast changes in the way he does his selling.

When you make calls with him, study what he does closely, instead of sitting there feeling alien. You might detect something he says or does that could be applicable to other salespeople. If you concentrate on looking for something that can be generally applied, you'll have less time to feel turned off.

Between visits call him on the telephone. Your contacts will make him feel appreciated.

⟡ 383

My advertising manager made some media decisions and then went on a week's vacation. When I found out what he'd done, I was appalled. I canceled the decisions and, when he got back, I told him what I had

done and why. He is furious with me, and tells me he can't work for me any longer. I hate to lose him over one mistake he made.

It was your mistake, too. You took unilateral action and thereby embarrassed, perhaps even humiliated, your ad manager.

By your action, are you telling him that he should have cleared the decision with you first? If he knew that, and didn't, you have a serious performance problem on your hands. If he didn't know that, you have a serious managerial problem to admit.

And if he didn't have to clear his decision, does he know the criteria that you applied to it? Is he operating in the dark as to what you approve of and don't? After this cancellation, he may feel he cannot confidently make a decision, and cannot trust you not to act behind his back.

So you see, this isn't some isolated event. What happened affects his performance and the relationship you have with him in the future. Sit down with him without delay and clear up the questions I've raised, and which must surely be plaguing him.

⇨ 384

When I close the door to my office occasionally, employees waste a lot of time speculating about what kinds of bad things are about to happen. How can I keep them from wasting a lot of time and getting themselves in knots just because I want privacy?

Be more determined to break your habits. Apparently, they have become conditioned to the sequence of the closed door and the bad events. When you close your door, something bad happens afterward. You'll have to be more casual about closing your door. Do it intermittently. If worried employees ask you whether anything is going on, answer, "No, I just wanted to work in quiet without interruption, that's all." As you break the pattern, you'll decondition them.

⇩ 385

The other night, after work, I was invited to join a few of my employees for a drink in a nearby bar. They were helping one of their coworkers to celebrate the birth of a new daughter. Actually we had three or four rounds. But my boss mentioned that he'd heard it through the grapevine that I'd been drinking with my people. I got the feeling he didn't quite approve. But I can't see any harm in it.

Some managers don't. I socialized freely with my subordinates for years, and, while we were equals away from the office, there was never any question about who was boss in the office. I still value the friendships I formed with some of these people.

But there are at least two other issues you need to think about. The first, and perhaps most important, is whether the culture of your organization discourages such socializing. If it is an unwritten rule that managers don't mix off the job with subordinates, then you may be seen as countercultural. You'll make other managers very uncomfortable, and they in turn will make you uncomfortable. If you don't mind being a maverick, do your thing. But be warned, however, that mavericks often get sidetracked. You may find out that you've hurt your chances for advancement, silly as it may seem. On the other hand, after a time, your colleagues may shrug their shoulders and accept you as being different.

The second issue is how your boss feels about it. If you believe he's the only objector, you may decide to continue to socialize on occasion, but inconspicuously. Bet that he'll be watching to see whether there are any negative consequences in terms of overfamiliarity, insubordination, and so on. Keeping everyone's performance high and the relationships appropriate will probably, in time, reduce the boss's fears.

Just remember that there are no hard and fast rules in management textbooks against socializing with subordinates. It's what you are comfortable with.

⇨ 386

I've been invited to the wedding of the daughter of one of my longtime employees. There will be several other subordinates there. I've never socialized with the people who work for me. Yet, I don't want to disappoint this man.

I assume that you've been invited to the wedding *and* the reception. Going to the wedding, it seems to me, would be gracious and not threatening for you. The reception is a different matter, since there will be a lot of mixing. When you say that you've never socialized with subordinates, does that mean that you've always been against it? If it does, there's no reason why you should feel forced to do something to which you're opposed. Go to the wedding, but plead that you're unable to attend the reception due to another obligation. If, on the other hand, you're not against socializing, and you've just never done it, consider it with the assurance that many bosses do socialize regularly with their people with no ill results. Some managers like the closeness; others don't. The choice really is yours. What are you comfortable with? If you'd like to experiment with this occasion, go to the reception and see how you feel. You can always leave. And if some of your people engage in heavy drinking, you may want to leave to avoid any unpleasant confrontation.

SIX

MANAGEMENT QUESTIONS, CONCERNS, AND ACTIONS
387–425

Management Style/Control

◊ 387

As branch manager for my company, one of my biggest problems is that people in the home office making requests or looking for information call my employees directly. They're really supposed to be relayed by me. My employees have their work schedules interrupted because, of course, everything that comes from the home office must be urgent, right?

Which of the two ends of the problem can you tackle with the best immediate results? It's possible that the home calls originate in several departments, which creates a control problem for you. If they all came from the same area, you could easily negotiate with the appropriate manager to direct them to your office.

But if you can't get them stopped at the home office end, work with your employees on telephone screening. First, the employee receiving the call should ask the caller whether or not the request is urgent. Regardless of the answer, the employee should then explain the timetable he or she will be working on to satisfy the request. If the caller objects to the schedule that the employee proposes, the employee refers the call to you. You can then decide whether the request takes precedence over the schedule your employee has proposed.

You can't shut off the calls, but you can train your employees in how to exercise control over their schedules. And you can back them up whenever possible.

◊ 388

I believe that when a manager pulls rank, he or she is admitting failure to get the job done any other way.

Ironically, he may be admitting failure, but I can see how that fact alone justifies pulling rank. If all else has failed and there is a need for action, use your authority. When employees are terribly demoralized or disorganized, when emergencies exist and don't allow time for participation or consensus, when a situation demands skills and decisiveness that others don't have, the manager steps in and exercises. "This is what we will do," says the manager.

Of course, the manager should ask himself or herself how the conditions came about, and whether he or she was responsible through poor planning or neglect.

◊ 389

I want to install an MBO program, but I'm getting some static from my boss, who says programs like that don't work. Do you believe they can be successful?

Yes, I believe they can and do work, primarily because they go with the grain of human nature. People need goals to commit themselves to, and the more specific and defined the goals are, the better, usually.

George Odiorne, widely considered to be the guru of MBO, has described many of the reasons why MBO plans fail in his books and articles. A few of the most common reasons: setting too many goals for people to keep track, forgiving failure to achieve goals and thereby sending the message that the goals really weren't too important, or simply not following up to see whether the goals were achieved.

I've always felt that the more participation by employees in setting goals, or in at least establishing the means to achieve the goals, the more commitment on their part. Simply mandating goals from above is not usually very compelling.

⋄ 390
I've always believed that it is undesirable to pull rank, but now I think there must be times when it's justified.

I agree that there are times when resorting to one's authority is quite in line. One situation that comes readily to mind is the case of immediate danger or emergency. For example, one employee's disregard of safety procedures, when the overall welfare or morale of the work group is threatened. One person is disruptive or generally causes trouble. One employee's behavior hurts another. You step in and demand a change when time is of the essence. A sudden change in conditions requires a fast mobilization to meet the challenge, when there's not time for consultation or consensus. The manager takes action.

Sometimes a manager must insist on making changes when he or she isn't permitted by higher management to explain why.

Basically, when there is a clear and immediate danger to the health, well-being, productivity, or survival of the work group, a manager uses clout.

⋄ 391

I sometimes have problems getting rid of people who come to my office to talk. I can't stand to do what others do, when they emphasize to visitors that they are so, so busy. They make the visitors feel small. How can I be more graceful in persuading people to leave?

I think it's within the boundaries of grace to flash signals to visitors and let them initiate the leave-taking. Discreetly looking at your watch usually does it. Or, when you feel that you've spent enough time, wrap up the conversation this way: "In the remaining couple of minutes, is there anything else we should cover briefly?" Or look at your watch and announce that you have to make a phone call in two or three minutes. Some people get up, walk around the desk, and lean on it, facing the visitor. In a moment, the visitor will follow suit, finding it uncomfortable to look up.

Other managers have agreed on signals to their secretaries: "Interrupt me after five minutes," and all that. Of course, that takes some of the control away from you. She'll buzz you in five minutes, even though you have decided in the interim that you want to continue. But should you say to her, "Yes, I know, but I think this is more important. Hold everything off," you've handed your visitor a very nice compliment.

◊ 392
When I hear all this stuff on good management, I think it sounds very good in theory. But it doesn't work in the real world.

Much of the stuff you talk about is the real world. It goes with human nature and not against it. People need and want work that is meaningful to them. Furthermore, most people want to do good work. They like to feel satisfaction over jobs well done. They like a sense of achievement. Self-esteem and the esteem of others are very important to them. People want goals. In fact, all human behavior is directed toward goals. Your employees will commit themselves to working for your goals if they can achieve their ends by doing so.

How do we know this? Through countless research projects, real-life examples, and feedback from workers themselves for the past 60 years in this country. Some of us who have been managers have applied the concepts, principles, and practices quite successfully. We're here to say they can work, because they have for us.

True, most organizations aren't run the way the experts advise. And the results they get suggest that something must be wrong. In a recent survey by Hay Associates in Philadelphia, more than two thirds of employees surveyed report that their companies, in their view, are not managed well. Those survey results are no surprise to management consultants who have been in the field for years. We know firsthand that few organizations are managed well. Few effectively use their people resources. But we also know of companies that through the years applied the stuff you regard with skepticism, and were run very successfully.

◊ 393

I hear a lot about MBWA—management by walking around. Is that a recommended practice? And what does it mean, anyway?

Basically it means getting out from behind your desk and seeing for yourself what goes on in your department or division.

Years ago I knew a man who practiced MBWA, long before it was written up. Every morning when he arrived at his factory, he would walk through the plant, greet employees, stop to talk with some of them briefly about anything they wanted to bring up. He believed that he kept his finger on the pulse with his daily walk-throughs.

It can be a good idea to get out and about, to talk with people and let them talk to you, to see and feel what is going on. But you must have a good and trustful working relationship with your people, lest they wonder whether you're on a spy mission. And your tours must be in proportion to your other activity, if you don't want employees to wonder whether you have any work to do yourself.

◊ 394

I'm a manager newly arrived in my company. The prevailing style of management is authoritarian, but I'm more participative. I've already begun to receive some criticism from my boss for my permissiveness.

Go easy and be quiet about your participative leanings. You're going against the culture, and most managements don't easily tolerate mavericks. In the eyes of your management, you are surrendering managerial prerogatives. In an authoritarian society, those prerogatives are dearly guarded.

Your employees may be enthusiastic about your increasing involvement of them at first, but if they perceive that you are subject to criticism from higher management on your level, they will probably become uncomfortable, knowing that you could be isolating yourself—and them, too. Isolated managers don't have much power and don't get in on the rewards that others enjoy. Employees look dimly at the prospect of not getting some of those rewards and of working for a relatively powerless manager.

Make your changes slowly, in bits and pieces. Start with decisions that aren't critical. How far you go depends on the tolerance you sense from other managers, especially those above you. I recommend that you abandon thoughts of an extensive participative style and aim for one that is comfortably between the autocratic and democratic.

At the moment, you are probably seen as a threat to the culture and to the power of management. Hope that, in time, others will view you as a rather harmless threat. When that occurs, you'll find it easier to inch toward more participation. Have patience.

▷ 395
I'm appalled at the way some of my people dress in the office. I've been thinking about setting a dress code.

The first rule of making rules is not to make a rule you can't enforce. Suppose you make a dress code. What will you do when someone breaks it? Someone will, intentionally or not. I doubt whether you can apply discipline. You can chastise, but if your chastisement is ignored in the future, you risk making a fool of yourself.

Be a model. Dress to the standards you'd like to see observed in the office. If you have a relationship of respect with your subordinates, you'll probably see some emulation. On the other hand, some subordinates might say, "With this boss, what counts is performance." That isn't a bad thing for employees to say about the boss, even if they do dress sloppily.

Firing

◊ 396

I recently fired a man for lying to me. Now he wants to give my name as a reference. What do I tell people who call?

Verify the dates of his employment. If he performed well apart from the dishonesty, you can decide whether you want to say yes when people ask you whether he worked well. When they ask why he left, you can respond, "What did he tell you?" If the answer is something you can reinforce, such as, "He said he had a conflict with you," do so, if you wish. But don't give the specifics.

If you want to be quite safe, simply stick to the dates of employment. Your refusal to go any further will convey a message, but you probably can't be sued for what you didn't say.

◊ 397

How much time should I be prepared to spend in a firing session?

As much time as is necessary for the employee to accept the reality and to understand why it has taken place, and for you to encourage the employee to start thinking about developing options. It could be 10 minutes, it could be an hour—or more. You have to judge how long an employee needs to absorb the shock and recover some stability. Some managers like to make it short and sweet, I suspect to cut short their own pain and embarrassment. But this is a time when you must service the employee's needs rather than your own.

There are some indicators that tell you to terminate the session. For example, the employee begins to argue with you to try to convince you to reverse the decision, when you've made it clear that the decision is not reversible. If the employee persists, bring the session to an end. Another indicator: The employee gets carried away by emotion and can't maintain control. You have to consider that further talking at this point is wasted. Assure the employee that you will be available later to continue the discussion. Or when the employee becomes abusive toward you, tell him or her that, for now, the interview is over, to be resumed when the employee is ready to talk without the abuse.

⟡ 398

I've been told that I must cut back on people—10 percent—in the next 30 days. It's part of a company-wide cutback. I've spent years building my team; I don't see anybody as expendable. How do I make the choice?

It's probably easier to start to choose the people you should not terminate: older employees who may have a rougher time getting relocated (and who are the most likely people to harass you with discriminatory action), people who are just short of vesting (it would be cruel to deprive them of pension benefits), and exceptional subordinates who could not be replaced by anyone else in the department (a cautionary note for you not to let anyone become irreplaceable in the future).

Whom do you have left? You might employ the LIFO principle: last in, first out. There are employees whose responsibilities could be assumed by others. If possible, concentrate on younger people who would not charge discrimination and who would have their lives least disrupted.

By all means, stay close to your personnel department to avoid running afoul of any antidiscrimination laws.

⇨ 399
When's the best time to fire someone?

I'm not sure what you mean by best, since there's not a time when it will be painless, for you or for the employee. Since the greater pain will be the employee's, reduce that person's pain as much as possible. Fire early in the day during the week. That way the employee can start telephoning agencies, personal contacts, and business resources, and can answer advertisements. If possible, arrange for the terminated employee to have an interview with your personnel department immediately following your talk with him or her, to learn about the status of employee benefits, severance, and so on. If you have outplacement services, make an appointment for the employee that day. Make it clear whether the employee will have access to an office and a telephone for a period of time; don't leave the employee wondering. Emphasize to the employee that it is important for him or her to get started on the job search.

Don't wait until Friday afternoon to deliver the blow. The employee will probably have a stressful, nonproductive weekend, with plenty of time to brood. Your former subordinate needs to begin immediately to regain some control over his or her life.

Rewards/Motivation

◊ 400

I get nervous when people talk about positive reinforcement and behavior conditioning. It all sounds like manipulation to me.

Manipulation in management involves deceit or withholding of the truth. The manipulative manager wants certain behavior from employees, but he doesn't tell them the reason he wants it, or he makes the reason obscure. To use an extreme example, a manager urges his employees to perform in an exceptional manner during a crisis so that they can qualify for a bonus. He has no intention or capability of paying a bonus. He is, instead, looking for a record that will qualify him for a promotion.

Positive reinforcement and behavior conditioning can both be manipulative if the manager uses deceit. But for the manager who is open about what he or she wants, the conditioning is quite honest and legitimate. Both positive reinforcement and behavior conditioning mean essentially the same thing: using rewards to encourage a particular kind of behavior in others. As a manager, I want my employees to be more effective. When they produce well, I reinforce them positively with rewards: money, praise, promotions, and so on. Employees understand that I want them to repeat the behaviors I've rewarded. That's behavior conditioning. It's very open and beneficial to all involved.

◊ 401

Is fear a good motivator? I know it's not a popular thought these days, but with all the cutbacks in

employment it seems to me that the thought of losing one's job would make people work harder.

Frederick Herzberg, the eminent social psychologist, calls what you are suggesting KITA management: kick-in-the-behind, to be polite. If you inspire fear in employees, their dominant motivation will probably be to avoid displeasing you. That isn't always the same as pleasing you. Managers who rule by fear often get just enough out of employees to qualify as acceptable performance. They seldom get more. And if the managers don't constantly monitor the activities of employees, they may not get even minimally acceptable performance. What's more, people driven by fear come to resent the person who inspires that fear, and the resentment surfaces in antiorganizational activity. Such employees tend to form strong informal groups that resist the efforts of management to achieve compliance with company policy and procedures. The results are definitely of the us-versus-them variety.

Managers who believe in motivation by fear frequently have to resort to threats; otherwise the fear dissipates. It never seemed to me to be the kind of activity in which I'd like to engage. Management should be fun, not the equivalent of guarding a prison.

◊ 402
How do you handle the subject of salary increases at the time of appraisal?

Announce at the beginning of the appraisal session that you will not be getting into matters of money or other rewards. That will follow, you say, in a few days. For the moment, you think it's essential to concentrate on doing the kind of evaluation that will help the employee become more effective.

⇨ 403

What are the pros and cons of discussing rewards at appraisal time? Some people say it ties the rewards closely to performance. Others say they should be dealt with on separate occasions.

I prefer giving appraisals on one occasion, and closely following them up with the announcement of rewards on another occasion. I agree with the principle of tying rewards to performance, but if employees know that you will announce their raises (or whatever you give as a reward) at the time of appraisal, they may not hear what you want them to hear while they await the good news. During appraisal, you want to discuss the immediate past performance, and how performance can be improved in the months ahead. You want the employee to note deficiencies and shortfalls in performance, and to set new goals. That's serious business. You can't afford to have the employee distracted by wondering how much money is forthcoming.

Training

⇨ 404

I have no training background, yet I've been asked to conduct certain kinds of training. What does it take to be effective?

Adult learning is different from that of children. For adults to learn and to be trained, they must see a value to them to undergo it. Make sure the purpose of the training and its benefits are clear at the beginning. People need feedback during the training process: how well or how poorly they are absorbing it. Finally, they need a chance to practice the new skills or to apply the knowledge to which they have been exposed.

Adults do little training in a vacuum, as children are forced to do. They commit themselves when they see that it is to their advantage to learn, and when they can see the practicality of it.

⬦ 405
The problem with assertiveness training, it seems to me, is that if everybody gets trained to assert himself or herself, it's all me, me, me.

I've often thought the same. Assertiveness training is undeniably useful in helping people to identify their needs and wants, and to express them in a way that is acceptable to others. But consultant Malcolm Shaw, author of the book *Assertive-Responsive Management*, adds a new dimension to the usual training: responsiveness. Assuming that the other person in a transaction brings needs and wants and resources, Shaw argues that each party, while asserting, should be responsive to those needs and resources. In short, "This is what I see going on, and this is how I feel about it," is coupled with, "What's your perception, and how do you feel about it?" On that base of information and understanding, the parties work to define a change that will provide a preferable situation. Thus, A-R is an effective negotiating and conflict management technique.

Here are the four steps of A-R:

1. Description of what each person sees as the existing situation;
2. How each feels about the situation;

3. What change in one or both is desirable;

4. The benefits of that change to one or both.

⇨ **406**

I run a small company. Some of my new supervisors need some training in how to supervise, but I don't have the money to send them away for workshops or courses. How can I accomplish this training on a limited budget?

Consider bringing someone in from the outside who can not only train your supervisors but train one or more of them to train, in turn, other new supervisors in the future. In-house training is usually far less costly than public workshops or seminars that may run close to $300 per day for each attendee. You can probably find a contract trainer to come in for $300 to $500 per day to work with all of your supervisors. Or, for a few thousand dollars, a trainer can design a self-study program suitable for your company.

Another possibility is to look for a retired manager in your community who might like to take on this training assignment for even less than you'd pay a contract trainer. Of course, you'd take a chance on the retired person's training skills.

A third option is to arrange for courses at your local college or university in supervisory skills. Once again, you take a chance, since the classroom is not the same kind of environment as that in which the supervisors work.

Even with compromises, you can achieve the needed training on a limited budget over a period of time. You may wish to supplement classroom work with discussions with you. No one provides more reality than you, since it is your company and your culture. Supplement course work with some of the newsletters, tapes, films, and books that concentrate on management skills.

⬦ 407

Every day my desk is covered with announcements of seminars and workshops. I'd like to send some of my people, but how can I tell in advance whether these programs are worth it? They are very expensive.

Yes, the costs of outside training have risen sharply. Those costs justify your doing research. For example:

- Talk to the potential trainees. Let them tell you whether they feel the workshops as advertised would be helpful to them, and why. This approach moves you away from the implication that you are sending them because you think they need training. Instead, you ask, "Would you see a benefit in attending this?"

- Check out the trainer's credentials. What are his or her qualifications for presenting this subject? You can get more information by calling the sponsoring organization and asking for it. They may refer you to the trainer, which gives you the chance to personally evaluate him or her. Talk to the trainer about your needs, and see how prepared he or she is to meet them. Don't, however, ask questions that suggest you might be looking for free consultation. Rather, you're trying to find out how familiar the trainer is with your kind of needs, and how experienced he or she is in dealing with them. You're looking for credentials rather than specific answers.

- Get a list of references: people who have attended previous sessions or who have sent others. You can discuss the session candidly with these people. What kinds of results did they get?

- Get advice from your in-house training department, if you have one. They may know about the program, the sponsoring organization, and the trainer.

Consulting

⇨ 408

My company has retained a consulting firm that will be studying the operation and making an analysis. Imagine my shock when the consultant who is looking over my shoulder is a man who used to work here and with whom I had deadly relations.

If sufficient time has passed, perhaps neither of you is interested in the painful history. However, if working with him presents an unpleasant prospect, so much so that you fear the results will be biased and unhelpful, talk to your boss about it. He may advise you that it would be unwise to make an issue of it, that you will, through your protest, not look good. On the other hand, he may agree that the consultant's residual bias toward you could skew the study.

You could always level with the consultant. Tell him that you realize the history between the two of you may threaten to make his work harder, but you want him to know that regardless of the past, you have confidence in his professional objectivity. Make your assurance simple: "I know it might be tough for you, but just in case you have any doubts, I'm confident we can work together and that your professionalism will be the guiding factor."

▷ 409

A valuable employee who has been with me for 10 years is leaving to enter private practice as a consultant. He wants to negotiate a contract with me. I'm sympathetic because I could use some outside help, and I'd like to provide him with some security during the transitional period. Still, I have questions about whether he's the right choice.

Draw up a pros and cons list. For example, on the pro side, he knows your operation quite well, and the two of you know each other well—and presumably trust each other.

On the other side of the ledger, he is still rooted in your operation. It would conceivably be better if he gained some other experience and then came back to you, ready to apply that diversified knowledge. And you might also ask, although this is not necessarily a major factor, why you're going to pay big money for him to tell you what he didn't when he was employed by you.

Or perhaps he did. Maybe he couldn't be effective in advising you because he didn't want to criticize other subordinates. You'll have to consider these questions. Possibly, you could give him some specific work that needs immediate attention, something that your employees cannot, for some reason, handle. That project will provide him with some transitional security. Then invite him to come back to you after a year or two to discuss more long-range work.

There's another important consideration: How well will the other employees, his former colleagues, receive him if they must cooperate with him? If you think long and hard about it—and you should—you might develop quite a list of things to consider before you commit.

⇨ 410

I'm at the point at which I must discuss fees with the consultant I want to retain. I'm not experienced in how to discuss fees with a consultant.

You're on firmer ground if you have some idea of the range of consultants' fees, which can be anywhere from $500 to $2000 per day, or even more. And there may be a considerable range in an individual consultant's charges, depending on the type of work, organization, length of time, and so on. For example, a consultant may set a fee of $1500 per day for work that will involve two or three days. But if you estimate that you will have, say, 20 days, he might be willing to take on the job at a per diem rate of $1000 to $1200.

The point is that most consultants will negotiate with you within reason. Don't forget to figure in expenses and travel time. If a consultant must travel long distances, he'll probably add travel time as well as the cost of travel.

If the job is lengthy and substantial, and if you can estimate the time required, you may be able to settle for a package rate, with additional per diem fees should the work take longer than the estimate.

⇨ 411

I've done some preliminary talking with a consultant on the telephone. He's coming in for an interview. He hasn't said anything about charging for that discussion. How do I know if he will?

If the consultant regards the clock as running from the time he enters your office, most likely he would have made that clear when he agreed to meet with you. I suspect that he is following a familiar practice of granting you one session before charging. If you have any doubts, you should call him and ask whether he charges for that initial call. If he plans to, and hasn't told you that, I'd think that you have some reason to wonder whether his lack of openness might cause you problems later.

If the session is free, don't expect him to start feeding you diagnoses, analyses, or recommendations. This is, in effect, a sales call to build rapport and to determine your needs.

⬦ **412**

I'm about to sit down with a consultant for the first time to evaluate his suitability to do a job for me. How do you judge a consultant?

Much as you might a job applicant. Allow time for talking in the beginning so that your intuition can work. You may be working with this man closely for a time, and you'll have to develop trust in him. What do your instincts tell you after your interview? Is this man someone you can collaborate with, and from whom you can take bad news and accept recommendations for improvement?

Talk about the situation with which he'll be working. Don't expect answers from him until the clock is running. He's too experienced to give you a free consultation. But look for signs that he is knowledgeable in the area of concern to you. For example, are his questions on the mark? Does he mention that he has worked on similar problems in the past? Again, he may not tell you how he resolved them.

Check his credentials in general. Has he had exposure to your kind of organization and industry? Has he published anything you might evaluate? Has he had actual experience as a member of an organization? It may not be absolutely necessary for him to have been a line manager if he is to deal with line managers, but it increases his credibility. What has been his history in the specialized areas in which you want him to work?

Finally, ask for references, preferably from clients who have had needs similar to yours. You'll want to be able to talk with two or three, as you would in the case of a job applicant. Don't simply accept a list of clients, no matter how prestigious. You really can't know what he did for them that would have any significance for you.

◊ **413**
I've been interviewing a management consultant for some work I need done. He has a list of blue chip clients a foot long, but I can't seem to pin him down to my kind of problem. When I start talking about my specific needs, he listens, then steers the conversation to something else. I have an uneasy feeling he doesn't know what to do with my situation.

First, let's dispense with the client list. Whenever a consultant has done work with someone, no matter how briefly, the client's name goes on the list. Lots of times the client list is hype. The consultant may have worked for the company, indeed, but that experience may have nothing to do with your needs.

Second, you have to be careful not to appear to be seeking a free consultation. If your questions are meant to evoke the consultant's diagnosis of your need or problem and get his suggestions for corrective steps or recommendations, they'll raise a barrier immediately. The consultant will say to himself, "This fellow wants to have me without paying for it."

Third, if you have a feeling of distrust, you and he will probably not work well together.

Finally, get a sense of his experience in general. Find out what his values are. Then you can decide whether this person seems sufficiently knowledgeable to work with you. However, you must be comfortable with him. He's probably going to have to say and do things you may not like. Ask for the names of clients for whom he has done related work, and talk to them.

Special Problems

⬦ 414

Recently I made a salary offer to an engineer from another company. It was more than he'd been making, but the other company made him a counteroffer. He decided to stay, even though I got the impression he wasn't too happy there. I don't want to get into a bidding war, but I'd like to stay in touch.

Phone him after a few weeks to let him know that you're still interested in him. When he got the counteroffer, he probably suppressed his dissatisfaction in the face of the blandishment of the higher pay. But in time his dissatisfaction will surface again, and it might be fueled by resentment over this employer's having raised his pay only under pressure.

Contact him every few months to tell him that you'd be happy to resume talks with him. If you don't want to raise the ante, assure him that you'll consider him for a raise at appraisal time. Meanwhile, get the message across that if he accepts your job offer, you'll work with him to avoid those factors that are causing him dissatisfaction in his present job. He may be happy to take your lower pay if he thinks he'll be happier and more satisfied working for you.

⬦415
I have to promote one of my employees to supervisor. I'm newly promoted to manager myself. What do I look for in an employee that helps me to know whether that employee would make a good manager?

It's almost impossible to divine whether an employee would make a good supervisor or manager. But there are some indicators that might help your decision along. First, does the employee really want to be a supervisor? Wanting is important in doing a good job. When people really don't want to be responsible for the work of others, they aren't happy being in a managerial position. Second, is the employee interested in the work and welfare of others? Does he or she work smoothly with others now? If the employee is highly competitive, subordinating that competitive drive will not be easy. Third, does the employee seem to think about the department as a whole, as opposed to his or her little piece of it? People who are preoccupied with their own tasks generally don't develop the overall perspective that managers and supervisors must. Fourth, does the prospective manager relate well to the people with whom he or she works? People who are abrasive and insensitive usually have a hard time encouraging others to work well for them. On the other hand, the employee needn't be well liked by everyone. Respect is a much better prescription.

The above are just for starters, but they are important. If you overlook or discount them, you may promote a lemon.

⬦416
I share a secretary with two other managers. The problem is that she gives preference to their work. I

seem to always be waiting for her to finish their stuff before she gets around to mine.

Your colleagues may indicate an urgency or importance that you don't when giving her work. If that's often the case, perhaps you'd better have a talk with your coworkers to work out some rules: When the work is really important, say so. Otherwise let the secretary work out her own priorities.

How do you find out? Ask her why it seems to you that she gives your work the lowest priority. Don't suggest that she actually does that, but rather that it is your impression that she does. She may not be aware of what she does. On the other hand, she may be following a pattern that should be broken. One manager I know found out that the secretary he shared did his work last because he was the newest member of the department.

Explain to her, quietly but firmly, that you are as concerned with getting your work out as are your two colleagues. She might be able to suggest new ways of giving assignments to her that all three of you should adopt. However, don't put pressure on her to give you more attention if the other two have been insisting that she give their work priority. That's the kind of evidence that demands that you work out an accommodation with the other two managers.

⍐ **417**

Top management in my company is tight with information. A couple of times I've told the president things that he didn't think were general knowledge, just to convince him that management might as well open up since there are no secrets. We have a good grapevine. He thanks me for telling him, but nothing happens. Am I being naive?

I think you are being logical, but the president is not. I doubt whether you will get the results you want, to persuade management to start giving out information. In fact, I strongly suspect you will get some results you don't want: Management is likely to try to tighten up even more. You are telling the president that top management has not been successful in withholding information. They don't get the "There's no use" message. Very likely they will take it as a challenge to do better at strangling any flow of information.

My experience with this kind of management has convinced me that they are strongly them-versus-us in their orientation. Information in this kind of organization is strictly a managerial prerogative that management has no intention of sharing with employees. Any time there is evidence of a leak, this kind of management expends tremendous energy trying to find out and punish whoever caused it.

I suggest that you and your coworkers forget any mission to convince management to loosen up, and work to strengthen your grapevine. It will probably, overall, be more accurate than the information you get officially from above.

◊ 418

I've heard that a manager can only delegate authority, not responsibility, to an employee.

Authority gives power to do something. Responsibility is accountability for doing something. As a manager, you can empower an employee to perform a responsibility. But you cannot rid yourself of the responsibility for doing the task or reaching the goal if it is something for which you are accountable. That's why many managers are reluctant to delegate. If the employee does the job poorly or fails completely, accountability is still the manager's.

♢ 419
How do you respond to people who are always saying, "We tried that and it didn't work"?

You may find it useful to ask them to tell you what "that" and "it" were. Their answer might reveal that they don't really understand your proposal. To them, it sounded familiar and they blew the warning whistle.

Even if what you are suggesting is similar to what was tried before unsuccessfully, the conditions are probably quite different today. The resources—money, technology, people—are certainly not the same. The economy and the market have undoubtedly changed. So, prepare your argument to show why what didn't work before may, because it's a different time, have a chance to work now. The more changes of circumstances and environment you can describe, the less forceful their negative arguments will be.

You may also want to prepare a worst-case scenario. What's the worst that can happen if we try this idea, even though a version of it wasn't successful before? When the worst is tolerable, further resistance vanishes.

♢ 420
I want to impress a subordinate who is a persistently poor performer. It seems to me that a memo has more permanence than the spoken word. Should I write a critical memo?

Generally, I advise against writing a memo that has a negative message. Negative words on paper seem to have greater wounding power than those spoken. In fact, what may seem to be justifiably critical in tone to you may be seen as hostile to the reader. And yes, the written word does have permanence. The recipient has every reason to fear that those written words exist somewhere in a file for all time. They can't be erased.

Your objective is to persuade the employee to correct a performance problem; it is not to arouse such resentment in him or her as to demotivate. Speak your criticism. Agree on a plan to improve performance. If you wish to reinforce the agreement, prepare a memo that outlines the plan for improvement. You need not refer to the problem in the memo. Keep it positive and future-oriented.

▷421

I hear a lot about obsolescence and I know it's a big problem. What are the early warning signs?

Obsolescent people tend to focus on the past. They measure their value by what they've done before. You might insist on their observing current standards, but they reply by pointing to the fact that they have always been known as good performers.

They become rigid. They'll reject new ideas with, "We've tried that and it didn't work," or, "This is the way we've always done it."

They also seem to stop learning. They make decisions on the basis of their experience. New data don't figure in.

When you see an employee who becomes fixed in a rut, rejecting help and challenge and seemingly content to coast on the past, you have a problem: an employee who is on the way to becoming obsolete.

◊ 422
Stress-interviewing of job applicants is big in my division. I'm trying to decide how I feel about it.

My feeling is that most job interviews are sufficiently stressful without the addition of stress by the interviewer.

If I were to use stress consciously, I would do so only for a job in which the candidate would be under unusual pressure. And then I would retain a professional who is thoroughly experienced in creating stress and handling its consequences.

You may lose qualified candidates who walk out of the interview saying, "Why should I work for someone who gives me such a hard time?"

Generally I believe that stress interviews may humiliate and embarrass people needlessly.

◊ 423
I made a popular decision, but now I know it was shortsighted. I have to reverse it, and I dread it. In fact, I'm not sure how to do it.

Be fast and open. If it was wrong, reverse it as quickly as possible before people get too accustomed to it. Present your evidence against the decision. Let the people involved have a chance to talk against the evidence or your thinking. Listen carefully. They may come up with a more moderate way to go, altering the decision to make it more workable. When you have the data, make your move. Confirm that the decision will be reversed or modified.

When all the data are in, you may be surprised to find that the people who benefited by the decision originally—or thought they would—agree with the need to undo it.

◊ 424
Some executives seem to radiate power. How do they come by it?

Some people project personal power. Probably more than anything else, it's based in competence and confidence. They are good at what they do, and they accept that reality. Actually it's more than being good; they know they are especially talented, skilled, or knowledgeable. Furthermore, they are convinced that they can handle most challenges that come their way. It's not necessarily arrogance, but rather one step this side: supreme self-confidence.

People with personal power often enhance their image by the elegant way they dress. They have cultivated a pleasing, authoritative voice. They stand erect. If you were to walk into a room and see a group of strangers, the person with personal power would stand out in the way that person relates to the others, and they to him or her.

◊ 425
Since I was promoted a short time ago, I sense that some of my old colleagues have wanted to continue to socialize with me. I'm not sure that that is in my best interest now that I'm on a higher level.

In some organizations mixing with former colleagues from a lower level used to be frowned on more than it is today. You may not want to get together with them as frequently and as conspicuously as before, but it is probably a mistake not to maintain contact with them as you move up. They are channels of communication for you. They may give you valuable information that some of your peers wouldn't for reasons of discretion or competition. Your old friends don't have hidden agendas that keep them from being open to you. Furthermore, your erstwhile peers can be a rooting section for you. As you climb the ladder, you need good PR, and you'll get it from them. They talk to their bosses about you, and those managers take note.

Finally, you can't overlook the possibility that one of those former peers will become one again, or maybe reach an even higher rung. A former ally may become your staunch friend in high places.

SEVEN

MEN, WOMEN, SEXISM, AND SEX
426–447

Affairs

⟡ **426**

How do I handle the problem of an executive two levels above me who is having an affair with my subordinate? I'm worried that she talks about how I run my department.

What do you worry about her saying? If you are doing a good job, why worry? Unless, of course, you do not have a good relationship with your subordinate.

I wouldn't talk to her about your worries. She may not realize that you know about the affair. I would, however, keep her on the straight and narrow regarding her performance. No one else in the department should have cause to suspect that you are easy on her because of her relationship with the executive. And she should not believe that she is entitled to special treatment.

If she does not perform well, and complains to her lover that you are hard on her, your documentation of her performance is your protection. Should your boss feel pressure and come to you to inquire what's going on, you can show him the evidence.

If your performance record is good, then you can quietly let your boss know that, should you be eased out because you are not sufficiently considerate of your subordinate, you'll sue on discrimination charges.

⇨ 427

At an industry association meeting, I met this gorgeous woman who works for a competitor. We spent time together and have written and phoned a lot since. In fact, we're making plans to take a week's vacation together in the Caribbean. My boss would probably kill me if he knew. Around here, anyone who gets chummy with the competition is a traitor.

Some managements are, understandably, paranoid about industrial espionage. For the sake of your conscience, you're going to have to restrict what you tell your lover about your company. That's a terrible way to have a relationship, but the damage that ensues from seemingly innocent information can be enormous. For example, if you were to tell her about an impending price increase that is a short time away, her company could clean up by feeding the information to its sales force.

For the sake of your job, you're going to have to keep this liaison a total secret.

It seems to me that you're putting quite a strain on the affair. Still, admittedly it adds excitement. It would undoubtedly be wise if you considered what job options might be available to you elsewhere should you be accused of betrayal. And you probably will be, since there will be some interest in your industry association in your networking.

◊ 428

Another manager who is a friend of mine invited me to have lunch with him and a woman who also works for our company. I suspect they're having an affair, and I'm supposed to be the beard, to throw anyone off the track. Now he wants to repeat the lunch, and I feel used. I'm just there to protect them.

The question is, in what are you being asked to collude? If the two of them are not married and are just reluctant to let the word of their true relationship get around, you're doing them a favor, unless of course, for some reason, you disapprove of the affair. If you don't, and if you enjoy their company, what's wrong with doing your friend a favor?

If your friend is married, and especially if you know his wife, you may have strong scruples. You are being asked to collude in an event to which you may have moral objections.

In short, if you do not disapprove, think of the lunch invitations as a request for a favor. If you do disapprove, tell your friend that you are not comfortable. You don't have to put it on the grounds of morals. Simply stick with your feelings, to which you have a right.

If he is a friend, he will understand and not want to cause you further discomfort.

◊ 429

One of my supervisors has begun an affair with a female employee who also works for me, although she doesn't report to him. There's gossip, and I know that, even in these times, some disapproval, especially since she is married. What is my role in this relationship? Do I have a responsibility?

Not to guard people's morals. If you try to dictate conduct, you may alienate two good employees. And you may make others uncomfortable, because they might wonder whether you would be repressive with them as well in other circumstances.

The best course of action is usually to ignore the romance, unless the couple's entanglement is affecting their work or their abilities to work with other employees. If either situation occurs, let your supervisor know that you're not about to tolerate any barriers to performance. Don't criticize the affair; concentrate instead on the signs of declining performance or conflict. Don't get drawn into a discussion of the personal feelings the two have for each other.

◊ 430
I'm a male supervisor reporting to an absolutely gorgeous boss. She's not married. When she's around me, I can hardly concentrate on what I'm doing. I think she might be interested in me. How do I get something going?

Are you sure you really want to try to launch an affair? If there are other supervisors, they'll generally have one of two reactions to the affair, which, I warn you, will not be a secret. One response will be to use you as a channel of information to her. The other will be to back off from you in fear that you might be relaying information about them in your pillow talk.

Management's reaction to her affair with you will probably not be positive. She may feel under pressure, and the only way she can effectively relieve that pressure would be to drop the affair or get rid of you. Neither option sounds pleasant or richly rewarding for you.

◊ 431

I'm a corporate trainer, a woman, working out of my company's home office. Lately I've been traveling to branch offices with another trainer, a man, to deliver sales training programs. We're both married, and we've talked about having an affair when we travel together. I'm very attracted to him, but I'm uncomfortable about the idea.

Stay uncomfortable. My advice is essentially the same whether you are married or single. Eventually, people in the home office will find out about your away-from-home dalliance, and some executive will say, "Why are we subsidizing their little romance? Besides, if they were working as they should, they'd be too worn out to play." It's quite possible that there would be some pressure exerted on your boss to split up the two of you, just because, even in our liberal times, there are many people who don't understand or accept the passion you feel.

Thus, most likely, your romance will be very temporary. Even if it isn't, and is tolerated, you're in for a lot of pain when your respective spouses begin to suspect.

Mentors

◊ 432

A young woman in the company has shown interest in getting to know me. At first, I wondered whether her interest was sexual, but I don't think so. I'm much older and not the romantic type. I really think that she seeks me out as a mentor, since I'm well placed in the

**company. I'm flattered, but at the same time I'm
worried that other executives will get the wrong idea.
How can I manage this without creating a scandal?**

I think you have to respond to more than flattery. A far more
important consideration is whether this young woman has the
talent and promise that would justify your investment of time as
her mentor. If others see her as such, they are less likely to ask
the question, "What does he see in her?" There is less likelihood
that you will be seen as an old fool.

Keep your contacts with her as open as possible. When she
visits your office, your door should be open. I advise against
socializing after work—no drinks. I'm not even sure about lunch,
although you may decide that so long as your discussion is
public, no harm is done. But don't arrange to have lunch at
some distance from the office as if you hoped to prevent the
two of you from being seen. You probably will be seen—and
suspected.

You'll find the telephone a good medium for your discussions.
It might be better if she visited you. If you went to her location,
you might constitute a threat to her boss. Take advantage of the
interoffice mail. Writing back and forth is acceptable form.

You must, of course, be very careful not to disclose confidential
information and gossip that could embarrass other managers.

Your reward is the satisfaction you get from helping to make
her a more valuable resource to the company. And no doubt
you will find something to learn in the mentoring process.

⇩ 433

**An older executive has become a mentor and a sponsor
to me. But in the last few weeks, he has been
suggesting that we go out for lunch and drinks after**

work. I am a young, fairly good-looking female. But I don't want to have a sexual relationship with him.

The first question that comes to mind is, Has this man been helpful to you? If he hasn't really, you have everything to gain by getting out of the relationship. The best way to do that is to make yourself unavailable. If, however, the man is powerful enough that you don't want to offend him, you might approach the problem this way: "I'm complimented by your interest in me. I have to tell you that I'm seriously involved, so much so that there isn't room in my life for another involvement. I want to be fair to you and not seem to lead you on." Even if you're not romantically involved with someone else, you are serious about your commitment to work. That simple statement, combined with your refusal to join him for quiet moments, should let him down. He is probably used to playing the field and not always scoring.

If he has been helpful, and if you'd like to continue the relationship in a nonthreatening way, use essentially the same approach—that you're involved—then add, "I value working with you, and I hope we can continue to do so. I just want you to understand that I'm not free to join you outside the office, and I know you can see why." If your mentor truly values your relationship, he'll respect your forthrightness.

⇨434
A male executive took an interest as a possible mentor to me, but then he made it clear that he wasn't interested in helping me unless I slept with him. I walked away from that, but now I hear he's saying all over the company that I wanted sex and he didn't.

I'd assume from his callousness and single-mindedness that he has done this sort of trading before, and he's probably been successful. If my assumption is correct, people will tend to discount his bragging. It's a hurtful experience for you, but maintaining your dignity will go a long way toward countering the effects of his malice.

To speak with him directly will be useless, and may even give him the content for another lie. If you can produce evidence that this man's behavior impairs your performance or deprives you in any way of getting ahead in the organization, you may wish to consult an attorney or your company's personnel director. Many companies are so wary of harassment actions that they don't require solid evidence. Your company's management may want to take quiet action to let your detractor know he is causing embarrassment for the company as well as for you.

⊳ 435

I'm a young female MBA, and I'm ambitious. An older executive in my company has taken an interest in me. We've had drinks after work three times, and I know he'd like to have an affair. He's married, but I think it would be fun, and I know he can help my career.

If you're looking for a complicated life, you're about to make the right choice. Once the news of your dalliance gets out— and it will—he may find that other executives frown on his relationship with you, especially since you're on a lower level of the hierarchy. With sexual harassment cases making headlines these days, managements get very nervous over the possibility that a female sex partner will later cry foul. Your boss will suspect that you are giving the executive information about his department, and will treat you warily. If you break up with your older lover, management will hesitate to promote you to a position in which you'll have contact with him.

If you are a protégé and report directly to your lover, it's possible that he will take you with him as he moves up. Remember, however, that his favoring you will not earn you a multitude of friends and allies, and the higher you go, the more you need friends and allies. Again, you have to keep in mind that the two of you might break up, and that's messy when your boss is your ex-lover.

Yes, it might be fun. But pleasure and satisfaction, for a time, might be your only rewards. Even in today's more liberal atmosphere, you're more likely to find that such an involvement will at least temporarily impede your progress rather than promote it.

Sexism

⬦ 436
I'd like to know how to get the men I work with to stop calling me "dear" and "sweetie." I think that, as a woman, I should be called by my name, just as the men are.

Let your male colleagues know that you want to be called by name. You can go the diplomatic route: "I know that you believe you are complimenting me by using terms of endearment, but I'm uncomfortable when you do. I would prefer that you call me by my name."

If the soft approach doesn't take care of the problem, be more direct: "My name is Jean, and I'd appreciate your calling me that. I'm not comfortable when you use a term of endearment, because you and I don't have that kind of relationship."

And finally, "I've asked you not to call me 'dear.' Please use my name. It's beginning to affect our working relationship, and I know that neither one of us wants that."

◊ 437

When I came to this department, I was the only woman supervisor. At first, the other supervisors would call me "dear," but I managed to convince most of them that I felt that was inappropriate. One man, however, still calls me that. But immediately after, he'll say, "Oh excuse me, I'm not supposed to say that." How can I deal with this man?

One way *not* to deal with him is to show your annoyance at his continuing to use a term of endearment. He is obviously needling you, and he gets a reward when you react. Grit your teeth and don't react. If you keep your dignity, it's possible that some of the other supervisors will ask him to stop embarrassing you, if only because his ostentatious and false concern for you embarrasses them. You may want to maintain a correct but cool demeanor toward him, sending the message that, while you intend to work with him, you cannot feel warm toward him.

If his offensive behavior continues, you may want to tell him straight out that you find working with him very difficult because of his offensive behavior. If your openness doesn't have the effect you want, drop the subject. Don't refer to it again. His hostility toward you probably runs deep. If you have a chance to be especially helpful to him on occasion, do so. Your helpfulness may soften him up. If it doesn't, then probably only time will cure him. He'll simply get tired of his game.

There's always the possibility that word of his inappropriate behavior toward you may reach your boss, and that the boss will put a stop to it. But think several times before you suggest that the boss take action. Your colleague may retaliate by finding another offensive game to play.

⇨ 438

My boss and I were walking down a corridor the other day when he casually put his arm around my shoulders. I've never seen him do that with the men. I didn't like it, but I was so startled that I didn't do or say anything. What should I do next time?

Move out from under the arm or stop walking. You probably won't have to say anything. If you want to say something, and if you have a good working relationship with your boss, smile and tell him that his putting an arm around you is not appropriate. You might add, again with a smile, "Haven't you heard about sexual harassment?" Unless he is terribly obtuse, he'll get the message.

If he doesn't, and repeats the intimacy, you'll have to say to him, without smiling, "I'm sure you are being friendly, but I'm not used to having men I work with put their arms around me. Please don't do it. We have a very nice working relationship, and I respect you very much. I wouldn't want anything to mar that relationship."

Special Problems

◊ 439

I'm very sympathetic with a young employee's situation. Her husband has left her for another woman. She has two small children. She needs someone to talk with, but I'm afraid other employees are beginning to talk about the time she spends in my office. It's very innocent.

When she is in your office, she isn't at her desk or workplace producing, and that's the most serious consideration. It's probable that the other employees are talking more about that aspect than what appears to be a budding scandal. To that extent, your talking relationship with this young woman is hardly innocent.

And, considering the way of all flesh, the relationship is going to get troublesome for you personally. She will probably rely more and more on you. She can unburden herself to you. You will find yourself increasingly swept into more intimate disclosures. You're undoubtedly already emotionally involved; it's just a matter of degree. If the involvement becomes what I'm sure it will, will you be able to cope with it? It's doubtful that you will be an effective manager of someone with whom you are deeply, emotionally involved. Furthermore, it's unlikely that the other employees are going to look with favor on that kind of relationship in their midst. It offers many opportunities for discriminatory treatment or favoritism.

The path ahead may look interesting from this vantage point. But it changes radically around the bend.

◊ 440

My boss is going through some bad family times, and he wants to talk with me often about what I think are very

personal matters involving his wife. I suppose he has singled me out because I'm a woman, but I'm uncomfortable about it and don't know what to do.

It's possible that he has singled you out because he hopes you will eventually show your sympathy in more intimate ways. Even if you want to give him the benefit of the doubt, that he seeks you out because you have a friendly ear, it is still an imposition on you. Not only may he be keeping you from your work, but he is burdening you with information that can only bring discomfort to you. It may, in time, also cause him distress that he has confided so much personal and potentially embarrassing information to you.

You'll have to get out from under this burden. Whether or not he's looking to have an affair with you, give him a clear but gentle signal. For example, "Walter, I know how much pain you're having. It frustrates me to no end that there is no way I can help you to ease that pain, and my frustration is beginning to affect my ability to work well. Besides, I think you need to talk with someone who can help you through this time." Suggest that he seek out professional help or at least a close friend who can offer the advice you can't and shouldn't.

If your boss doesn't take the hint, and again brings personal matters up, remind him that you do not feel you can help him, and therefore would rather not discuss it.

◊ 441

One middle-aged employee sees himself as a real Lothario. He's always coming on to new female employees. He never makes a pass, but he interviews women to find out whether they'd be willing to have a

fling. I don't worry so much about harassment, but it's unseemly.

I don't normally recommend the humorous approach to a problem, but I think I might want to use it in this case. The man is making an ass of himself. It is probably annoying to the women, but not terribly threatening. When you see him after such an interview, you might say something such as, "Another interview, huh? How'd it go?" Don't smile. Be matter-of-fact. His response will probably be one of surprise. He hasn't realized that his behavior is so transparent. If he wants you to explain, tell him that the women in the department talk about what he does.

If it comes as a surprise to him, you probably won't have to say any more. If he thinks that what he does is a big joke, let him know that he's the only one who thinks that way.

⬦ 442
A very pretty young subordinate embarrasses me by her flirtatiousness. I think that other people in the office are laughing at her. I don't want them to laugh at me.

People do what they feel rewarded for doing. It's probable that your pretty young subordinate has done very well for herself by being a flirt with men. If you want her to ease up on that behavior, you have to be sure not to appear to reward it. Don't respond to it. Don't laugh at the flirting. Don't give in to her requests because she has become the pleading little girl (it works a lot of the time with a lot of men). And don't show disapproval. That may challenge her to try to break down your defenses.

Ignore the flirtatious side of her behavior. Eventually, when you've shown no reaction, she will give up. And other subordinates will increase their respect for you.

◊ **443**

At a recent convention where my company was exhibiting, I found out by accident that one of my top salespeople occasionally provides call girls to his best customers. One of the customers called my room by mistake to make arrangements. I don't think this kind of thing is compatible with our image or our ethics. Yet I don't want to lose the salesman.

Level with him. Tell him about the phone call and your feelings about it. If he denies that he provides women for his customers, accept the denial even if you don't believe him. By denying, he shows that he has understood your warning. He may not stop the offensive practice, but he now understands that he'd better not get caught.

If, instead, he admits the practice and defends it, tell him of your objections. Add to them that you believe higher management will also disapprove. He may not see anything wrong with what he has been doing, but he can hardly ignore the weight of management's intolerance. You may also threaten him with termination if he continues to procure women. Such activity is against the law, so you should have no problem in making the termination stick.

Be aware that you may not succeed entirely in stopping the distasteful procurement, but you will have put him on notice that you will not tolerate it further—if you see evidence of it.

Caution: Do not terminate without clear, indisputable evidence. If you act on circumstantial evidence, you may find yourself involved in a lawsuit.

◊ **444**

My boss is an attractive woman of around 50. We have a good but not necessarily warm working relationship.

Last night we had some drinks after work, continuing a business conversation that had started in the office. She got smashed, and I took her home. Instead of getting out of my car, she kissed me passionately and asked me to come into the house and make love to her. I managed to get her into her house, but I didn't follow her. I'm very embarrassed and afraid that this will hurt our relationship on the job.

You are probably the key to the continuing relationship. Try to bury your embarrassment and act as you did before the seduction scene. If she doesn't remember much of what happened, she'll have a vague uneasiness, which will be dispelled in time by your acting as if nothing exceptional happened. If she does remember, she'll probably be as embarrassed as you. She may hope that you don't remember, and she'll be comforted when you act as if you don't. If she apologizes, accept it as if it were no big deal. Be kind, and be discreet. Everyone has an unguarded moment now and then. It might be a good idea, however, not to make yourself available for future after-hours drinking sessions.

If her everyday behavior is as it was before, you can forget about the incident. But if she now makes little hints, even refers to the incident and seeks further intimate moments, act as if you are not getting the signals.

⬦ 445

One of my employees is spreading the word that another made a pass at him when they were having drinks after work. They're both male. I like both of them, and I hate to see the accused man get hurt. No one knew he was gay. Should I step in as a manager?

What would you do? This is essentially a private matter between two of your employees, although one has made it public. It's plainly not your business to intervene unless it causes a performance problem. If the accuser comes to you with the story, you can firmly respond that you don't want to hear such reports, that you disapprove of spreading gossip that can damage a person's reputation or ability to work with others. With the accused, be normal. Relate to him as you always have, and hope that subordinates follow your example.

⬦ 446

My boss asked me to take an important client to dinner. We mixed business talk with personal subjects. We were man and woman enjoying each other's company. After dinner, he suggested that I go to his hotel room where we could continue the business talk. He explained that it was quiet, that we could get more done. I begged off, saying I was tired and that I would prefer meeting him early in the morning at our office, or over breakfast. We did meet the next morning, but he was noticeably cool. I'm afraid I've offended him, and that my boss will be upset.

He probably assumed you were part of client service. It's possible that he was miffed because you declined to go to his room, but think how much worse it might have been, for both of you, had you found yourself in an unwanted wrestling match in the privacy of his hotel room. In order to get away, you might have had to do more than make him cool.

Level with your boss, who needs to know what happened— or didn't—just in case the client wants to continue to pout or decides to threaten. A reasonable boss will not expect you to perform that kind of service to keep the business.

Suppose the time comes when you do decide to become involved with a client? Remember that it's not a good idea to mix business with pleasure. And other people, namely your boss, might be confused as to what you are willing to do with clients.

⇨ 447

I'm a good-looking young single male. Some of the younger women in the office pal around together and have adopted me as their male mascot. We go to lunch together or have drinks after work. Lately some of the other guys have referred to the women as my harem. It's harmless, I think, but maybe it is affecting my image in the office.

You can be sure there is a lot of envying and fantasizing going on among your male colleagues. If you have ambitions to be taken seriously, you'll want to shed the possible playboy image that you may have developed. Find ways to be more discreet and less frequent in your socializing with your female friends.

EIGHT

YOU AND YOUR CAREER
448–500

Getting Ahead

▷ **448**
**This organization is so political. I doubt whether I'll
ever get far here, because I'm not.**

Every organization I've encountered is political. You don't have
to do the equivalent of shaking hands and kissing babies to get
ahead. People often do so quietly by drawing on the sources of
power that are readily available to them. For example, your
competence forms the most important block in your power base.
The better you are at what you do, especially if what you do
meets the organization's needs, the more power you have. What
resources can you offer the organization that aren't plentiful? If
you have resources that others want and can't get elsewhere—
knowledge, experience, skills—you have resources power. If
you are close to a power center, such as an executive who has
clout, some of that can rub off on you. When you take on an
important delegated task, you can build assigned power, especially
if the responsibility comes down from a higher level. When you
are active in your peer group and belong to a strong informal

organization of managers or specialists, you may find that you have alliance power.

Power is there for you. You don't have to be seen as a politician. But when people see that you have quietly accumulated power in a legitimate way, you'll find they see you as being political. Without that power, you can't get much done.

⇩ 449
How do I conduct a publicity campaign for myself?

The first place to begin is to publicize the significant achievements of your employees. Their records praise you. Your good producers are your monuments. The more you get public credit for them, the more they will spread the word that you are an outstanding manager.

Be visible in the organization. Get out and talk to people. Be seen. Build your alliances. Volunteer for challenging, even risky work.

Look for opportunities to get your name in print. Write an article for the organizational newspaper or magazine. Get active in community or volunteer work, and make sure that articles are published in the local press.

If you have an industry or professional association, seek visibility there, too, and write for their publications.

Write memos to your employees praising their work, and send copies to your boss.

If you can play the role of a mentor/sponsor to a fast-track person, you'll share some of the glory as that person moves up.

⇩ 450
I feel stuck in my career. I'm essentially doing what I've been doing for several years, with a bit more

responsibility and money every so often. My boss talks to me about what I should do or where I might go from here, but he hasn't been much help.

I hate to do you an injustice, but it sounds to me as if you are placing primary responsibility on your boss for planning your career. You need to be clear on what you'd like to do and where you'd like to go. Here are some questions to ask yourself:

- What do I like best in my present job that I'd like to do more?
- What would I like to do less?
- What do I do well?
- What do I not do well? (There ought to be a correlation between these first four questions, because generally what people like to do is what they do well.)
- Where would I like to be in three to five years?
- If I had my ideal job, what would my day be like five years from now?

These are starter questions to help you determine what you'd like to have as a goal. Then you must plan what it would take for you to achieve your goal. At that point, you approach your boss, discuss your thinking with him, and see how realistic you are, given the constraints of your organization. If your boss agrees that your plans are feasible, enlist his help in making them a reality.

⇨ 451

I'm a new manager in the company. What's a fast way to get people to recognize me? I don't want to be an outsider.

Learn the names of the people you want to know and be known by, then use those names each time you pass them in the hall or join them in an elevator. People feel complimented when near-strangers take the time and trouble to learn their names. Before long, people you've greeted will be asking, "What's that fellow's name?"

⇧ 452
I'm bored with the work I'm doing. The other day, I was offered an exciting job, one that would really turn me on. Yet, the salary is smaller, and it would be a comedown.

In what way would it be a comedown? You must be careful that you do not peg your worth to the dollar: so many dollars, so much worth. It's easy to do that in corporate life. Many highly paid managers say they feel diminished in worth when they get fired or when they retire.

Perhaps you feel that others would look down on you for having taken a lower paying position. The truth might be, however, that at least some of those who knew the circumstances would envy and respect you for having had the courage to leave perks and security to take on a job that excites you. Most of them, it's safe to say, wouldn't exhibit such daring, and they know it.

Money is nice, no question about it. But you know the clichés about what it won't buy. Think about yourself, your health, your happiness, and your growth as a person. If the new job can offer all those wonderful things, the difference in salary is the investment you've made in yourself and your future. And think ahead to how good you'll feel when you are happy with your work again.

⇨ 453
I want to get into management, but I have no experience. I'm not even sure I would be a good manager. How can I find out?

One way you can find out whether you'd be a good manager, and get some experience at the same time, is to take a position of responsibility in a volunteer organization: a charity, a community group, the P.T.A., a professional association, and so on. Most of these groups are happy to get people willing to take leadership positions, and they often don't require a management background. Managing volunteers is perhaps the most difficult management challenge there is. The people who report to you don't have to do what you ask them to do, and they don't have to stay if they don't care for the relationship with you. Thus, you'll learn a great deal about how to influence people to do what you want them to do when you have responsibility but no real authority. Since most managers in most organizations possess more responsibility than authority, you'll be learning under realistic circumstances.

If you do a good job managing the work of volunteers, chances are good that you'll do well with employees in paid reporting relationships.

⇨ 454
I'm being asked to take on much more responsibility than I have now. It's going to be a lot more work, and I want more money. But management says that the budget is tight and I have to wait. Should I take the job?

Would the new responsibilities be an investment for you? If they provide you with the means to acquire more prestige, skills, knowledge, and experience, they may be bankable. While you aren't getting any money now, it's possible that you are being rewarded with more responsibility because of your work record.

For many people, money is the measurement of their worth. But the reality is that your worth is tied to intangibles such as what you can do, what you know, and what kind of person you are. Money is a poor indicator of what you are worth. Look at the new responsibilities in terms of the intangibles above. The money will surely come later.

It won't hurt, however, to try to pin your boss down to a date when you will be considered for a raise. As the date approaches, remind your boss that you are looking forward to sitting down with him to discuss an increase.

If the new responsibilities are not really new, that is, merely an extension of what you are already doing, then ask another question: Am I doing management a favor by taking on the extra work without more pay, and will they remember this favor? If you believe the answers are negative, then decline the responsibilities, so long as it will not hurt your standing to do so.

◊ 455
I'm happy in my present job, but yesterday a search person called me, and I don't know how, or even whether to respond.

You may be hesitant because you don't want your paradise to be disturbed or because you might feel disloyal if you did respond. If the first is your reason, then you shouldn't go any further. But you can bet on being shaken up somewhere down the road. You can hardly isolate yourself from the outside world indefinitely.

As for disloyalty, reality is different these days from what it might have been a decade ago. The old bonds that tied employees to their employers have frayed. Many people who depended on their organizations to be loyal to them and provide security have since had to find other jobs.

Your initial response will land you an interview with the search specialist. How far it goes beyond that is up to you or the specialist. What can you gain from pursuing the contact? You can learn more about the job market, what people like you are being paid elsewhere, what advancement opportunities might be out there, and how other people size you up. In short, you can learn a lot about you and the world. If after your investigation you get a job offer, you can always turn it down. But the stroke to your ego is richly satisfying. You may emerge from the process with a different sense of worth. That will hardly hurt you.

◊ 456

A month ago my boss left this company to take a better job in another one. Now he's calling me up to suggest that I join him there. I'm happy where I am, but I wouldn't mind bettering myself. And I like to work for him. Should I go?

It's a very seductive situation. And it sounds very simple. You've worked for him, know him, like him. He's in a better job, ergo. . . . Those are the knows. Now look at the less-certain questions. For example, how well established is he in his new company? Is he working out? Does he truly have the clout to bring you in at a good level? Is the company one that you would like working for as much as the present one? What are your comparative routes for advancement?

In short, what would you give up, and what would you gain? You might have your ego stroked by your boss's invitation, but you might also be letting yourself in for much uncertainty and high risk. Your former boss hasn't yet set a track record for himself. He hasn't really been in his new job and company long enough to know whether he likes it or not.

Make up a pro and con list. If you don't know your career path where you are, this is the time for you to try to find out. You also need to talk to your former boss to see what your career path in the new company might be. List everything, no matter how minor.

One word of caution: If your former boss is vague in his answers, put that fact in your con list. You need definite, reassuring answers before you leave a good position.

▷ 457

I've never worried much about clothes, and I was surprised the other day when a woman friend in the company told me I should pay more attention to what I wear if I want to get ahead. I don't know how much weight I should give to what she said, especially since I think women are more concerned with these things then men.

You ought to give quite a bit of weight to what she told you. Clothes are important in getting ahead. Clothes don't substitute for intelligence, maturity, skill, and other managerial talents, but they do make a positive impression on others. If you pay attention to your clothes and grooming, you'll find that others pay closer attention to you. Furthermore, wearing well-tailored, tasteful suits will make you feel better about yourself.

You don't have to follow the uniform notion, where everyone winds up wearing the same kind of suits. But you should look at how the powerful, successful people in your organization dress. If the preference runs to dark suits, that gives you a clue as to how you might build your wardrobe. You may not wish to be a slavish imitator, but observing the significant people in the hierarchy can help you set boundaries. Always wear suits, not sports combinations, unless you work in an industry in which trendy clothes are the norm. And always make sure that what you wear is tailored well and is spotless.

Invest in expensive shoes. They look it, and, if cared for, they last.

⇨ 458

I've known men who were very flashy in presenting themselves, although in some cases they did mediocre work. Nevertheless, they were the guys who always bragged about the calls they got from headhunters. Is the system as screwed up as I think?

I suspect that the bragging they do is part of the presentation of themselves. They know the value of creating an image. The image is what others remember when search people ask for names. Incidentally, the number of calls received is not as important as the number of job offers made. There's a big gap between the two.

Just because the system may not be working for you is no evidence that it is screwed up. If you hunger for search calls, you'll have to work to achieve more visibility. Headhunters have to find out about you. Look for ways to increase your publicity. Can you get your name in print? Headhunters don't necessarily read articles about you or written by you, but others do, and may recall you at the right time. How can you increase contacts with others who are influential in your field or industry? As a hint, people who hold offices in trade or professional associations often get search calls. It could be risky to indicate that you would be happy to look at other positions—word could get back to your employer. But when people know you are receptive, they will keep you in mind should they get search calls.

If you're good at public speaking, line up as many engagements as possible. Getting up before an audience is a good way to publicize yourself.

Promotions

▷ 459
I've just lost out on a promotion I wanted very much. My pride is hurt. I'm thinking about resigning.

You're making what could be a dangerous assumption—that you lost out on the promotion because the organization doesn't value you. You need to know precisely why you failed to get promoted. Sit down with your boss and explain that you believe it would be helpful for your development to know what were the criteria applied to the candidates for this promotion. Incidentally, first make sure that you were indeed considered. You may find that no one regarded you as a potential in this case.

If you were a candidate, you want to learn what you have less of, and what the person who was promoted had more of. Turn the conversation to other promotion possibilities that may develop in the near future, and what your boss believes will be the applicable criteria in those cases.

If you believe the promotion was arbitrary, you have the options of quitting or fighting hard for the next one. This time, you'll have some idea of what you have to fight with. You can always quit; that's a last resort. But never quit until you have made your boss sharply aware that you want to be seriously considered for promotion, and he or she indicates indifference.

⇨ 460

I'm a financial executive in a division of a large corporation, and my husband has a successful law practice. The home office has beckoned. It's halfway across the country. Naturally, I want the promotion, and I'd like my husband to go with me. But he says it would take years to build a new practice. It's so painful we're hardly talking to each other.

You're mobile; he is not. It's surprising that you never seemed to anticipate this eventuality. Or perhaps you did and simply didn't want to plan for it.

What are your options? He might be able to get a position in a law firm or as a corporate lawyer with another company in that city. It would be a different kind of practice. If he is willing to talk about it, ask your company to work on it.

If he isn't willing to change, and you insist on making the move, you can start negotiating a long-distance marriage. Many other couples are practicing such an arrangement in these days of the two-career couple. You live and work there, he lives and works here, and you join each other on weekends and holidays, sometimes halfway between your two domiciles. It's expensive. It creates much tension. And it should be negotiated completely, even to the point of agreeing on whether you'll have social lives with others.

⋄ **461**

A new position has just opened up in the company. It sounds very exciting, even though I haven't had much experience in that kind of responsibility. But I have a good track record, and friends are urging me to go for it. I think I'm bright enough to take it on, even with my lack of background. Is it too big a risk?

If you don't have the appropriate background, you're obviously going to have to do a lot of learning in a short time. How much time would you have? If you're expected to function effectively very quickly, you're asking for a great deal of stress. And you're also inviting failure. If you do fail, what will that mean to your career? It would, of course, be nice if others in the company applauded you for taking the leap even though you failed or didn't perform well. But they might not. You could be stamped as a failure, even though the odds were greatly against your immediate success.

Assuming that you would be given ample time to learn the new responsibilities, where would you get this knowledge and the right skills? Are they easily available to you?

Another consideration is where the job will lead you, if you are reasonably successful in it. Does it point to a career path you'd like to follow?

There are just a few starter questions to help you assess the degree of risk involved in taking on the new job.

⋄ **462**

The company is asking me to become assistant to a man I know is incompetent. They're giving me a small raise, but it's not adequate considering I'll have to do his work as well as mine.

If you can't get monetary compensation, then you have to look at what other benefits there might be to taking on what sounds like a thankless job. The point is that in reality it may not be thankless. Look first at what kind of deal you might be able to cut with higher management. How long will you be expected to be assistant? What will happen at the end of that time— another change, promotion, more responsibility, a better title, a chance at a job you'd like? Sometimes management is willing to negotiate when they want an unfavorable assignment filled. Of course, you must accept a risk: What they negotiate now, they may not be able to deliver later on. Times, conditions, and people change.

Look next at what you can get out of the job. For example, if you do much of this man's work, will you learn new skills? Will you acquire new knowledge and experience? Those could be chips you cash in later. What will the job title and responsibility look like on your résumé? Will you enjoy a reputation in the company for having taken on such a position and performed it well and discreetly?

There's usually no joy in working for an incompetent. You just have to measure what the job is worth long-term. If you can't see the value, turn it down. It could be a dead end.

▷ 463

There are two of us competing for a promotion, and the decision is going to be made soon. I have some dirt on him. I've heard that in another job he was accused of having embezzled some money. It could be a bombshell. Should I use it?

You could become a victim of the blast yourself. Suppose he is able to prove that the accusation was never substantiated. What will you do then? Not only will you have slandered him, you will have embarrassed any manager who followed up on your gossip.

You can use the information in a more honorable way. Go to your competitor and tell him what you've heard. Reassure him that you would not, under any circumstances, repeat the gossip, but you can say that you assume others could have access to the same rumor. You can add that you wanted to warn him of that possibility. If the gossip is true, he may decide to ease up in the competition. But there's a risk in doing so. He may interpret your words as a threat. He may not believe you wouldn't use the information against him. He may then decide to find a way to strike back at you.

It's a big risk. I think I would choose to find other ways to conduct my competition.

⬦ 464

I'm being offered a promotion within the company. It's a nice title, more money, and a lot of prestige. But I wonder whether it's a job that I'll enjoy doing. I worry that it isn't. How much risk is there in turning it down?

You have to compare two kinds of risk: You incur one if you turn down the promotion, but you create the other by taking on the job and not doing it well because you can't commit yourself to it. You'll have to determine which is the greater of the two, depending on how your boss and/or the organization regards managers who turn down what is offered. If you believe you must accept, consider whether you can negotiate aspects of the new job to make it more palatable. For example, can you get an estimate of how long you'll have to occupy the position? What more desirable responsibility might be there for you after your tenure? Can you change the job, adding or subtracting responsibilities, that would make the new position more desirable and interesting? Often we take just what's handed to us, when we really could tailor the offer a bit to fit us better. If you have an empathetic boss who wants you to succeed, you can indulge in some give and take.

If you can't change the job, and if you believe the risk is tolerable should you turn it down, the reason you offer might be that you don't believe you will do as well as the position deserves. You're saving the company some disappointment. If your higher management is enlightened, they'll appreciate your candor—and the disappointment you have saved them.

◊ 465
I recently turned down a promotion in the company because it didn't seem right for me. But now I'm worried that I'm not going to get another chance. I see myself sitting here for the next 10 years.

You may be right. What can you do about it? It's possible, you realize, that you may not get another offer because management isn't sure what you'd accept—or is of the opinion, mistakenly, that you don't want more responsibility. Do you know where you'd like to advance? If you're not clear, you can hardly expect management to be omniscient with respect to your career path.

Define options for yourself. Look at the company to see where you could exercise those options. If you have a good rapport with your boss, and there is reasonable trust between you, you might want to schedule time with him or her to discuss some of these options. If you are hesitant to put the interview on the basis of, "Here's what I'd like to do," you can suggest that, with the boss's help, you are exploring possibilities. Ask the boss to realistically evaluate your options. You might emerge from the session with one or two possibilities for which you can develop strategies.

It's also possible that you will emerge with no encouragement. If so, begin looking at your options elsewhere.

Advancing Ideas

◊ 466
I get defensive when people argue against ideas that I propose. Usually I wind up frustrated because I don't get what I want, and angry with myself because I've lost my cool.

Train yourself to handle opposition as a good salesperson would. The minute you sense resistance in what the other person says, relax. Sit back and adopt a posture that suggests you are not tense and threatened. This tends to disarm the other person, who expects you to fight back. Listen to what the other person says about your idea. The more you hear, the more you can understand to what the person is objecting. Thus, encourage the other person to talk freely. When you believe you understand the resistance, you can follow one or both of the following tactics. The first is to acknowledge the objection: "Yes, I can see that that is a consideration." Then sell another benefit of your idea: "And here's another consideration. The cost figures that I cited should decline by about twenty-five percent after the first year." In short, use the yes-and approach rather than the standard but offensive yes-but. When you've completed your sell, sit back and ask the other person whether your idea makes better sense than before.

A second technique that can be used is to ask, "How do you think we could make this work?" The salesperson says, "What stands between us and doing business?" Concentrate on what could make it work rather than on the fact that the other person seems to be opposed. Don't be surprised if your resister joins with you in looking for a better version of your proposal.

◊ 467
When I send ideas up the line, they sometimes get lost, delayed, or watered down. How can I have more influence over what happens to them?

A good salesperson, talking to a contact who is not the decision-maker, will ask to meet with those who can say yea or nay. You might do the same. Ask your boss whether you can meet with the higher executives who will consider your idea. You'd like a chance to present your case cogently and be there as a resource when the questions are raised. Your boss may be relieved not to have to do the selling for you.

As a good salesperson would do, discuss with your boss how you can most effectively play an influential role in the meetings, given the personalities involved.

◊ 468
I proposed what I thought was a good idea to higher management. They discussed it, but they tabled it. It's not dead, and I'd like to revive it without being a pest. How can I do that?

What new information regarding the idea can you provide? Perhaps the original circumstances surrounding the submission of the idea have changed. For example, there is a new urgency. Costs have improved. A competitor has adopted something similar.

Or you have found a way to better the idea and its application. Whatever new slant or information you can come up with justifies reopening the discussion.

Mentors

▷ 469
How do I make myself interesting to a potential mentor/sponsor?

Have an outstanding performance record. Conduct a good PR campaign for yourself. Publicize your achievements. You have to do these to get some attention.

Ask questions of the potential mentor about the operation, specifically his or her part in it. Seek advice for yourself. People are flattered to be sought out for counsel. Express those interests of yours that seem to coincide with your potential mentor's.

Basically, you sell yourself to the mentor. You must answer the question he or she asks: "Why should I take interest in this person?" You may believe you are exceptional and worth the mentor's attention, but you must see yourself through his or her eyes. You must also appreciate, especially in the case of a sponsor, that he or she must receive some gratification from helping you along. Your success must be a form of validation for the sponsor.

▷ 470
I've had a good relationship with my mentor for three years, but I've reached a level in the organization at

which I don't think I need a mentor. Am I being arrogant?

No, mentor relationships change and that's normal. But your mentor can still be useful to you. You are arrogant only if you toss him or her aside.

Maintain your contacts with your mentor, although perhaps not as frequently as before. Steer the conversation away from your individual concerns, talk instead about more general company developments or industry trends. Gradually your mentor will be eased out of an advisory role and into one as a conduit of information. He or she may not even be very aware of the change in your relationship. The point is that you find him or her useful, although not necessarily in the same way as before. If your mentor offers advice, listen respectfully. You don't need to follow it or report back on it, as you might have done in the past.

⇨ 471
Where do I find a mentor/sponsor?

The two are not necessarily the same person. A mentor is someone in the organization who can coach you in advancing in your profession, in the organization, or in your job functions. Depending on your priority, you look for someone who is knowledgeable, has the time and will to guide you, and with whom you can share confidences. The person you choose must not have interests that compete with yours. If you want professional help, look for a more senior or advanced person in your field. Or if you want someone to advise you on career paths and power realities, a more senior manager could fill your need, so long as he or she would not be threatened by your progress.

A sponsor is usually someone in a position of power and prestige, whereas a mentor, who only coaches you, need not have a great deal of clout in the organization. A sponsor wants the ego gratification that comes with bringing along a young high potential. He or she is usually building a power base, and that can be accomplished by placing protégés in responsible positions. A sponsor can mention your name at the right moment, and prepare the way for you.

If you're fortunate, you'll find both roles in the same person.

◊ 472

For the past few years my sponsor, an older man in the company, has done a lot for me. But now he's not in a position to help me much, and I'd like to ease out of the relationship and just be friends. I suspect that he may feel the change is a comedown for him.

Continue to talk with him, have lunch or whatever, from time to time, but perhaps not as frequently as before. Avoid questions that might make you appear to be seeking his help. Talk instead about the organization, or the industry, or the economy—very general areas in which he might have opinions.

He may sense that your need for him is not as strong as it was. Find ways, through maintaining contact with him and showing warmth, to convince him that you still have a need for him—that is, for his friendship and for what he knows about the organization and the field.

He remains a resource for you, to be tapped from time to time, but now in ways different from in times past. And he may still be capable of alerting you to developments that could mean opportunity for you, and to continue to mention your name in the right places at the right times.

◊ 473

I'm a protégé of an executive who is generally regarded as the heir apparent to the presidency. My position is highly visible and highly vulnerable. How do I protect myself?

Let's cover the obvious first. Your competence is the core of your power base. You are somewhat shielded from covert politics if you continue to perform satisfactorily in achieving organizational goals. Protégés frequently run into trouble when they rely too much on associative power—that is, the power reflected from their sponsors. What is probably your next most relevant source of power is alliance with other managers, even though some of them may see themselves as competitors. Your working relationships with them should be positive and helpful—to all involved. You should be accumulating as many IOUs as possible, to be called in later should you get into a power struggle. The greater the number of managers who regard you as a valuable and respected colleague, the wider your power base. A third source of power lies in the resources you control. What knowledge, skills, or talents do you possess that the organization needs and cannot easily find elsewhere? Study the needs of the organization to determine what you may have to offer that others do not. Your study should extend to the future. What will the organization's future requirements be, and how can you prepare to supply them?

Keep your communications channels open at all levels. Many rising managers neglect their former sources of information as they move up in the hierarchy. That's a mistake. People at lower levels have much gossip and rumor to pass along to you. You can never have too much information, and you must never assume that your power base is strong enough. Keep adding to your store of knowledge and your power. Eventually many of your would-be competitors will decide you are simply too strong to take on in a race.

Personal Problems

◊ 474
I've had so many problems with my three teenaged children—drugs, drinking, truancy, problems with the police. I wonder how I could be such a miserable failure as a parent.

You may not be blameless in the conduct of your children, but take comfort in these words. First, parents who truly are miserable failures often don't consider themselves to be. They blame the children, or influences on the children, but usually not themselves. Second, these days many good people are undergoing or have undergone many of the trials and tribulations you describe. Third, many children who resemble yours have grown up to be fine, law-abiding adults.

A friend of mine, whose experiences with his adolescent children were horrifying, now looks proudly at his offspring and says, "There were times when I was afraid I would see all of them in jail."

I doubt whether parents of previous generations faced the enormous and painful challenges that contemporary adults experience. It takes a lot of love when you don't necessarily like your children. It takes patience. You're always there for them, even when you sometimes resent having to be. Most of these youngsters will pull through just fine, and yours will probably tell you later that you were a good parent.

◊ 475
I've been traveling a lot lately for the company, and my wife and I seem to fight constantly when I'm home. She think's I'm a wimp for being so committed.

The conflict you're having is quite common among ambitious people. There's a big gap between your priorities and those of your wife. You want to get ahead in the company, please your boss, and show that you are gung ho. Your wife asks, "Why aren't you gung ho about me (and the kids)?"

The gap will not disappear by itself. Quite the contrary; it will widen. And you'll find yourselves another statistic in the divorce tables.

It's time for some negotiating. Explain to your wife what is important to you. Don't put it in terms of what others make you do, or that she should accept this as a good wife (after all, doesn't she spend the money?). Stick strictly with what you want. Then ask her what she wants. Keep the shoulds and ought-tos out of the conversation as much as possible.

Then ask the questions, "What can we do to help both of us get what we want?"

At that point, the negotiations are just beginning.

⬦ 476
I've accepted a transfer that I am sure will boost my career. But when I told my wife about it, she hit the ceiling. She's threatening not to go with me.

These days more and more people are insisting that they be part of their spouse's career decision-making. Too bad you didn't talk everything over with her and get her feelings before you accepted. She may not be rebelling against your decision so much as she is against your having made it without her.

Sit down with her now and hear her out. Then ask that she hear you out. You may be able to negotiate, especially when you promise her that she will help you think through your next move.

◊ 477

It's hard for me to take a vacation because so many things go wrong or happen while I'm away. My wife gets unhappy with me, and I try to explain to her that when you reach the level of responsibility I have, time isn't your own.

I suspect you have fulfilled your prophecy. When you go away, matters at your office will require your attention. You make sure of that by not training your employees, or not giving them the authority, to handle those matters. It's a human failing. No one likes to be dispensable. I remember when, from time to time, I would call my office while I was away on a business trip or vacation, and discover that people were handling everything skillfully. One has mixed emotions about that.

You are cheating yourself, your wife, and the people who report to you. You deprive yourself of the rest that you need, you deprive your wife of the pleasure of being alone with you, and you deprive your employees of the chance to show you the stuff of which they're made. Before you go away on your next trip, assign responsibilities to your staff: "John, if the Everstone account has a delivery problem, here's what I'd like you to do"; "Jean, if the boss wants the data on the northwest sales, here's where you can find it." Then leave your number in case of an emergency. Of course, if training is called for, provide it. You are developing the effectiveness of your people resources for the long run.

You should be in control of your time—and your life. That's a distinguishing mark of a good manager.

◊ 478

I'm going through some painful times with my family, and it's affecting my work. I know I'm not doing as

well as I can. Should I tell my boss and my subordinates?

There is no management textbook answer to your question. Much depends on your relationships with the people with whom you work. If you've had close ties with your boss, for example, go with your intuition. If you feel comfortable talking with him or her about it, do so. Your boss will probably be quite understanding and appreciative of the fact that you know you're not as effective as you want to be. Nothing says that you have to be detailed with the boss about the nature of the problem. Again, unless you're good friends, the boss will probably be just as content not knowing too many of the specifics.

Essentially the same thing applies to the people who report to you. If you have been informal and forthcoming, then, when you are inattentive, impatient, or forgetful, you might have no hesitation about apologizing and asking for their understanding.

It's a case of how easy it is for you to talk with others about your problems. If it doesn't feel right to you to disclose personal matters, you shouldn't feel as if you must. At the same time, if you have been insensitive to others or have wronged them because of your emotions, simply apologize without explaining.

Résumés

◊ 479

Because of my company situation, I think I should get my résumé up to date. But I haven't made up a résumé for 18 years. It's hard to get started.

Your hesitation and floundering are good reasons never to have to get started on making up a résumé. I've long advocated that managers keep résumés up to date, culling old outdated accomplishments and adding more contemporary, relevant items. Such a résumé could be ready for printing or duplicating in a day or so.

Keeping a résumé on yourself also gives you a continually fresh perspective on yourself—what you've accomplished, what you do well, and where your work and talent are taking you. The résumé thus becomes not only a record but a planning tool.

◊ **480**

I'm sending you a copy of my résumé, which I've been sending out for the last few weeks with disappointing results. Perhaps you can tell me why.

I can only tell you why I might not respond to you. You're obviously trying to get a job with this résumé, and that may be partly to blame for the lack of action. I'll explain. There are several steps to the job-hunting process. A cover letter should be designed to persuade the employer to read the résumé. The purpose of the résumé is to arouse enough interest in the employer to take your phone call when you try to get an appointment. Your phone call sells an appointment: "See me. It will be to your benefit." The appointment, or interview, presents you as a candidate for the job.

Your résumé is a closely packed two pages. You're trying to do too much selling at once. If you slow down and think of getting the employer's attention, you'll produce a very different document. I suggest, based on my experience in having read résumés much of my professional life, that you confine your life to one page. Remember you want to catch my interest, and if you make the résumé too hard or forbidding, I'll put it aside unread. Summarize your key accomplishments in such a way that you highlight your chief skills. I must be able to see at a glance whether you have skills and knowledge that would apply to my operation. I do not wish to read through a paragraph to find out whether you are an interesting prospect.

Leave plenty of white space—wide margins, and gaps between paragraphs. Make your résumé inviting, and make it possible for me to skim it easily in seconds.

▷ 481
How long should a cover letter for a résumé be?

Short. Remember that the primary purpose of a cover letter is to persuade me to read the résumé. Include the kind of information that is persuasive: why you were impelled to write me. It might be the reputation of my company, the fact that we know the same people, that what you've heard about me specifically has attracted you, or that you have a special skill you know I'm in need of at this moment. It's a simple selling job. You know I'll get the letter and ask, "Why should I read this?" You'd better answer that question in your first paragraph.

In the second paragraph, you might highlight a significant part of the résumé. For example, you've just turned around an un-profitable division of your company and have the same skills to offer me. You might be concerned that I would miss that in the résumé, or wouldn't even look for it.

The short (or shorter, because all paragraphs should be short) third paragraph should tell me when to expect your call to make an appointment.

◊ 482
What are the characteristics of the most effective résumés you've ever read?

The chief thing I look for in a résumé is a dare: It practically dares me to ignore it. Very few résumés have ever dared me. Most of them make it very easy for me to throw them aside for reading later, which I probably won't.

A résumé should immediately arouse my interest. I want to see, upfront, the proven skills and accomplishments of the writer. Each one should be described in a short paragraph that explains the results of applications (outputs) of the skill. Unfortunately, most descriptions suggest inputs rather than outputs. "I was responsible for organizing a training program for 800 people. . . ." That's an input. And output would be, "I designed a training program for 800 employees that increased average departmental productivity by 18 percent."

As a skimming aid, each paragraph should have a one- or two-word run-in head summarizing the skill. For example. "*Business start-ups.*" The paragraph might then go on to describe successful launchings of business units by the sender.

Emphasis should be on your most recent experience. What you did in 1972 doesn't have much impact now.

Follow the paragraphs with an outline of your work history. If you reported to significant people of stature, reputation, or position, tell me that.

And education, degrees, and professional affiliation. Don't bother me with health, number of children, hobbies, or references. We'll cover that later in an interview.

Above all, unless you are remarkably experienced and accomplished, confine your résumé to one page. I know people who have never read any résumés that went beyond one page.

Writing

◊ 483

I've read things in people's memos that I'm sure they never meant to say, or regretted afterward. It almost makes me scared to put anything in writing.

When you have something important or sensitive to put on paper, I suggest that you write a rough draft and place it in your desk drawer for at least a day, and preferably two or three. When you take it out, you'll be looking at it with fresh, less-involved eyes. You'll see things that you didn't suspect were there: ambiguous statements, cloudy meanings, and so on.

Even after you've cleaned up your copy, show it to someone you trust, if you can. A more objective pair of eyes can detect shades of meanings that are unintentional but potentially very embarrassing.

◊ 484

I feel at this point in my career that I need to do some writing to establish and publicize my credentials. Would you advise my doing a book or perhaps writing a few articles?

If your objective is to spread your name around, articles work just fine. In fact, since many people don't buy books regularly, articles may do the job better.

Pick the journals or magazines that are interested in the subjects about which you want to write. Send a query letter to the editors of those publications, describing the article briefly. Any editor interested will probably ask you to do your article "on spec (speculation)," meaning that he or she isn't obliged to accept it. It's seldom that an unknown author will be commissioned to write an article for a fee. In fact, for anyone, a fee, if offered, is payable on acceptance or often not until publication.

Many periodicals offer reprints or permit the author to duplicate his or her article. You can then circulate the reprints or duplications to the people you want your name to reach.

◊ 485
At the end of each month, I have to prepare a status report, and that involves a lot of writing. It's a job I hate. Tell me how I can get through it with less loathing.

I use two techniques that I find useful in getting me through a tough day or a task for which I'm not in the mood. One is to visualize how I will feel when the task is done or the day is over. I feel myself experiencing relief and a sense of achievement. I can actually see the results of the day's work. For example, if I'm writing, I imagine the pile of manuscript pages. If I'm conducting a workshop, I hear the people tell me that they enjoyed the session. I conjure up how I look forward to relaxing afterward, perhaps with a drink or dinner with a friend.

While I'm doing the task, I reward myself for having finished segments. If I'm writing, I'll have a cup of coffee after finishing two more pages. When I complete another segment, I'll have some lunch. All day, or through the entire task, I set subgoals or time limits, after which I take a few minutes to do something I like to do. I remember vividly doing a book in a condo at the beach. Just walking down a block or so to look at the ocean was a break—and a reward for having completed my segment.

Between the rewards and the visualization, I've been able to get through almost anything distasteful.

◊ 486
I have a very good idea for a book on management techniques with which I've been successful. How do I find a publisher, and what's involved?

Look for publishers who do the kinds of books you're thinking of writing. You'll find a list of publishers and their specialties in the *Literary Market Place*, which you will find in your local library. Or make up your own list from the management books you see.

Describe your book's theme and highlights in a paragraph or two, and send your letter to the publishing houses you select. Specify also the audience for your book. If the publisher is interested in your idea, you'll receive a request for an outline and perhaps two chapters (to make sure you can express yourself on paper). If your work is attractive to the publisher, you'll get an offer of a contract.

I would not recommend that you write the book before soliciting a publisher. Each publisher may have a different perspective on your book, and you may find yourself rewriting it totally. Nor would I suggest that you waste time looking for an agent. There is so little money to be made from the kind of book you plan that agents generally are not interested.

◊ 487
Sometimes when I read some of the business books that are selling today, I think I could do as well. What are the chances of becoming a successful author?

Success is measured in various ways. Some people would say that simply getting a book written would be their criterion for success. If you're thinking of making a great deal of money writing a business book, that's probably unrealistic. The business book market goes in cycles that produce occasional best-sellers. But no one really knows why a particular book takes off. For every book that makes its author rich, there are thousands of books that sell no more than a modest number of copies. Of course, you could always get lucky—and luck is mostly what it is.

It's more realistic to aim for writing a book that people find interesting and/or useful. And if it's well written in the bargain, you'll take just pride in it. It's great for the ego to see your name in print, but the excitement of having people tell you that you have produced a good book has, I think, few parallels.

If your book can enhance your reputation, especially in your profession, it can be a worthwhile expenditure of time and energy.

The main thing is to be clear about what the book will accomplish for you: satisfaction from achievement, help for others, prestige for yourself, and so on. Making you rich is not a realistic goal.

▷ **488**

I really hate to write, but I sometimes have to produce reports and analyses. It's part of my job, and yet often I just can't get started. When I have a writing job to do, it spoils my day—or week.

Writer's block is a very common ailment among managers. My theory is that most people experience the block because they force themselves to write before they are ready. That is, they're not clear about what they want to say, or they are not on top of the data they have to present. Good writing is good thinking. When you have the material well organized in your mind, it flows out onto the paper.

If you are creating information, for example, proposing and justifying a project, take time to brainstorm with yourself everything even remotely related to the subject. Then, as you look over your notes, organize the material in terms of what is the most important thing you want to say, what is the next most important thing, and so on. Or use the KEY formula: K stands for key point, E is for explanation or elaboration, and Y is for the windup (remember the keys that used to make toys move before batteries became commonplace?).

If you are working with data, become so familiar with it before you start writing that it seems to fall into place in your head. Sometimes material just seems to organize itself when you're thoroughly acquainted with it.

Now that you're on top of your data, it's organized in your head, and you know what you want to say, start your writing when your energy curve is on the upswing. If you're a morning person, that's when you start. Professional writers usually confine their starts to when they are up.

Special Problems

⊹ 489

When I was a younger manager, I always had a fear that other managers in the company did not take me seriously, even though my record and my appraisals were good. Even today, as a successful man with a fine

track record, I still find myself wondering whether people will take me seriously, whether I have credibility. Am I weird to feel this way?

The self-doubt phenomenon you describe is anything but uncommon among people who are successful by objective standards. Unless your hesitations and reservations about how other people regard you impede your effectiveness, I'm not sure I would worry unduly about them. I once sat in amazement as a man I had known for 20 years as a confident, supremely self-possessed management authority with a score of well-known books behind him confessed to me that only now did he really believe he knew what he was doing, that he had something to offer. I sympathized with his words, which tells you something about me.

You can always go into therapy to find out why you feel this way, or how you can get rid of the self-doubt and the wondering. But perhaps it will help to know that others whom you admire also ask questions about themselves and how others perceive them. Such questions, I've come to believe, serve to keep us level-headed. Remember Spencer Tracy's wonderful advice to young actors: "Take your work very seriously, and yourself not at all."

⬦ 490

I like to develop as many sides to an issue as possible. But I was shocked the other day when, during a meeting, I started to respond to someone else's idea and another manager said, "We know how you think. You're against it." I asked him how he knew that, and he said, "You're always negative." How can I get out from under this negative image?

You may see yourself as developing all sides of an issue, but that's not the way at least one of your colleagues sees you. Put your talent to work: Develop more than one side of an issue and speak to each. Apparently you've been speaking to the negative side only. Next time, say something such as, "Well, I see a plus and a minus." Describe both.

The problem with being seen as playing a limited and predictable role is that, when you talk, people tune you out because they're sure they know what you are going to say. Shake them up; be unpredictable on occasion.

▷ 491

Sometimes I get so tired of the politics and the pettiness of corporate life. I fantasize about going out on my own as a consultant. How do I know whether it is a realistic fantasy?

If you're dreaming about going into private practice, as opposed to joining a consulting organization (which could mean more bureaucracy and politics), know that it can be a lonely life, especially at first while you're trying to get started. Many people can't take the loneliness. They discover that they like to be among people.

Going it alone can also produce much anxiety. Not having that weekly or biweekly check coming in automatically is a wrenching experience. Even in these insecure times of cutbacks, you'll be surprised at how much security you felt in the company. That will be a thing of the past.

You must be highly motivated to work on your own. Some people would say highly disciplined. Either way, you have to get up in the morning and head for your desk or office, even when you don't feel up to it, just as you did in corporate life.

The only difference is that now there is no boss to whom you are accountable—besides yourself.

Are you a good salesperson? There's a good amount of hustling, looking for prospective clients. You'll have to work the phone and make cold calls, perhaps. Many consultants agree that the selling aspect of private practice is the most burdensome.

On the plus side, you can relish your freedom, which grows as you become more successful. You can choose your clients and the type of work you take on. You are freer from politics, although you'll find that the same nonsense goes on in your clients' organizations, affecting you somewhat. When you're on your own, you work for a boss with whom, presumably, you get along well. The achievements are yours. You don't have to share them or worry that someone else will try to steal the credit.

It can be a good life because, to a large extent, you create it and you own it.

◊ 492

I hate my job so much that it's hard for me to get up in the morning. Yet I make so much money I can't seem to walk away from it.

Either you make a choice now to leave your job or you will probably have it made for you later. Eventually the stress you experience now will cause you to have health problems, or your dislike will show in your work and prompt your boss to take action—perhaps drastic action. You may believe you cannot afford to leave your job, but it's more likely that you cannot afford to remain.

Start preparing to make a change to something you will enjoy doing. You will find out once again that you can be happy. Your body will benefit, your family will benefit, and your work will be of a much better quality. Most of all, you will like yourself again; you probably don't now because of what you're forcing yourself to do.

⬦ 493

Recently I made a switch from being a field salesman to joining the inside marketing staff. Most of the others have MBAs, and I don't. I can tell they don't accept me as an equal. In fact, some are quite cool toward me. How can I convince them I can do the job?

Don't waste time trying to convince them. Just do the job. They probably have a negative stereotype of salespeople, which tells them you aren't capable of doing the thinking work that they do. If you don't know marketing, concentrate for now on learning as much as you can. Granted, you have a perspective that they lack: practical experience in the field. But you must be diplomatic about offering that perspective. Unless they are ready to listen to you, you'll be wasting your words. Read, talk to experienced marketers, and attend courses and workshops to acquire some expertise.

Be friendly and open. Eventually some of your new colleagues will respond. Form working friendships with them. In time, they will let others know that you actually have something to offer. Widespread acceptance will take a while, but once your colleagues have gotten over their disdain, and once you have begun to demonstrate skills in your new work, others will begin not only to hear you out but to ask, "What was your experience in this when you were selling?"

◊ 494

I know I should read more, but I never seem to have time.

Managers seem to solve the reading-time problem in various ways. Some take the quiet-time route. For a half or full hour each day, usually early in the morning, they close their doors and ask subordinates not to disturb them unless it's an emergency. To ensure uninterrupted time, some of these managers come to work before the working day commences.

Other managers take reading breaks between sections of work or tasks. Ten or 15 minutes of reading time can relax you and help you collect your energy for the next segment of work.

I favor reading when my energy curve dips, usually between noon and two o'clock. I don't work as efficiently during those hours as I do the rest of the day, so, for me, it's a perfect time to do my reading.

But making sure you read is more than fitting it in your schedule. You must believe, as I do, that reading is a necessary part of the managerial function. Reading must be a high-priority item on your to-do list. Only then will you find time to do it.

◊ 495

I tied one on at an office party the other night, and I shot my mouth off about some of our executives. I'm not clear about some of the things I said, but I'm sure they were not flattering. I'm very nervous about the consequences.

People probably knew you'd had too much to drink, and they may have more tolerance toward your shooting your mouth off than toward your intoxication.

Act as you normally would in your contacts with others, including those whom you may have maligned. If they have problems with you, they'll bring them up. If that happens, just say, "I'm sorry, but I have a fuzzy memory. I had too much to drink. If I offended you in any way, I apologize. I ask you to overlook an unfortunate situation."

Some of the offended people may treat you warily for a short time, but if you don't have any more lapses, they'll forget about it.

▷ 496

I'm afraid my company is going to be bought out or merged. If that happens, there will be some cutbacks. I may be one of them.

Your thinking is sensible. These days, with the demise of what we used to consider job security, it's just realistic to anticipate that we might have to make occasional unplanned changes in our jobs and careers.

My answer is, therefore, plan on it. If you have to go out the window, what kind of a net can you have there waiting for you?

Who are your contacts elsewhere, in other organizations? Or, taking a more basic view, what are the organizations in which you might be qualified to work? Start your list now, if you don't have one. Watch the advertisements in newspapers and magazines, both the commercial and help-wanted types. Who hires for what? Who has the kinds of specialized functions with which you're involved?

Is there an industry or professional association for which you're qualified? If you've not been active, become so now. So many high-level jobs are gained through word of mouth. So many jobs are never advertised but are available to people who solicit them or who are referred by others.

Begin or update your contingency lists now. Don't wait until the disaster strikes to get your resources together. In the meantime, just knowing that, when the worst happens, you'll know where to turn will ease your tension.

⇨ **497**

I no longer like my job, the man I work for, or the company. I've been hanging on until I get vested in another 18 months, but I'm beginning to think it isn't worth it. What advice can you give me?

Much depends on how old you are. If you are in your 30s, perhaps it isn't worth the wear and tear on you to stick around. You'll have time to get vested elsewhere. If you are in your late 40s or early 50s, you might want to take advantage of your present employer's pension plan.

If you decide to hang on, put the next 18 months to good use by planning where you want to go, and what you want to do. Such thinking ahead will serve at least two purposes: One, it will help you mount a serious, intense job search when you are free to do so; and two, just planning for your release should reduce the stress. You know you'll be getting out.

⇨ **498**

I recently came back from a six-week course for middle managers. It was great, but now I'm having problems remembering a lot that I learned. Problems come up and I can't always recall the solutions that I picked up

during the course. I'm afraid I'm going to lose it all, or look like a nincompoop.

You aren't a nincompoop. You're experiencing a normal phenomenon: the plunge of the retention curve. You've had a lot of information given to you in a short time without the opportunity to apply what you've learned as you learned it. Educators predict that within a few months you will lose a vast portion of what you covered in the course.

Don't try to retain everything; it won't be possible. Go back and review those areas of the course that had the most meaning for you, probably because they covered problems or deficiencies that you most frequently experience. Also review the most relevant portions that were concerned with the most serious challenges you encounter. Whatever your criterion, reexamine the suggested solutions and techniques that are most valuable to you. When you feel you are knowledgeable in those areas, pick some others and repeat the process.

It's also important for you to have a retrieval system. A useful step to take is to develop a card or a computer file. When you meet a particular problem or concern, you can find some suggested options to consider as solutions.

⇧ 499
How do I know when to pick up the tab at lunch?

Lunch etiquette depends on the circumstances of the invitation and the relationship of the people who are lunching. If the relationship is largely business, a good rule to follow is that the person who issues the invitation is prepared to pay for lunch. But there are exceptions. Even though a client initiates the lunch invitation, you'd be well advised to be prepared to pay, unless the other person makes a genuine fuss and *insists* on treating you.

Most friends meeting for lunch expect each to pay as you go. They split the check equitably. Others alternate picking up the check, which amounts to the same thing, ultimately, but is a nice gesture, especially since the alternation suggests that the lunches will continue.

If you think there will be a dispute about the check, arrange ahead of time for the maitre d' or waiter to present you with the check. If you are not sure who is going to or should pay the check, and would like to be safe as well as gracious, quietly place your credit card on the table where the waiter can see it. If the other person is determined to bear the expense, he or she will make it known at that moment.

⇨ 500

Frequently I have trouble making myself understood when I'm talking to others. I get enthusiastic or wrapped up in something and I talk very fast. Sometimes I can see that people aren't getting my meaning. Or I'll talk for about five minutes and find out they've been confused.

Break up your speeches. Simply stop after a few sentences and ask listeners whether you are being clear or making sense. Don't ask them whether they understand. Put the burden on yourself, instead, to be understandable. Another question you can ask is, "What kind of a reaction do you have to what I'm saying?"

Asking such questions will help you to involve your listeners more.

INDEX